Henry Morris Myers, Philip van Ness Myers

Life and nature under the tropics: or, Sketches of travels among the Andes, and on the Orinoco, Rio Negro, and Amazons

Henry Morris Myers, Philip van Ness Myers

Life and nature under the tropics: or, Sketches of travels among the Andes, and on the Orinoco, Rio Negro, and Amazons

ISBN/EAN: 9783337208394

Printed in Europe, USA, Canada, Australia, Japan

Cover: Foto ©Andreas Hilbeck / pixelio.de

More available books at **www.hansebooks.com**

VICTORIA REGIA.

THE TROPICS;

OR,

SKETCHES OF TRAVELS AMONG THE ANDES, AND ON THE ORINOCO, RIO NEGRO, AND AMAZONS.

BY

H. M. AND P. V. N. MYERS.

NEW YORK:
D. APPLETON AND COMPANY,
90, 92 & 94 GRAND STREET.
1871.

TO

PROFESSOR ASA GRAY, M.D., LL.D.,

CORRESPONDING MEMBER OF THE ROYAL BAVARIAN ACADEMY, ETC.,

WHOSE EMINENT LABORS

HAVE DONE SO MUCH TO ADVANCE AND RENDER POPULAR THAT DEPARTMENT
OF NATURAL HISTORY TO WHICH HIS LIFE HAS BEEN DEVOTED,

THIS VOLUME

IS, BY PERMISSION, MOST RESPECTFULLY INSCRIBED

AS A SLIGHT TRIBUTE OF

PROFOUND ADMIRATION AND GRATITUDE.

" Nowhere does Nature more deeply impress us with a sense of her greatness, nowhere does she speak to us more forcibly, than in the tropical
world."—*Humboldt*.

" It is a goodly sight to see
What Heaven has done for this delicious land !
What fruits of fragrance blush on every tree,
What good prospects o'er the hills expand :
But man would mar them with an impious hand."

CHILDE HAROLD.

PREFACE.

THE following pages are a narrative of a scientific expedition from Williams College to the tropical regions of South America. The Lyceum of Natural History of this institution has sent out several expeditions to different localities that have presented themselves as favorable fields for new and interesting research. The one whose history is given in this volume was sent out in the summer of 1867. Upon its first inception, Prof. A. Hopkins was intending to accompany the expedition; but business and educational relations having rendered this impossible, an invitation was extended to Prof. James Orton, of Rochester University, to take charge, and was accepted.

Colonel P. Staunton, Vice-Chancellor of Ingham University, Leroy, N. Y., accompanied the expedition as its artist; the party was also joined by F. S. Williams, Esq., of Albany, N. Y.; Messrs. A. Bushnell, W. Gilbert, R. H. Forbes, and the authors, were the members from Williams College. The expedition was formed into two divisions: one, consisting of three members, Messrs. Gilbert, Forbes, and H. M. Myers, proceeding from Caracas, upon the northern coast, penetrated to the Amazons, by the courses of the Orinoco and Rio Negro; the other party crossed the continent from the west, first ascending the Andes to Quito, then descending the slope of the Eastern Cordillera to the Rio Napo, and, by a canoe-voyage down that stream, reaching the Amazons, which was followed to its mouth.

As the scientific results of the western branch have been given to the public by Prof. Orton, we have made brief the portion of our narrative referring to that division ; yet, while divesting it of details, we have made sufficient notings of our experiences and observations to give completeness to our history. Portions of the work have been taken, with but few incidental corrections, from articles written by us while upon our tour, or after our return, and which have appeared in different papers and periodicals. Neither part is distinctly that of either author; but in the preparation of the work we have freely interchanged notes and suggestions.

While giving, in our boyish way, mainly the results of our own observations, we have not failed to avail ourselves of the labors of others, and have carefully examined the few works within our reach relative to the regions traversed. In the first portion of our work we have been guided by the " Travels " of the eminent German naturalist, Humboldt, to whose observations we have made frequent allusions in the course of our narrative; to the graphically-written work of Paez we are also indebted for many suggestions; upon Ecuador, Hassaurek's " Four Years among Spanish-Americans " has been almost our only guide. The greater portion of the volume is devoted to the Orinoco, Rio Negro, and the Andes. We have given but two chapters on the Amazons, for the wonders of that river have been made known by such writers as Agassiz, Wallace, and Bates, and many earlier travellers, and to these writers we would refer those of our readers who may desire a better knowledge of the valley of the Great River. The desire of many that a complete narrative of the expedition from our college should be given in a permanent form, and our own wish that others might share with us the pleasure we experienced in viewing a tropical Nature in those equatorial regions where she presents herself in forms so strange and grand, coupled with the fact that so little has been written upon those interesting portions of the continent to which sections our work is principally devoted, are the only considerations that could have led us to undertake the preparation of the present volume. We are conscious that our work has all the imperfections incident to a first effort, and that its kind reception can come only through the kindly indulgence of our readers.

The illustrations which embellish the work are principally from our own sketch-book, and are, for the most part, representations of natural scenery. In this connection we would express our especial indebtedness to Miss F. A. Snyder, to whom our sketches were submitted to be prepared for the engraver.

The expedition is under deep indebtedness to the Smithsonian Institution, which provided instruments for making meteorological observations, and secured transportation of collections, besides giving essential aid in other ways.

We desire to express our kindest thanks to Dr. Asa Gray, for the identification of many of our plants ; to

Don Ramon Paez, of Venezuela, for valuable assistance
rendered us in the preparation of our work; to Señor
E. Staal, of Valencia, for much information kindly
given us; to Mr. James Henderson, of Pará, J. F.
Reeve, Esq., of Guayaquil, and Dr. William Jameson,
of Quito, for many favors. We would also express
our deep obligations to Prof. A. Hopkins, for valuable
suggestions and kind encouragement in our work; to
Dr. J. Torrey, for the examination of plants submitted
to him; to R. H. Forbes, our fellow-traveller, for notes
generously placed at our disposal; to Albert Bushnell,
also our friend and companion; to C. P. Williams, Esq.,
of Albany; to W. P. Palmer, Esq., and Cyrus W. Field,
Esq., of New York; and to R. B. Hall, Esq., of Ash-
field, Mass. Nor would we forget to acknowledge our
indebtedness to Captain Lee, of Guayaquil, to Captain
Raygado, of the Peruvian steamer "Morona," to Commandante Cardozo, of the Brazilian steamer "Icamiaba," on the Amazons, and to the many other friends
that have aided us, and whose favors are gratefully remembered.

THE AUTHORS.

WILLIAMS COLLEGE, November, 1870.

CONTENTS.

CHAPTER V.

VALENCIA AND PUERTO CABELLO.

CHAPTER VI.

OVER THE MOUNTAINS TO THE LLANOS—AFLOAT IN THE FOREST.

CHAPTER VII.

BAUL AND SAN FERNANDO.

CHAPTER VIII.

AFLOAT UPON THE LLANOS.

CHAPTER IX.

URBANA.

CHAPTER XIV.

FROM PANAMA TO BODEGAS.

CHAPTER XV.

CROSSING THE ANDES.

CHAPTER XVI.

QUITO.

CHAPTER XVII.

MOUNTAINS ABOUT THE VALLEY OF QUITO.

CHAPTER XVIII.

OVER THE EASTERN CORDILLERA.

CONTENTS.   xiii

INTRODUCTION.

SOUTH AMERICA is a part of the world about which little, comparatively, is known. Owing to the disturbed political state of the country, commerce has sought other channels, and enterprise has looked elsewhere for its reward. A large capitalist said to the writer, many years ago, "Convince me that money can be made, and I will put a steamer upon the Magdalena at once." This was when General Mosquera had lately been elected President of New Granada, or, as it is now called, Colombia, and when religious toleration had just been secured in that republic. At that time the prospects for Colombia, politically and religiously, seemed to be brightening, and the students of Williams, wakeful to "the signs of the times," pledged five hundred dollars to one of the officers of the College to assist in the exploration of the country. The idea was, that feasible points should be selected—points that could be occupied as centres of a higher civilization and better type of Christianity. Some years later, one of the students, Frederick Hicks, proposed to realize this idea on his own responsibility. After looking the ground over, travelling somewhat extensively both in Colombia and Ecuador, he returned to Panama and built a commodious chapel, regarding that as a point which was central, and from which an influence might be exerted northward as well as southward. Frequent communications from Mr. Hicks have fanned the South-American spirit on this ground for a long time, and rendered the Lyceum of Natural History the more willing to undertake an expedition in that direction; so that, when Prof. Orton, with whom a correspondence had been opened by the Lyceum on the subject of an expedition, expressed a decided preference for South America, the thing was at once agreed to.

It is obvious that the expedition, by dividing as it did at New York, was able to secure far more important results than could have accrued from a joint expedition. It is especially obvious that the branch of the expedition which struck the northern shore of the continent, exploring first the Orinoco, and then the Rio Negro at least eight hundred miles farther than Humboldt had done, has performed a very valuable service in the interest of geography, natural science, and ethnology.

Prof. Orton has published an interesting account of his observations in connection with the western branch of the expedition. The northern branch now gives its report to the world. Some independent observations made by a member of the western branch of the expedition will also accompany the present volume.

We have no Royal Geographical, Geological, or Astronomical Societies in this country; but no doubt many curious eyes will be eager to read, and many interested ears to listen, while our young friends tell the story of their explorations, and their adventures in a region purely tropical, where every thing in Nature and man differs so widely from any thing we see—a region, too, for the most part, until recently, almost unknown.

A. HOPKINS.

WILLIAMS COLLEGE, *December*, 1870.

LIFE AND NATURE.

CHAPTER I.

FROM LA GUAIRA TO CARACAS.

First View of the Tropics.—Silla—La Guaira.—Fortifications.—Custom-house "Reasonableness."—Ascent of the Cordillera.—Picturesque Scenery.—Arrival at Caracas.

It was on the afternoon of July 27th, after a voyage of twenty-five days from New York, that we caught our first glimpse of the tropics. Far to the southward could be seen what appeared to be a mass of clouds piled one upon another, which, to the unpractised eye, differed not from those that encircled the entire heavens. That dark pile, whose outline was so distinctly marked far up from the horizon, was a branch of the Andes, that mighty range of mountains which traverses our sphere almost from pole to pole, and, although over sixty miles away, the irregular contour of its lofty summit could be distinctly traced upon the sky. We were not permitted to watch long the scene before us. Clouds soon gathered in around, and the darkness of approaching night veiled the land from our sight.

By three o'clock, next morning, we were within five miles of La Guaira, where we were obliged to wait for day and a favorable breeze to carry us into port. The wind, as is usual here in the early morning, blew but feebly, so that we entered with some difficulty. At length we gained the haven, and dropped anchor about three hundred yards from shore. Directly before us, rising abruptly out of the sea, looms up Silla, the highest peak of the northern Cordillera of the Andes. Its rocky and precipitous side, rising to the height of nearly nine thousand feet, looks as if one of those convulsions of Nature, which so often shake this unstable land, would overthrow the towering heights and bury forever in its ruins the town La Guaira, which lies closely nestled at its base. Clinging to its rugged slope, far up its side, is a scanty, scrubby growth of bushes, with here and there, in some ravine, a clump approaching somewhat to the magnitude of trees. Interspersed throughout this undergrowth, and towering above it, are cactuses, some attaining the height of thirty feet, and resembling at a distance leafless and nearly branchless trees. Higher up the mountain-side we see only Alpine grass, and this in turn gives place to barren rocks which crown the lofty summit. To heighten still more the grandeur of the scene, the morning is clear and beautiful, and the sun, as it rises from its ocean-bed, gilds the few fleecy clouds which float over the crest and along the flank of Silla, presenting a scene not often witnessed at this season, when clouds and storms prevail in the tropics. One of the first things which will attract the attention of the traveller, if he has never before visited the equatorial regions, will be the palms scattered along the coast, and which by their tall, straight trunks, thirty and forty feet in height, topped with a cluster of gigantic and elegantly-formed leaves, will impress him at once with the strangeness as well as beauty of vegetation within the tropics.

The port, or, rather, roadstead of La Guaira, opens

LA GUAIRA.

directly into the sea, with nothing to break the force of the
winds or waves. In the absence of a breakwater, which
might easily be constructed, wharves are, of course, useless.
Vessels are therefore obliged to anchor some distance
from land, and unload their cargoes by means of lighters.
The position of the town, wedged in between Mount Silla
and the sea, on a strip of land scarcely three hundred
yards in its greatest breadth, backed by an enormous
rocky wall, reflecting the heat of the sun on the red-tiled
roofs and stony pavements, renders it, according to Humboldt, the hottest place upon the earth. La Guaira has a
population of about eight thousand. There are a theatre
and two churches; one of the latter, the temple of San
Juan de Dios, is one of the most elegant edifices in Venezuela. As we wander through the long, narrow streets
of this antiquated city, we meet groups of every shade
of complexion and in every variety of costume, from the
gayly-dressed señora in her flounces and extended trail,
with a black-laced mantilla over the shoulders and a veil
upon her head, to the negro boasting of pants and hat,
and the urchin clad only in Nature's simple garb.

Leaving the narrow and crowded streets, we clamber
to the fortifications which lift their battlements above the
town. A few cannon frown defiantly through the embra-
sures and over the parapets. Soldiers in almost as many
different costumes as in number, with "arms at will," are
lazily guarding the works. From this stand-point, we
have a fine view of the city and its environs; but we cannot tarry long, for twilight is already deepening, and we
are reminded that in the tropics darkness quickly succeeds. We therefore hastily descend to our hotel, stopping for a moment to view the evening muster of the soldiers within the fortifications that line the shore. These
works are quite formidable as well as those overlooking
the town on the mountain-side, and if well manned would

render the place impregnable to an approach from the sea, which is the only side upon which an attack can well be made.

We cared not to protract our stay on the hot and arid coast of La Guaira. We were also admonished, by the death from yellow fever, the day before we arrived, of one of our countrymen who had been for some years a resident of the place, that it would not be well for us to remain long where that epidemic was raging. We therefore determined to leave on the morrow for the more genial and salubrious clime of the table-land of Caracas. That beautiful and fertile valley is situated directly over the mountain from La Guaira, at an elevation of some four thousand feet above the sea. There are two roads leading to it from the coast, the shorter but more precipitous of which is a mule-path, leading over the summit between the peak of Naiguanata and the Cerro de Avila, the two forming what is called the Silla, or saddle, of Caracas. The other, and the one we preferred, is a carriage-road which reaches the capital by a circuitous route of fourteen miles. The old road, which was in use at the time of Humboldt's visit to the country, was between the two we have mentioned. Before allowed to take our departure for Caracas, we were what they termed subjected to the inspections and extortions of custom-house officials. Our arms, ammunition, and some other articles, which were pronounced subject to duty, they were willing, in consideration of the object for which we visited their country, to allow to pass upon the payment of what they termed the reasonable amount of forty dollars, although they claimed that much more was rightly due them. Such "reasonableness" we hope it may be our good fortune not often to meet with. Our coach, with three abreast, at the appointed hour, is at the door of our hotel, ourselves and baggage stowed within, and all is ready. It is two P. M. as we take our departure. The rays of a tropical sun pour down without mercy, and are reverberated by every stone and rock until the very air we breathe seems as if drawn from a heated furnace. We lay aside our outer garments and make ourselves as comfortable as circumstances will permit. The road leads out of the town on the north, skirting the base of the mountains, between which and the sea there is for some distance scarcely room for the coach to pass; then the space widens, and we find ourselves riding through the village of Marquitia with its beautiful cocoa-nut grove; then turning up the mountain-slope, we wind along the eastern side of the Quebrada de Tipe, a large ravine, the aspect of the landscape varying at every turn. Here the maguey, a plant with agave leaves, finds its native home and adorns by its unsurpassed beauty these rugged wilds. Its lofty arboreal form, with its thousands of drooping liliaceous flowers, presents a sight of which the traveller never wearies.

As we continue our journey, slowly winding up the zigzag road, we find ourselves rising into a purer atmosphere. We breathe more freely, and no longer feel that languor and debility experienced while amid the burning sands of the *terra caliente*, or hot land below. Reaching what is called the half-way station, we stop and change horses. There are two or three other wayside inns we have passed, and which afford resting-places to the traveller and trains of animals that daily pass over the road between La Guaira and Caracas. Our garments, removed at the outset of our journey, we now gladly replace, for we have attained an altitude of nearly five thousand feet above the sea. Above us and along the summit heavy clouds are gathering, and, as they come sweeping down the mountain-side, threaten to soon envelop us in their gloom. From this point, the view, which the traveller has spread out before

him, is one of surpassing loveliness and grandeur. To his
left and far below he beholds the terminus of the deep
ravine of the Quebrada de Tipe, which running down the
mountain-slope, spreads out at its base into a plain of exu-
berant fertility, covered with beautiful estates of growing
corn, bananas, and other productions, sustained by irrigation. The extension of this plain, or, rather, low ridge of
land, into the sea, forms the promontory of Cabo Blanco,
whose white, barren shores glisten in the distance.
Farther to the right, and almost beneath his feet, lie the
village of Marquitia and its grove of cocoa-nut trees,
which so impresses the traveller as he approaches from
the ocean. Looking to the right and southward are seen
vessels in the port, riding at their anchorage. And there
is La Guaira, encircled by the sea on the one side, and by
an amphitheatral wall of rock on the other, while beyond
the ocean stretches to the horizon, striped by lines of
billows which come rolling in toward the shore.

From the half-way station the ascent is much easier,
owing to the sinuosities of the road, and the less precipi-
tousness of the Cordillera as we approach its summit.
The scenery also grows wilder and vegetation less luxuriant as we ascend. The clouds through which we pass
give forth a drizzling rain, and the increasing cold renders
our overcoats necessary for comfort. Respecting the
change of temperature experienced in passing from the
tierra caliente to the *tierra frio*, as the high elevations are
called, one is liable to form a wrong estimate : for it must
be remembered that the traveller in his ascent passes in a
few hours from the burning sands of the tropical coast to
an altitude of some seven thousand feet, the highest point
of the range over which the road passes. This elevation,
although not great, has a temperature so cool, that, in
entering it suddenly from an extreme of heat, there is experienced a sensation that leads to an erroneous conclusion.

The same may be said in regard to the temperature of La Guaira. The thermometer seldom rises above ninety degrees Fahrenheit; yet, as the variation during the twenty-four hours, and even from one season to another, is comparatively slight, one can easily conceive that the quantity of heat received must be very great. The intense suffering, therefore, in the tropics, results, as Humboldt observes, not from an excess of heat, but from its long continuance at a high temperature.

The summit of the Cordillera is at length reached, and over it we ride rapidly, and commence the descent at a still greater pace. The first view of Caracas, which lies just at the base of the mountain where the road makes its descent into the valley, is obtained at no great distance. It is nearly dark as we enter the capital of Venezuela. Our lumbering, three-horse vehicle rattles over the rough, stony pavement of the streets, and stops in front of a posada, kept by Madame St. Amand, who welcomes us in English, and shows us at once to a fine suite of rooms, which, like all the apartments of the house, open upon a court-yard in the centre, containing beautiful shrubbery and a maguey-plant in full bloom.

Upon the evening of our arrival, we were met by Mr. Wilson, the minister from our country, who gave us a most cordial reception. We were also happy in making the acquaintance of Profs. Ernst and Gearing, two distinguished German naturalists. The rich and varied flora of the tropics, comparatively but little known to the botanist, had enticed Mr. Ernst from Europe to this his adopted country. For three years he had been engaged in his favorite pursuit, confining his researches to the district of Caracas and vicinity. During that time he had collected and classified over three thousand species of plants, which is more than twice the entire number described in the Natural History of New York. The result of his labors will in due time be given to the public, and will constitute, if we except the published reports of Humboldt and Bonpland, with those of some minor travellers, the first botanical work that has ever been issued on that region. Mr. Gearing had been in the country about a year, and had succeeded in making a most valuable collection in the department of ornithology. The researches of these gentlemen in Northern Venezuela will add much to the cause of science, and increase largely the facilities for others who may desire to make investigations and collections in the natural history of this country. Often did we in the course of our travels have occasion to be grateful for information imparted to us, as well as many valuable suggestions received from them during the short time we remained in the city.

CHAPTER II.

In the southern portion of Colombia,* the Andes, which
sweep along the western coast of the continent, through
Chili, Peru, and Ecuador, with a breadth of sixty to four
hundred miles, yet with a rigid preservation of their unity,
divide into three distinct ranges. The most western of
these branches runs close along the Pacific shore of Colombia, and enters the Isthmus of Panama; the second traverses the centre of the republic, until it touches the shores
of the Caribbean Sea; the third takes a more easterly
direction, and, upon finding the ocean, skirts the northern
shore of Venezuela, terminating at the delta of the Orinoco. One of the most interesting features of this remarkable and unparalleled mountain-system, aside from its
volcanoes, is its lofty table-lands and beautiful valleys,
lying between its longitudinal ranges. Far to the south
we find the Thibetan highlands of Bolivia, lying about
the shores of Lake Titicaca; under the equator the beautiful plains of Quito; and, advancing still farther north, we

* Called New Granada, until September 20, 1861, when a new consti-
tution was adopted, and the name changed to United States of Colombia.

find ourselves surrounded by the smiling vales and verdant plains of Bogotá. If, from the tripartition of the system in Colombia, we journey along the eastern branch until we reach the sea, then follow the range for one hundred miles, as it sweeps along the coast, bathing its feet in the waters of the Caribbean, we find ourselves in one of the most beautiful valleys that fancy could depict.

Here, lying between two parallel ranges of the Cordillera, at an elevation of nearly three thousand feet (2,924) above the Atlantic, is the picturesque valley of Caracas. This plateau runs east and west, having a length of ten miles, and a breadth of six or seven. On the south is a range of hills which separates it from the valley of Tui, while on the north are the high mountains of Silla and Avila of the coast-chain. The Rio Guaira, taking its rise in the mountains of Higuerote on the west, flows through the valley, irrigating the soil, and maintaining a most luxuriant growth of vegetation. The climate is that of perpetual spring. What place can we conceive to be more delightful than that where the temperature of the day is never above eighty degrees, and at night seldom below sixty;* where vegetation is always green, flowers ever blooming, and fruit in the greatest abundance and variety at all seasons? Here, growing side by side, are the banana, the cocoa-nut, pine-apple, orange, grape, peach, Indian corn, and strawberry. There is no particular season for seed-time or harvest. Fields of maize may be seen in every stage of growth, from the young and tender blade just shooting upward into light, to the full and ripened ear of harvest-time. From the same shrub or tree may be enjoyed the fragrance of its flowers and the flavor of its fruit.

Not less beautiful is Nature in her wildness than when under the controlling influence of domestic culture.

---

* The average annual temperature is 71°.

CARACAS.

Trees of magnificent growth, festooned with hanging moss and pendant vines, their trunks and giant limbs covered with parasitic plants of rich, brilliant hues, stand alone in their majestic grandeur, or, by their united crowns of fadeless green, bedecked with flowers of rare delicacy and beauty, form picturesque bowers and arcades. Towering and crested palms, with their plumes wafted by the breezes, adorn alike the forest and the plain with their stately, graceful forms. Giant vegetation, in that variety and beauty elsewhere unknown, springs up on every side, while amid and beneath all—

> "There spring the living herbs, profusely wild,
> O'er all the deep-green earth, beyond the power
> Of botanists to number up their tribe."

Enclosing this beautiful valley, are lofty, rugged, and barren mountain-cliffs, which break the strength of the equinoctial winds, and shut out the burning atmosphere of the plain on the coast. The contrast presented by these barren ranges, and the stern, forbidding aspect of their chilling peaks which rise into the region of the clouds, only add to the loveliness of the valley which lies encircled within their embrace. Here the sweeping pestilence is seldom known, for those lofty Cordilleras, which serve as a barrier to the winds, also prevent an approach of those malignant diseases which are the scourges of southern ports. It seems scarcely possible that a spot within the equatorial regions, less than five miles in a direct line from where the earth is parched by the burning heat of a tropical sun, could possess such a cool, salubrious climate, and the luxuries of both temperate and torrid zones.

At the western extremity of the valley, situated upon a steep slope which inclines toward the southeast, is Caracas, the capital of Venezuela. At the base of this declivity, skirting the suburbs of the city, runs the Rio Guaira, while crowding the town on the west are rocky and sterile hills, which present a wild and gloomy aspect. Rising abruptly on the north, is the Cerro de Avila, down whose rugged slopes pour rushing torrents into the streets of the city, whenever a storm sweeps over the valley. Why Caracas was built in this wretched corner, when so large and beautiful a plain lies spread out before it, we cannot conceive. Could the town have been placed farther to the southward amid the charming scenery of the valley, it would have occupied a site in every way far preferable to its present position. Caracas in its greatest length is about one and a half miles, and is of nearly an equal breadth. Its area, although small, has crowded within its limits a population of fifty thousand inhabitants. Intersecting the city are deep ravines, some of which are dry, others the channels of small rivers, the Catuche, Caroata, and Arauco, which descend from the mountains. The ghastly appearance of these immense gullies, with their unsightly weeds and bushes, impresses the traveller still more unfavorably with the situation of the town. From the Rio Catuche the city is supplied with water, which is brought from a reservoir about a mile up the stream on the slope of Avila, and furnished the inhabitants at public and private fountains.

Caracas, like all Spanish-American towns, is regularly built, with narrow streets crossing each other at right angles. These are well paved, and slope toward the centre, thus making a sort of canal, which dispenses with the need of gutters at the sides. The sidewalks, which are found only on the principal streets, are flagged, and scarcely wide enough to allow two persons to pass. The houses enclose pleasant court-yards, are mostly one story in height, and solidly built, so as better to resist the shocks of earthquakes, which are frequent along this coast. Inside the court-yard, along the upper story, where such exists, runs an open gallery, while a corresponding veranda generally extends outside, along the front of the building. The roofs are tiled, and project far over the walls of the houses, shading the narrow streets, and affording protection to the pedestrian from the sun and rains. The windows, unglazed, and covered with an iron grating, protrude into the street, giving the house a gloomy, prison-like aspect. The only way of ingress and egress, the one used alike by man and beast, is through a large archway, which leads into the court-yard. The massive folding-doors, with their clumsy iron hinges, bolts, and fastenings, seem as if made for a fortress. The house internally is as scantily and antiquely furnished as the exterior indicates. The parlor of the Venezuelian boasts no carpet upon its brick floor; the walls are scantily ornamented with a few small pictures; one or two cane-bottomed sofas, some plain chairs, and still plainer tables, complete the furniture, useful and ornamental. The house has no chimney, the smoke and steam finding their exit from beneath the raised roof.

On the east side of the Grand Plaza, or great square of the city, stands the new cathedral, the largest and finest architectural structure in Caracas. It was founded nearly three centuries ago, but has since been modernized, being completed and consecrated during our visit at the capital. It is two hundred and fifty-feet in length, by one hundred and fifty in breadth, and is supported by two lines of gigantic columns. The floor is a marble mosaic, while the walls are hung with tablets bearing Latin inscriptions, and with paintings illustrative of Scriptural history, or of Roman Catholic mythology. This structure, although the pride of Caraquénians, will compare but unfavorably with similar ecclesiastical efforts in countries where civilization has made greater progress; but we must consider that it has been erected by a people struggling against all the evils which beset this unfortunate republic.

The government-house, which stands on the side of the plaza opposite the cathedral, presents nothing attractive. A Venezuelian flag floating from a short staff, and a few soldiers guarding the front and entrance, alone indicate that it is the capitol of the republic. On the south of the plaza is a university, founded in 1721, which ranks as the finest institution of learning in the country. The north side of the square is lined with dwellings and *pulperias*, or shops. A Venezuelian store is one of the curiosities of the country. The low, narrow room has two doors, for the admission of persons and light. The stock of the *pulpero* embraces, in kind, if not in quantity, sufficient to establish a country fair. A few pieces of calico and cotton cloth must occupy a prominent position upon his shelves. He must have groceries of every description, including hams, sardines, sausages, a few rounds of *cassara*, the bread of the country we have yet to describe, butter brought from Europe, some strips of dried beef, a coil of native tobacco resembling tarred rope, some bottles of Madeira and German wines, and also *aguardiente*, an intoxicating drink made from the fermented juice of the sugar-cane. Then there are articles of hardware, such as nails, knives, and machetes, a huge knife with a blade nearly two feet in length, the indispensable implement of the Spaniard. A dozen stalks of sugar-canes, a few bundles of finely-split wood for fuel, and an armful of green corn, occupy the corners. These, with a thousand other articles, render the collection as unique as a college museum.

There are scenes of a different nature that will interest the traveller as he wanders through the city. On every side will be seen traces of that terrible earthquake which destroyed the town in 1812, and buried in its ruins over ten thousand persons. Walls of buildings, overgrown with vines and parasitic plants, still stand as silent witnesses of that dreadful catastrophe. It is sad to reflect that this beautiful valley should ever have been the scene of such a fearful visitation, and a living sepulchre to thousands of its inhabitants. The frequent threatenings of these convulsions of Nature tend to keep the people in a constant state of alarm for their safety. Happy, indeed, is the man who is not distrustful of the soil upon which he lives. Among the few buildings which survived the general destruction of the city, were the government-house, the old cathedral, and the church of Altagracia, which is not far from the Grand Plaza. The last mentioned, however, bears evidence of the powerful agency which desolated the place. Its massive walls withstood uninjured the violence of the shock, but its enormous tower, about one third of the distance from the top, was twisted and jutted over the lower part, where it will probably remain until another earthquake shall complete its downfall.

The destruction of Caracas occurred upon the 26th of March, 1812, Ascension Day, or Holy Thursday of the Church. The country was engaged in a desperate struggle for its independence, and the ignorant and superstitious people, with their fears augmented by the priests, whose sympathies were with the mother-country, were led to regard the calamity as the vengeance of Heaven for their attempts to sever themselves from the crown of Spain. The day is represented as perfectly calm, with not a cloud in the heavens. Although at long intervals quite severe shocks had been felt at Caracas, an almost entire immunity from any of destructive force had inspired a feeling of security, and led the people to believe that, in their elevated valley, they were safe from such fearful visitations, as frequently laid in ruins the cities of other districts.*   No one had any apprehension of danger. The festivities of Holy Thursday had filled the churches. Suddenly the earth trembles.   The bells of the churches toll as though "rung by an invisible hand."   Caracas is doomed.   For four seconds the ground quakes, then rocks with a sea-like movement, and in six seconds more the city lies heaped in ruins.   Heavy thunderings rolled beneath the earth, and rocks were hurled from the sides of Silla.   Of fifty thousand inhabitants, ten thousand were killed upon the first overthrow of the city, while thousands afterward perished from injuries, hunger, and exposure.   Beneath the walls of San Carlos six hundred soldiers were mustering.   The barracks, says a chronicler, hurled from their base, left not a man of the regiment. Terrible scenes has our earth afforded; but none more fearful than Caracas presented when the clouds of dust, which at first veiled the ruins, lifted from the fated city. The imagination alone can picture that scene of ghastly ruins, terror, and consternation.   So great was the number of victims, that, interment being impossible, for days the survivors were employed in collecting and burning the bodies upon vast funeral-pyres.   Humboldt, in his graphic account of the fearful calamity, alluding to the tolling of the bells by the short tremor which preceded the final shock, pens the following thrilling sentence: "It was the hand of God, and not the hand of man, which rang that funeral-dirge." †   This passage possesses a peculiar interest.   While illustrating how powerfully Humboldt was impressed by the contemplation of this phe-

* The earthquake of Caracas was the culmination of a series of convulsions during the years 1811–'13, felt through the West Indies and over a large portion of the Mississippi Valley.

† "*Es war Gottes, nicht Menschenhand, die hier zum Grabgeläute zwang.*"

nomenon, it also shows, as Agassiz, in an address given upon the hundredth anniversary of the great German naturalist, has remarked, that Humboldt was a believer in a personal, superintending Providence. This fact has been so often denied, and Humboldt even pronounced an atheist, that we feel the cause of truth justifies us in making this slight digression.

Dr. Tschudi, in his "Travels in Peru," uses the following language in illustrating the effects of an earthquake upon the residents of the country and upon travellers: "No familiarity with the phenomenon can blunt the feelings. The inhabitant of Lima, who from childhood has frequently witnessed these convulsions of Nature, is roused from his sleep by the shock, and rushes from his apartment with the cry of '*Misericordia!*' The foreigner from the north of Europe, who knows nothing of earthquakes but by description, waits with impatience to feel the movement of the earth, and longs to hear with his own ear the subterranean sounds which he has hitherto considered fabulous. With levity he treats the apprehension of a coming convulsion, and laughs at the fears of the natives; but, as soon as his wish is gratified, he is terror-stricken, and is involuntarily prompted to seek safety in flight."

The inhabitants of Caracas, ethnologically and socially, present but few interesting features. The entire population of the city, as near as can be estimated, is fifty thousand; while that of the whole republic, including Indians, is one and a half millions. It consists of whites, mainly of Spanish extraction, negroes, and the various classes produced by the intermingling of these. The descendants of the foreign element, of whatever color, are denominated Creoles.

The negroes were formerly kept in slavery; but by virtue of a law which compelled the master to give freedom to a slave who should offer him three hundred dollars; by the voluntary bestowment of liberty, which was common; and by the proclamation of 1854, they have all become emancipated. The Indians we shall have occasion to speak of, when our journeyings lead us where man as well as beast exists in a state of nature.

In dress, the upper class follow the European styles; the man of modest pretensions considers himself equipped when supplied with pants, *camisa*, which is worn outside of the former, wool or panama hat, and leather sandals. The children of the lower class are not inconvenienced by clothing, until they have attained the age of eight or ten years, when a camisa constitutes their outfit.

Education, although provided for by law, is sadly neglected among all classes. Besides the university in Caracas, already referred to, there has also been founded a military academy. The need of books is much felt. None are printed in Venezuela, and the foreign supply is small and not of the highest order. It is, however, gratifying to state that much has been done of late to meet this want of the people, and that no country has contributed more to supply the deficiency than our own. School-books, as well as others, published in the Spanish language and sent out from the United States, have been widely circulated, and are now doing much toward the advancement of educational interests in Venezuela. There are in Caracas two printing-presses, each of which issues a daily newspaper on a single sheet. Much difficulty is experienced in preserving records, books, or papers, owing to the ravages of termites, or "white ants," as they are called, which possess an insatiable appetite for literature. This was more particularly brought to our notice afterward at Valencia, where we found it difficult to procure, for the use of our herbarium, any papers which had not been more or less damaged by these voracious insects.

There are eighteen churches in Caracas and three convents; the last are merely tolerated, as no monastic institutions are permitted by law in Venezuela. Here, as in every Roman Catholic country, the Sabbath is but little regarded. The services in the churches, the same as those for the other days of the week, continue for one hour, from five to six o'clock in the morning, when the religious exercises of the day are over. All places of amusement and public resort are then opened and thronged as they are at no other time. The card and billiard tables are frequented, but the cock-fights and bull-fights call together the greatest crowds. Sabbath afternoons are especially consecrated to the latter amusement. The cock-fight partakes more of a domestic character, and there is scarcely a family that has not its cockpit. All day long the shops are opened for traffic, mules and donkeys laden with merchandise wend their way through the streets, soldiers parade the city, and, to destroy still more if possible the quietness and sanctity of the Sabbath, the bells are in an eternal jingle. In the evening the theatre affords the closing entertainment of the day.

Caracas has six Catholic cemeteries, the largest, which is said to be the finest in South America, is north of the city, upon the slope at the base of Cerro de Avila. It is enclosed by a high wall, on the inside of which are niches, or receptacles for the dead. Upon the payment of a certain sum, coffins are allowed to be placed within, where they may remain three years. At the expiration of that time they are taken, if not removed before by friends, and the bones cast in the *carnero*, or common sepulchre. Those who do not desire, or cannot afford for their deceased relatives, these funereal niches, bury at once within the enclosure of the cemetery. There are also two Protestant burial-grounds, German and English, situated south of the city.

CHAPTER III.

EXCURSIONS ABOUT CARACAS.

Trip to the Cave of Encantado.—Railroad.—Thunder-storm.—Petaré.—A
Hopeful Student.—Experience at a Posada.—The Cave.—Pineapple-
Plant.—Calabash-Tree.—Yuca-Shrub.—Death of Mr. Wilson.—La
Valle.—Cerro de Avila.

DURING our stay at Caracas we made many excursions
to places of interest in the valley; the first of which was
to the Cave of Encantado, four leagues east of the city.
On the morning of our fourth day in the capital, we set
out for this place. The sun had not risen, yet the streets
of the city were already bustling with life — for the
Spaniard is an early riser, the morning being, more from
necessity than choice, the business part of the day. Scores
of water-carriers hastened along with their immense earth-
en pots, balanced upon their heads—burdens are seldom
carried in the hand; while donkeys, so completely buried
beneath their loads of maize, that they seemed like piles
of herbage endowed with locomotion, pushed stubbornly
through the street.

Crossing the Arauca, the stream which forms the
eastern boundary of the city, we passed at our left a line
of railway. The track, which was overgrown with grass
and weeds, terminated a short distance farther on. It had
been purposed to carry it to Petaré, but, like all Venezuelian enterprises, the affair had come to an untimely end.

At our right was a large coffee-estate, the shrubs shaded by gigantic trees whose trunks and brawny arms were clothed with parasitic plants, and hung with long, tangled tufts of Tillandsiæ, that gray moss which so ornaments our own Southern forests. On either side, the road was hedged with trees and bushes, thickly interlaced with vines and creeping plants. These at length gave place to rows of mango-trees, whose arching boughs, spread with dark-green foliage, formed a most beautiful arcade. The mango, which to us seemed possessed of no particular gustatory virtues, is considered by the natives as one of the finest of tropical fruits.

About ten A. M., while enjoying our breakfast of oranges and bananas, we were forced by a sudden shower to seek shelter in a way-side pulperia. A thunder-storm in the tropics is an incredible exaggeration of a northern tempest. The rain does not spatter down in drops, but falls in almost unbroken sheets of water, which in a few minutes completely flood the earth. The thunder and lightning which accompany these showers in the elevated regions of the country are generally "moderate in quantity but inferior in quality;" yet on the llanos of the interior they are in good keeping with the terrific storms which sweep over those plains.

Our visit to Caracas was during the rainy season, which commences about the last of April, and continues until November. It must, however, not be supposed that even during this season the sky is continually overcast with clouds which are incessantly discharging their contents upon the land. The showers generally last only a few minutes, seldom half an hour, when they cease as suddenly as they commence. The annual fall of rain is about thirty-five inches; the time of greatest heat is during the wet period. This regular alternation of the seasons in the valleys of Caracas and Valencia is not, however, the same everywhere within the tropics, for in certain localities various causes tend to modify essentially the tropical seasons, which in sections often not far separated, but perhaps upon opposite sides of mountain-ranges, are frequently the reverse of each other.

Late in the afternoon we reached Petaré, a town of four or five thousand inhabitants; and it being still a league farther to Encantado, over an unfrequented road, requiring a guide that could not be had until morning, we determined to spend the night here. After considerable difficulty we at length found a house labelled "Posada," where accommodations were offered us. While dinner was preparing, which was promised *luego* (presently), we strolled about, making a general inspection of the establishment. In the largest apartment, and in reality the only respectable one, was a billiard-table, which seemed the centre of attraction to a crowd of men and boys, among whom was an Englishman, who was wandering about the world with apparently no fixed object, and had happened into this out-of-the-way place. He was not inclined to give much of his history, leaving us to draw our own inferences. There was also a young Spaniard of quite an intelligent and prepossessing appearance, who, learning we were Americans, brought us a copy of an old English book of poetry, and repeated from it long sections that he had memorized, but of the meaning of which he had not the vaguest conception. He informed us that he was desirous of acquiring the English language; and for that purpose he was committing to memory the contents of the volume. He said that he found the task an exceedingly difficult one, and that he had as yet made no very satisfactory progress. We did not doubt the truth of his statement. He, however, seemed confident of ultimate success, and expressed a desire to obtain from us other English books, that he might prosecute his studies. A more hopeful student under such adverse circumstances we have seldom met with.

From the long time which had intervened since our order for dinner, we began to apprehend that, perhaps, our host had forgotten the wishes of his hungry guest; but, upon inquiry, we were comforted with the assurance that it would be ready *luego*. Another hour of waiting, and again we seek the cause. "*Paciencia, señores, luego;*" but that was long since exhausted. A traveller in this country will have abundant opportunity to exercise his *paciencia*, for *luego* and *mañana*, presently and to-morrow, are words in frequent requisition among the Spaniards, and are used in their broadest signification. Never punctual, never in a hurry, are prominent characteristics of this people. The meal was finally announced. In a small room, upon a small table, was the food, which had cost them so much labor and us so much patience. We allow that the best had evidently been done to meet our wants, but confess that we formed no very high opinion of the ability displayed in the preparation of the meal.

Early the following morning, having passed the night in unsuccessful efforts to protect ourselves from the persistent attacks of fleas, we gave a consideration of three dollars, for the annoyance and suffering we had endured, and, taking our guide, started for the Cave of Encantado. Our road was simply a narrow foot-path, which led around the base of densely-wooded hills, and then over a mountain-range, the summit of which we reached just as the sun was appearing over the top of Silla. We shall not soon forget that glorious prospect. Clouds, with their upper surface brilliant with the rising sun, filled the valleys beneath us, while, piercing this sea of mist, the cragged peaks of Silla rose majestically above the lower mountains, which here and there scarcely pushed their summits above the surface of the vapor-ocean. From the mountain we descended into a valley through which rushed a broad, rapid torrent, on whose opposite bank, directly in our front, rose a perpendicular wall of limestone, in the face of which, fifteen feet from the base, was the entrance to the Cave of Encantado. Clambering up the cliff, we found ourselves within a large, irregular, arched chamber, adorned with beautiful stalactic formations. Diverging from this chamber, are dark, contracted passage-ways, leading to smaller apartments, the principal of which we entered, often obliged to crawl upon hands and knees to gain admittance. Swarms of bats, disturbed by our intrusion within their haunts, hovered around us, making the place hideous with their unearthly screechings. Shooting one of the creatures only tended to arouse the others the more, while the deafening report of our gun, reverberating through the cavern, fell with stunning effect upon our ears. Having explored the cave, we dismissed our guide, purposing to remain through the night, and return to Caracas on the following day. We spent the night within the cave, where upon our rocky beds, softened by wild-canes, we, undisturbed by our companion bats and owls, enjoyed a rest, free from the fleas of Petaré.

Our visit to Encantado afforded us a most glorious harvest of plants, the first gathering for our tropical herbarium. Not a single species was familiar; yet some were so closely allied to varieties in our own land as to pleasantly recall many a botanical ramble there. Our return-trip also introduced us to several interesting products of the mountain valley of Caracas, among which was the pineapple. There is, perhaps, no production of the tropics which is so generally and deservedly esteemed by the people of the North as this; yet of none have they such vague ideas, as to manner of growth and propagation. The pineapple-plant (*Ananassa sativa*) is indigenous to tropical America, growing wild in the forests, but cultivated largely in those regions, in the West Indies, and on the Eastern Continent. It has fifteen or more long, serrated, ridged, sharp-pointed leaves, springing from the root, and in its general aspect resembles the century-plant, but is much smaller. In the centre of this cluster of thick, succulent leaves, springs up a short stalk, bearing a spike of beautiful flowers, which in time produce a single pine-apple. On the summit of the fruit is a tuft of small leaves, capable of becoming a new plant, which, together with suckers, is the means by which it is propagated, as the cultivated fruit seldom produces seeds. It flourishes best in a moist and warm climate, but is able to survive a long drought and extreme heat. There are several varieties, differing in their leaves being more or less spiny on their margins, and in the shape, size, and color of the fruit. Great care is requisite in its cultivation; otherwise it will be coarse, fibrous, and deficient in saccharine matter. Nothing can surpass the rich and delicate flavor of a pine-apple which has been properly cultivated; or of the wild fruit of the forests, which we always found equal, if not superior, to the domesticated ones.

Of the arboreal productions of these plains, especially interesting is the calabash or crockery-tree (*Crescentia cujete*), which is seen growing by the side of every Venezuelian hut. In size and appearance it resembles an apple-tree, and yields a hard, roundish, ligneous-shelled fruit, from three to twelve inches in diameter, which supply the natives with cups, dishes, and many useful utensils. They are sometimes fancifully carved, or highly polished, and by the natives of the Amazons * are beautifully tinted with various colors, both mineral and vegetable substances being employed for the purpose. But another more indispensable plant which

* This name in Portuguese is *Amazonas*, and when Anglicized the plural form should be retained.

we here found is the yuca,* or mandioca (*Manihot utilis-sima*), a shrub some ten to twelve feet in height, from the large tubers of which are made the cassava of the Venezuelian, and the farina of the Brazilian. The tubers are first grated upon a concave board, thickly set with sharp pieces of quartz gravel. The pulp is rendered still finer by grinding with stones, and the pulverized mass subjected to pressure for the purpose of removing, as far as possible, its poisonous juice, which contains hydrocyanic or prussic acid. The substance is then formed into round cakes, two feet in diameter, and a quarter of an inch in thickness, and baked upon concave plates, over a brisk fire, which expels the remaining volatile juice. Farina, the same as the mañoca of the Rio Negro and Upper Orinoco, is made by roasting the root, grated, into a coarse flour-like substance. In these forms the yuca constitutes an excellent and nutritious food, which retains its sweetness for a long period. The mandioca, or yuca, is extensively cultivated throughout the continent of South America, and, with the plantain and banana, constitutes, in many sections, the principal support of the people. Tapioca of commerce is the sediment, obtained from the expressed juice of the mandioca. This plant must not be confounded with the yuca dulce, or sweet yuca (*Manihot aipium*), a species similar in appearance, but which contains none of the poisonous property of the first. The former is preferred for cassava and mañoca, as it is richer in fecula, while the latter is largely eaten as a vegetable.

Our return from Encantado was followed by the death of Mr. Wilson, our minister, who contracted a fatal fever while attending diplomatic business at La Guaira, upon the coast. He was buried at Caracas, far away from home and those he loved. But a few weeks previous to his death, his family, who had been with him, returned to

* Sometimes misspelt *yucca*, a plant to which it is in nowise allied.

their country, where he expected to join them soon. The tidings of his death and burial, carried by the departing steamer, were the only greeting for the waiting ones.

Among the many places of interest in the vicinity of Caracas, that will repay a visit, is La Valle, half a league south of the capital. Leaving the city by the route which leads to the plains of Ocumare, the traveller crosses the Rio Guaira, and ascends a gentle slope, which brings him to the summit of a low range of hills. This road passes over the ridge by a deep cut, made through the soft micaceous rock, rendering the ascent an easy one. Emerging from this gorge, there opens before the observer a most fertile plain, presenting a beautiful picture of waving grass and cultivated fields, dotted here and there with haciendas and hamlets, nestled beneath the shade of graceful palms. The posada and few houses which bear the name of La Valle lie just a little distant from where the traveller catches his first glimpse of the valley. Botanical and zoölogical attractions led us to make several excursions to this picturesque spot, from which we always returned richly laden with collections.

The ascent of Silla promised excitement enough to awaken a strong desire in us for a climb to its summit; but the continuous rains which prevailed during our stay at Caracas, rendered impracticable the scaling of the steep, slippery heights of the mountain. But the accessible slope directly under Cerro de Avila, clothed with magueys and cactuses, and traversed by the wooded ravine of the Catuche, was a most interesting spot, especially to the naturalist; accordingly we planned a trip there. Following up the river, the ascent was easy to the *Toma de Agua*, a large reservoir from which the city receives its supply of water. From here the gorge was deeper, and more densely wooded, and we advanced with greater difficulty. The trees attained no great size, yet some of the smaller forms of vegetation were of gigantic proportions. We found a species of equisetum which was twelve feet in height, and we were assured by Mr. Ernst that it frequently attains a height of over thirty. Epiphytes, usually called air-plants, so covered the limbs of the trees, that it was often difficult to determine whether what they concealed was alive, or in a state of decay. Some of the flowers of these orchidaceous plants are of exceeding beauty, resembling in shape, and surpassing in the brilliancy of their colors, winged insects. The butterfly-flower (*Orchidium papillio*) is one of the most beautiful, and is so similar in appearance to the insect whose name it bears, that it not unfrequently deceives persons unacquainted with it. Others look like humming-birds, glittering with metallic lustre. Many animated objects of Nature are thus imitated by Flora's kingdom of the tropics.

We followed the ravine until the steepness of the ascent and the density of vegetation rendered farther advance exceedingly laborious; when we climbed the high banks that enclosed the gorge, and emerged upon the open slope. The contrast between the vegetation in the deep glen, and that of the sunburnt side of the mountain, was no less striking in the different degrees of luxuriousness than in the specific peculiarity of distinct forms. In this rocky soil, which for several months during the year is not moistened by a single refreshing shower, thrive only plants that are capable of enduring a long season of drought, such as the maguey and cactus. The straight, cylindric, and spiny trunks of cerei rise thirty and forty feet in height amid straggling opuntias, whose grotesque forms lend such a peculiar physiognomy to this tropical landscape. A species of this consolidated form of vegetation, the prickly-pear cactus (*Opuntia tuna*), is cultivated by the Venezuelians for the sake of its edible fruit, and is also employed for hedges, its spiny, branching stems admirably adapting it to that purpose.

There are two varieties of the maguey, differing in the leaves of one being serrated while those of the other are entire. The spreading panicle which shoots up from the cluster of fleshy, sharp-pointed leaves, five to eight feet in length, has straw-colored, liliaceous flowers pendulous from the branches. At a distance the giant flower-stalk resembles a tree in foliage, but on a nearer view the arborescent plant exhibits its true nature and beauty. We measured the stem of one, which was twenty inches in circumference at the base and thirty-eight feet in height, a growth it had made in six or eight weeks. The maguey is not only admired for its beauty, but also valued for the uses to which it can be applied. From the fibres of its leaves are made twine, rope, cloth, and hammocks, while the thorn which arms their extremity, when removed with a bundle of the attached fibres, furnishes a needle and thread. The leaves furthermore yield an excellent detergent, that washes equally well with salt water or fresh. From the flower-stalk is obtained an excellent beverage, while the pith of the stem, which contains silica, makes excellent razor-strops. This plant, the *Yucca acaulis* of Humboldt, and the *Codonocrinum agavoides* of later botanists, is often mistaken for the *Agave Americana*, or century-plant, which it resembles in its leaves, but from which it differs essentially in its flowers and inflorescence; those of the latter terminating the branches in erect clusters, instead of being scattering and pendulous, as we have observed, in the former. We did not see the *Agave Americana* in Venezuela, although it is said to grow in some districts of the littoral mountains.

CHAPTER IV.

VALLEYS OF ARAGUA AND VALENCIA.

Departure from Caracas.—Scenery of the Rio Guaira.—Beautiful View from Mount Higuerote.—The "Garden of Venezuela."—Victoria.—Spanish Extortion.—A Word on Mules.—Venezuelian Coaches.—Maracai.—Castilian Etiquette.—Fast in a Stream.—Entrance into Valencia.—The City.—Lake Tacarigua.

AFTER two weeks spent in the beautiful valley of Caracas, we left the capital for Valencia, the second city of Venezuela, situated a hundred miles to the westward, upon the shores of the picturesque lake whose name it bears. Unfortunately, we were in the midst of the rainy season, and the roads were now impassable by the stages which run between the two cities. Moreover, the country was suffering from one of its chronic revolutions, and roving bands of outlaws interrupted communication, respecting the persons or property of neither friend nor foe. However, we determined to undertake the journey, arming ourselves well, in case of emergency. In lieu of stage-conveyance, we contracted for mules to Victoria, a town midway between Caracas and Valencia, paying ten *pesos* * for each, just one-tenth the value of the beast, and an equal amount for a *muchacho*, or muleteer, which proved near his whole valuation.

* The peso is the Spanish dollar, whose value is eighty cents.

At three o'clock, upon the morning of the 15th of August, we were riding rapidly through the streets of the slumbering capital, scarcely able to keep pace with our *muchacho*, who ran by the side of the baggage-animals. Our course led us along the Rio Guaira through a most charming valley, whose beauty was enhanced by the light of a full moon, which threw weird shadows down the broken slopes of the precipitous mountains that rose upon either side. Just as we were falling into a poetical mood, we were aroused by the imperative demands of a toll-gate official, to whom we paid twenty-five cents for each mule, which exorbitant exaction destroyed our good-humor for the remainder of the day. The river, along which we journeyed was bordered with *caña brava*, a gramineous plant (*Gynesium sacharoides*), which attains a height of fifteen to twenty feet, and is much used in the construction of fences and buildings. The declivities were covered with magueys, the last we met with in the country. Often have we recalled the giant form of this arborescent plant, which lends so strange a beauty to the landscape of its mountain-home.

At length we commenced the ascent of Higuerote, still following the course of the Guaira, which takes its rise among the elevated peaks of this mountain-range. In places the road led through deep ravines along the stream, then over rugged summits, and on the steep side of precipices, while far below we beheld the rushing torrent of the Guaira as it went plunging and foaming down the heights through rocky gorges worn by the incessant flow of waters for many ages. After an easy ascent, but one difficult and wearisome when made with a coach, we arrived at the summit, where we were greeted with one of Nature's finest pictures. Beneath us was one of the far-famed valleys of Aragua, bounded by wooded slopes, upon which here and there a hut was nestled in some quiet nook amid growing corn and bananas, while far down in the lovely glen there flowed a rivulet, which added its waters to those of the larger stream that bears the name of the picturesque and luxuriant valley through which it passes. The extent of the prospect was not so great but that the whole could be embraced at a single glance, and every portion, even the most distant, was so distinctly seen that it appeared like a vast picture set in bold relief before our vision. Many were the glorious scenes we enjoyed in our tropical wanderings, some wilder, more romantic, surpassing by far, in grandeur, any we ever beheld in our own land; yet this view from Higuerote seemed to excel them all, and left an impression upon the memory which the lapse of time can never efface.

Along the southern declivity of the mountain-range, bounding upon the north the valley we have described, is the road, cut from the soft micaceous rock, which leads by a gentle descent into the plain below. About half the distance down we halted at a wretched *venta* for rest and breakfast. With hunger half appeased by a scanty meal, we again mounted and were on our way. The mountain-side along which we were travelling received the full benefit of a tropical sun, and, as mid-day approached, the heat became most oppressive. We were often tempted within the cool retreat of some shaded glen, such as were frequently crossed as we zigzagged down the Cordillera into the valley beneath us. But our destination for the night was a long journey ahead, and we urged our animals forward.

The descent was at length completed, when we entered the valley, which, narrow at first, gradually widened as we advanced, spreading out into a broad and beautiful plain, which is one of the great coffee-regions of the world. The valleys of Aragua have been fitly called the " Garden of Venezuela." Their elevation is nearly two thousand

feet above the sea, one-half that of the table-lands of Caracas, and the average temperature during the day is 70°
to 75° Fahr., falling at night to about 60°. The soil is
most fertile, and every product of the tropics, with many of
northern latitudes, flourishes luxuriantly. Coffee is, however, the great staple of these regions. As we approached
Victoria, we passed extensive estates of this shrub, shaded
by gigantic trees to prevent the rapid absorption of moisture from the soil, and to protect the ripening berry from
the burning heat of the sun. Great care in cultivation is
bestowed on these coffee-groves, and the harvest yielded
is proportionally fine; the berry being of a superior quality, and the quantity greater than in most other places
where the shrub is cultivated. Wheat was formerly raised,
and produced, according to Humboldt, nearly sixteenfold;
but, notwithstanding this large return, the greater profit
from the culture of coffee, cacao, and cotton, has caused
the cultivation of wheat to be wholly neglected, and the
demand for it is now supplied from the States. We saw
none of this cereal growing in the country, but were
informed that in the provinces of Merida and Trujillo
there is sufficient raised to supply the demands of these
districts.

It was nearly dark when we entered Victoria and
reined our jaded animals up in front of quite a respect-
able-appearing posada. Weary and sore from our journey
of sixteen leagues over a rough mountain-road, we gladly
alighted from our saddles. A call for dinner was answered
by eight o'clock, when we sat down to our meal, which we
enjoyed with a keen relish, notwithstanding the successful
efforts of the cooks in destroying the natural flavor of
every dish with the inevitable garlics.

In our wearied condition we were not, perhaps, in the
best humor to spare the feelings of our precious *muchacho*
—we recalled our paying ten pesos for his invaluable ser-

vices—who had lost by the way one of our herbariums, filled with choice plants. The loss was an irreparable one; for many of the species were known only to the high table-land and mountains of Caracas, where they had been collected, and consequently could not now be replaced.

The imposition again practised upon us in making arrangements for the prosecution of our journey was the next thing to destroy our equanimity, and to persuade us, if not already convinced, that Venezuelian officials and *posaderos* possess the fewest virtues of any mortals we were ever privileged to meet. Our mules, which had been engaged only to Victoria, were not allowed to go farther, and others could not be obtained. We therefore made a trial of coaches, which our post, who monopolized this business in Victoria, furnished us for the moderate sum of sixty pesos. This was the price of a single day's ride in one of the miserable, wheeled arrangements of the country. Nor did this include the keeping of the driver and horses by the way. Such is Venezuelian extortion to which the traveller in these fair lands is subject.

We will here add, for the benefit of any who may follow us over this route through Northern Venezuela, that complete arrangements should be made for the entire journey at Caracas or Valencia, whichever place may be the starting-point. If you are not familiar with the Spanish language, procure an interpreter, who can always be had, to make the bargain for you, being particular to mention every thing, and have all agreed upon, even to the feed for your animals, and also the toll which may be extorted by the way. An occasional cigar and glass of *aguardiente* will also be expected by your muleteer. The journey is most easily performed by mules. Be contented with allowing the beast to choose his own time for accomplishing the distance. Like his counterpart, his master, he is a subtle animal; if not deceitful above all things, at least desperately wicked. With a little experience, however, you will soon learn to manage the creatures, so that no difficulty need be apprehended. You cannot change his wily nature; but do not call it forth by placing yourself in violent opposition to his will.

Punctuality is not one of the virtues of Venezuelians; we were, therefore, not surprised that it was fully an hour late in the morning when the wretched conveyance, in which we were to be dragged to Valencia, was ready for us. The prospect of a discomforting journey in no way allayed our feelings of indignation which we entertained for Venezuelian swindlers in general and our Victoria posadero in particular. The coach in question was a shambling affair, drawn by three horses abreast, which were from the roaming herds of the plains, and, before our journey's end was reached, gave evidence that their wild and fractious nature had not been wholly subdued. Stowing ourselves and baggage as best we could inside of the concern, the driver cracked his long raw-hide whip, shouted at his fiery steeds, and away we dashed over the stony pavement of the streets with noise sufficient for a train of artillery. Victoria is an unattractive town of seven or eight thousand inhabitants, and of but little commercial importance, although situated in the midst of the rich.growing valleys of Aragua, and upon one of the great thoroughfares of the republic. The valley here is a league in breadth, but widens as it approaches the Lake of Valencia, until, embracing that beautiful sheet of water, it expands into the broad plain bearing the same name.

The villages of San Mateo and Zurmero were passed, when we came in sight of the Saman de Guere, an enormous tree of the mimosa family, whose large hemispherical top looks more like a forest-crowned peak than the summit of a single tree. The height of this giant of the vegetable kingdom is only about sixty feet, with the cir-

cumference of its trunk thirty, dimensions less than those
of other trees of the same kind growing in the vicinity.
But its beauty and attraction consist in the extension of
its branches, which spread out on every side to the distance of nearly a hundred feet, making a spherical summit of about six hundred feet in circumference. Its small,
pinnated leaves form a most delicate foliage, which con-
trasts curiously with the gigantic size of the tree, and add
greatly to its beauty. The age of the Saman de Guere
must be very great, for tradition only tells of its antiquity. It was held in great veneration by the natives at
the time of the Spanish Conquest, and is now carefully
preserved by the government. Humboldt makes mention
of it, as seen by him during his visit to the country in
1800, when it was, he says, in the same state of preservation in which the first conquerors found it. It has since
been observed with increased interest and attention by
travellers, and no change has been noticed in its appearance during the half century or more that has followed.
But there it stands, green and vigorous, as in the days
when first the aborigines of the country reclined in the
shade of its forest-top, even then rocked by the blasts of
many ages. It is more than probable that it will withstand for centuries yet to come the fury of tropical tem-
pests, an object of wonder and reverence to the traveller
who shall journey through the valley of Aragua.

Four leagues westward of Turmero, and six from Victoria, is Maracai, a town of some eight thousand inhabitants, where we stopped for breakfast. For the first and
only time while in the country we saw a woman seat herself at the table in company with men. Among the better class of Venezuelians it is customary for ladies to take
their meals in their rooms, having them brought by servants; while among the middle and lower classes the
women wait until their lords have eaten, when they take

possession of the table with what may be left, or, as is more commonly the case, they crouch with the children upon the ground in the corner, where from the iron pots they take their food. The wife of our host, disregarding this custom of Spanish etiquette, placed herself with us at the festive board, and together we enjoyed a pleasant repast.

After our mid-day siesta we left Maracai, and soon after caught a glimpse of Lake Valencia, or Tacarigua, its Indian name. The road thus far had been tolerably good, but now became outrageously bad, so that our progress was slow and laborious. Swollen streams rushing from the mountain-sides crossed our path, occasioning us oftentimes no little difficulty in fording. To add to the perplexities of the situation, our horses were weary, and began to exhibit signs which forboded evil. We were making our way over the plain which borders the lake upon the north, at times riding quite briskly over a smooth patch of road, and then floundering through mud hub-deep, when suddenly we came to a halt. Putting our heads out of the open sides of the coach to learn the cause of our stopping, we discovered ourselves in the middle of a broad stream; the horses standing composedly in the water with a malicious look of self-satisfaction at our ludicrous position. Yes, there we were, and no amount of coaxing or lashing could induce the obstinate brutes to budge. To the repeated blows of the driver, they responded with kicks, throwing mud and water in a most spiteful manner in every direction, until one at length threw himself completely out of the harness. Seeing that our present mode of procedure was not likely to avail us much but kicks and a liberal sprinkling with the contents of the stream, we concluded to alight, in hopes that the rebellious creatures might then, perhaps, be induced to extricate the concern. This was no sooner done than their ugliness took a new direction, and, with a spring, they started forward, purposing no doubt to leave us to our reflections, which, just at that crisis of affairs, were in no very solemn strain. Our driver, however, being on the alert, the creatures were checked in their career until we could regain our seats, when the lines and the whip were both given, and away we dashed wildly over the plain.

At five P. M. we reached the small village of San Joaquin, distant from Valencia six leagues. We had been so detained by the badness of the roads, and the refractory performances of our steeds, that we concluded to pass the night at this place. At the early hour of three in the morning we were served bread and coffee by our pompous host, who, to lessen the trouble of dressing, had wrapped himself in his blanket. We were soon on our way, riding rapidly over the bed of an ancient lake, which formerly covered the entire plains of Aragua and Valencia. Leaving the rich and beautiful regions of Aragua and Maracai, we entered upon a broader plain, formed by the receeding of the hills to a greater distance from the lake. Bushes and stunted trees, alternating with belts of grass-growing land, were the features which the landscape now presented. We drove for miles, meeting with only an occasional hut on a cultivated plot. Within half a mile of Valencia we passed to our right the Mono, a rocky and precipitous semi-isolated hill, from whose summit can be obtained one of the finest views of the plain and lake.

It was eight A. M. when the rumbling of our coach through the streets of Valencia announced to its inhabitants an arrival, which is not an every-day occurrence, but an event to be signalled by a general cessation of business, and a simultaneous appearance of a multitude of heads from windows, doors, and balconies. Crossing the Rio de Valencia, a stream which flows through the city, we passed up the principal street amid staring crowds, and stopped at the posada of La Bella Alaza, on the eastern side of the Gran Plaza. Immediately the posadero, guests, porters, cooks, and a whole retinue of attendants, came rushing out, and besieged us on every side, so that with difficulty we forced an entrance to the apartment we were to occupy. Our baggage was seized by three times the number needed to carry it, and was followed by as many more, who came thronging into our room, which they so filled that we were scarcely able to move. Their curiosity becoming somewhat satisfied when they had seen and examined every thing it was possible to get hold of, they gradually withdrew, until we were at length left to ourselves.

The city of Valencia is situated in the midst of a most salubrious and fertile valley, which, including the basin of Aragua upon the east, and the grassy plains stretching out upon the west, is about twenty-five leagues in length and five in its greatest breadth. It is difficult to conceive why Caracas, which is farther from the geographical centre of the republic, and so difficult of access from the coast, with only an open roadstead for a port, should have been preferred as the capital of Venezuela to the more accessible and in every respect more desirable place of Valencia, which is only fourteen leagues, by a splendid road, from one of the finest harbors in the world. Valencia has been a favored city; it has never been sacked by an invading army, never thrown down by an earthquake. It was even spared by the tyrant Lopez de Aguirre, whose name spread such terror throughout the republic; and the wild Carib tribe, which came up in hordes from the Orinoco to lay waste the place, were turned back before they had crossed the borders of the plain. Contending parties in the political convulsions of later times have also chosen other places in which to shed each other's blood. Notwithstanding, Valencia has advanced but slowly in growth and prosperity. Its population of ten thousand, three-quarters of a century ago, has scarcely doubled. The most prominent part of the place, as of every Spanish town, is the Gran Plaza, upon the north side of which stands the cathedral, built more than two centuries ago. On the south is the government-house of Carabobo, of which state Valencia is the capital; the remaining sides of the square are occupied by hotels, shops, and private residences. The city has four churches, and two others in process of erection, but which it is more than probable will never be completed. There is one regular newspaper, but in times of revolution, which is the normal condition of the country, two or three are issued.

Our first visit from Valencia was to the beautiful Lake of Tacarigua, which, when the city was founded, in 1555, was one-half league to the eastward, but, by the rapid desiccation of that body of water, it is now distant over two and a half leagues. Leaving the city by the road which leads to Victoria, we soon reached Guias, a little village one and a half league from Valencia; and here, abandoning the main highway, we followed a crooked trail, which took us through a forest tract, then across flourishing plantations of maize, bananas, and groves of cocoa-nut trees, broken by stifling jungles of reeds and bushes. It was noon when we reached the western shores of the lake; when, oppressed by the heat of mid-day, we threw ourselves beneath the grateful shade of trees at the base of a wooded hill, which was at one time an island of the lake, and enjoyed a view that has but few rivals in beauty or interest upon either continent. Formerly, the shores of the lake were the mountains which now form the boundaries of the valleys of Aragua and Valencia; the geological formations of the mountain-slopes, and their fresh-water fossils (*ampullaria* and *planorbis*), embracing species now inhabiting the lake, are unmistakable evidence of the extent of its ancient borders.* How rapid the change of level was previous to the nineteenth century, we have no exact means of estimating; but, judging from the increase in the rapidity of its shrinking since that date, we infer that its rate of diminution formerly was much slower than at present. The historian Oviedo states that when Valencia was founded, in 1555, it was one-half league distant from the western shore of the lake, and Humboldt asserts that, according to his own measurement, in 1800, the town was a little more than twice that distance from its borders, and that the lake was ten leagues long, and nowhere over two or three leagues broad. The last accurate observer also makes mention of there being, at the time of his visit, fifteen islands, and also adds that many formerly such had become, by the retreating of the waters, attached to the main-land, forming promontories. The lake at present is about eight leagues in length, with its width proportionally contracted. Within the last three-quarters of a century, no islands have become attached to the shore, by the lowering of the waters; but, instead, seven new ones have appeared. The height of the lake above the sea is nearly twelve hundred feet. The water has a temperature of 75° to 80° Fahrenheit, and is perfectly fresh, although stated by Eastwick as being brackish. We used it exclusively during our stay upon its borders. Humboldt found that the water upon evaporation left only a small residuum of carbonate of lime, and a little nitrate of potash.

The desiccation of this great basin of Valencia has excited general interest, and is a matter of no small importance to the inhabitants of those regions. During the last half-century the process has been going forward with

* These fossils we found in strata often several feet in thickness; in the vicinity of the lake, the soil, in places, is largely composed of them.

increasing rapidity, and immense tracts of land, which were formerly inundated, are now fertile and cultivated plains; as the country bordering the lake is so low and level, that the lowering of a few inches in the surface of the water lays dry a wide belt of land. The same nature of the circumambient plain also causes considerable portions to be submerged during the rainy period of the year, preventing the planting of maize at that season.

There are twenty-two streams, some of them of considerable size, that flow into the lake, but, as it has no discoverable outlet, the waters must be removed wholly by evaporation. Of the quantity of water which empties into the basin of Valencia, some idea may be formed from the calculations of Cordozzi, in his *Resúmen de la Geografía de Venezuela*, published in 1841. This writer gives the size of the lake as twenty-two square leagues, and the area of the valleys of Caribobo and Aragua, which, from their configuration, give their waters to the basin of Valencia, as eighty-six square leagues. This, united to the twenty-two of the lake, gives a surface of one hundred and eight square leagues, over which it is said there yearly fall seventy-two inches of rain. This estimate will enable us to conceive how rapidly evaporation goes on in the dry and heated atmosphere of the tropics. Certain local causes have tended to greatly accelerate the desiccation of the lake. The mountains which enclose the basin were formerly covered with forest, which retained the moisture of the earth, and produced copious springs that fed the streams. This natural protection to the soil has been removed, the land has become parched, streams dried up, the heat of the valley augmented, and evaporation has consequently become more rapid. The Pao, which was the largest river that flowed into the lake, was, at the close of the seventeenth century, diverted from its original channel for the purpose of irrigating the country to the southward, and its waters allowed to escape in the Llanos. The low depression of the hills at the passage of Bucarito was the outlet of the ancient lake; a rise of the water forty feet above its present level would cause it to discharge as heretofore. In less than a century, at the present accelerated rate with which its shores are receding, desiccated plains, covered with growing crops and luxuriant verdure, will mark the spot the lake now occupies.

CHAPTER V.

Hacienda of Mr. Glöckler.—Coffee.—Cacao.—Tiger-Hunt.—A Tropical Forest.—Lost on the Mountains.—A Cheerless Night.—Exit from the Wilds.—Return to Valencia.—Descent to the Sea-coast.—Papaw-Tree.—"Cow-Tree."—Thermal Springs.—Discomforts of Life at a Hacienda.—Cocoa-Palm.—Mangroves.—Puerto Cabello.

WHILE at Valencia, we made the acquaintance of Mr. Glöckler, the German consul from Hamburg. Mr. Glöckler was the owner of a large estate about two leagues from the city, and thither he invited us for the purpose of a tiger*-hunt among the mountains. The pleasing diversion which such an excursion promised, besides the opportunity presented of making valuable collections from the high altitudes of the Cordilleras, toward whose lofty summits we had often cast a wistful eye during our abode upon the plains, induced us to accept the proposal.

Leaving Valencia upon the road which leads to Puerto Cabello, we soon abandoned it, and, turning to our left, crossed a ridge of hills which brought us into a finely-cultivated, lateral valley, opening upon the larger plain of the lake. It was noon when we alighted at the *hacienda*,† one of the largest and finest we saw in the country, where

---

* The *Felis onça* of naturalists; generally known as the jaguar, or American tiger.

† Hacienda is a term used to designate alike landed estate and the usually large dwelling situated upon the same.

we were kindly received and hospitably entertained. The house, a low two-story structure, occupied one side of a large court-yard of about half an acre in extent, which was enclosed on the remaining sides by high walls, and the small dwellings of the laborers of the hacienda. Outside of the enclosure were cocoa-nut, orange, banana, and lemon trees, loaded with fruit in every stage of perfection. Of the last mentioned there are two species cultivated in Venezuela; one (*Citrus lemonium*), the kind so well known in commerce, the other (*Citrus lumia*) a sweet lemon, in which the acidity that belongs to the other is entirely wanting.

The estate, which stretched far up the mountain acclivity, was devoted principally to coffee-raising. How much might be written of coffee—its growth, uses, and the influence which it exerts commercially, socially, and physically! The temperate valleys of Valencia and Aragua seem peculiarly adapted to its cultivation, the yield being large, and the berry of a superior quality. The site for a coffee-plantation must be such that it can be irrigated during the dry season; and the shrubs need to be shaded by large trees, to protect them from the scorching rays of the sun. If grown from the slip, they will produce their first crop the second year; but usually not much is expected until the third. The average annual yield is one and a half or two pounds from each bush, although sometimes as many as fifteen pounds are gathered from a single plant. The berries grow in fascicles, or clusters, at the end of the branches, and, when ripe, resemble an oblong cranberry.

Another product of these temperate valleys, one which thrives most luxuriantly and forms one of the chief exports of Venezuela, is cacao (*Theobroma cacao*), the chocolate-tree. The cacao is a native of Central and South America, and was unknown to the inhabitants of the Old World, until introduced after the discovery of the New. Among the ancient Aztecs and Incas it was used as a medium of exchange, besides affording them a most delicious beverage and nutritious food. Bananas and the erythrina are planted at the same time with the cacao; the former, which is a very rapidly-growing plant, protects the cacao during the first stages of its growth, being removed as soon as the latter tree attains sufficient size to afford the requisite shade. The cacao-plant seldom rises higher than twenty feet, and commences to bear at the age of six or seven years, yielding two crops annually for an indefinite number of years. The manner in which the fruit grows, attached to the trunks and large limbs of the trees, will strike one as a little curious. It resembles a short, thick cucumber, four or five inches long, and two and a half or three inches in diameter, and contains thirty or forty large, flat beans of a dark-brown color, enveloped in a sweet pulp. One or one and a half pound is the average annual yield of a single tree. Notwithstanding this small return, it is an exceedingly lucrative branch of culture, as a plantation, when once established, requires but little attention beyond the harvesting of the crop.

Toward evening of the same day of our arrival at the estate of the consul, we climbed the mountain to an upper hacienda, also owned by him. On the way we were shown some hieroglyphics, sculptured upon the rocks, the work of a civilization prior to the conquest. The designs were those of animals and various other objects in nature, rudely executed and still in a good state of preservation, notwithstanding the rocks upon which they are carved have been for centuries subjected to the destroying agencies of a tropical climate. On the old road over the mountains from Valencia to Puerto Cabello, and near the latter place, are upon the rocks similar engravings, which must be referred to the same origin and antiquity.

Spending the night at the upper hacienda, at early dawn we were preparing for the excursion of the day—a tiger-hunt among the mountains. Hastily taking our coffee, we mounted our saddles, and were on our way up the Cordillera, attended by two natives and the hospitable German who had charge of the hacienda. From time to time in the ascent we caught a momentary glimpse of the country below through openings in the white fleecy clouds, but, as the highest point of observation was reached, the mist was dispelled, and we had before us a picture that we shall long remember. As we cast our eyes downward, almost beneath our feet we beheld the charming valley we had left, and beyond, separated by a range of wooded hills which appeared scarcely elevated above the surrounding level, was the fertile plain of Valencia, and still farther on the Golden Valleys of Aragua. There was the city of Valencia, and beyond, in the midst of forest and cultivated grounds, was that gem of lakes whose waters glistened under the light of the morning sun. To our left and far distant rose semi-isolated mountains with barren slopes and sharp summits, while to the southward were the sierras of Nirgua and Guique, and beyond, range after range piled itself against the sky. Rarely, indeed, does the eye behold a more glorious prospect than is gained from the lofty mountains of Valencia.

Leaving the animals in charge of one of the natives, with instructions to wait until our return, and taking the other with us for a guide, we plunged into the dense forest. He who is acquainted only with northern woods can have but a faint conception of the primeval forest of the tropics. Gigantic trees rise to a height unknown in temperate regions, displaying the greatest variety in the form and aspect of their foliage. Towering and crested palms shoot upward straight as an arrow, waving their pinion-like leaves in the breezes. Arborescent ferns and grasses, thirty and forty feet in height, add their colossal forms to the greater monarchs of the forest. Parasitic plants cover the huge trunks and limbs of the trees, and vines interlace their wide-spreading branches, forming a thick, tangled mass of verdure through which no ray of the sun ever penetrates. Beneath, constituting what might be called the lower stratum of vegetation, are bushes, ferns, and creeping plants, which are so thickly interwoven as to make a net-work that is almost impenetrable. The earth is densely carpeted with leaves, mosses, and lichens, and strewn in the greatest profusion with thousands of fallen flowers. Such was the forest into which we had entered. Our guide preceded us, opening a way with his *machete*, and the party followed in single file. We had not penetrated far in these deep solitudes before we discovered the fresh tracks of a huge tiger deeply embedded in the soft earth. After several hours of fruitless travel in these tangled wilds, finding pursuit with any prospect of success impossible, we abandoned the attempt, and determined upon our return, taking a different course from the one we had come. But this soon brought us into difficulty, for our circuitous mode of travelling bewildered the guide, and, although he endeavored to keep the fact from us, we were not long in making the rather unpleasant discovery that, for aught we knew, we were plunging deeper and deeper into a boundless wilderness. We would descend one mountain-ridge but to mount laboriously another. We ascended the highest peaks, and climbed to the tops of the tallest trees, only to be rewarded by the same cheerless, interminable line of waving forest. Once were we gladdened by a view of the distant Lake of Tacarigua, but in our wanderings in the inextricable labyrinth of woods our direction was again lost. Nearly every step of our progress had to be cleared with the machete. Slowly we toiled along, dragging our aching bodies wearily up precipitous cliffs, and, bruised and exhausted, would land at the base of the opposite slope. Under these severe exertions one of the party gave out completely, and another was bitten on the hand by a *mapanase*, a venomous serpent, the effects of which caused a frightful swelling of the wounded member, but was prevented from proving fatal by the application of liquid ammonia, an antidote we always took the precaution to be provided with.* Excepting coffee, early in the morning, we had taken nothing since the day previous, and we had brought nothing with us; all our outer garments were left behind, and those we wore were not the better after our experiences of the day.

Darkness at last terminated our wanderings, when we threw ourselves down upon the stony bank of a mountain-torrent which came thundering down from the granitic rocks that were piled above, with a roar that made the surrounding hills tremble. Our scanty clothing protected us but poorly against the chilling atmosphere of the mountains, so that we suffered severely from the cold. The spray from the stream rendered more chilly the air, and a heavy storm, whose rising was indicated by a deeper darkness and stronger gusts of wind through the forest, threatened, for a time, to add to our discomfort; but fortunately it swept over with only a slight dash of rain. Morning at length came. One of the party during the night had unconsciously crawled to the edge of a precipice, and there stretched himself upon some bushes and tangled vines, where a single incautious move or an open-

---

* This specific is employed with success by the natives for the bite of all venomous serpents. It is also useful for the stings of poisonous insects, and no traveller to the tropics should be unprovided with this simple means of security against the evil effects of venomous creatures which inhabit those regions. Dr. Fayrer, of Calcutta, has, however, in a very interesting series of experiments, shown that ammonia cannot counteract the virulent poison of the cobra.

3

ing of the treacherous couch would have let him into the gulf below. Picking up our rusty guns and ourselves, wet and stiff from the rain and cold, we followed down the bed of the torrent, climbing over the huge bowlders of granite which blockaded the narrow gorge, forming cascades and rapids, as the waters went leaping down in their haste to reach the deep valley beneath. Whether the stream flowed into the plain of Valencia or the Atlantic, we knew not, but were certain that it must be in one, and, in either event, by following its course, we would extricate ourselves from the forest. About the middle of the forenoon we reached Trinchara, a hamlet about midway on the road from Valencia to Puerto Cabello. The stream which had been our guide, descending the Cordillera to the northward, emptied its waters into the ocean.

Trinchara was seven or eight leagues from our hacienda by the main road, but by the trail over the mountains the distance was much shorter. The hope of gaining time led us to choose the latter course, which for a while was well defined, but at length became lost in a tangled thicket. We cut our way through dense jungles of reeds and matted woods, climbed precipices, and crossed range after range, until we reached a hut buried in the wilderness. Learning from the occupants the nearest exit from the forest, without further difficulty, save a long and wearisome march, we reached, toward the close of the second day of our setting out, the hacienda of the consul. The native left with our mules had returned with them on the previous night, bringing the tidings of our mysterious absence, which caused no little anxiety to our friends. Our wearied condition induced us to accept proffered hospitality and pass the night at the hacienda, dispatching a servant for our baggage which we had left upon the mountain. On the following morning we returned to the city, and thus ended our unsuccessful and long-to-be-remembered tiger-hunt in the mountains of Valencia.

Our excursions having now embraced most places of interest upon the elevated table-lands of Caracas and the valleys of Aragua and Valencia, we commenced preparations for our journey to the *Llanos* of the interior. We determined, however, before starting, to visit once more the *tierra caliente* of the coast, in order to acquaint ourselves more fully with its botany and zoölogy, and that we might also forward to the States the results of our labors thus far, together with the unnecessary baggage, which would prove an encumbrance to us in our long journey to the Amazons. Accordingly, upon the morning of the 7th of September, we left Valencia for Puerto Cabello, reaching the summit of the Cordillera, over which the road passes, just in time to witness a glorious sunrise. Leaving the crest, we commenced the descent toward the sea through a deep and at first narrow ravine, the road at times running along the steep slope, overlooking deep gorges, and then descending and following the stream below. The sides of the sierras were clothed with a dense and heavy forest. The trees were hung in drapery of long, gray moss, and decked with garlands of convolvulus, passion-flowers, and an endless variety of parasitic plants. Stately monarchs of the forest, stripped of their branches, and covered from base to summit with climbing verdure, rose like huge green columns in the surrounding woods. Palm-trees, of all tropical vegetation the most majestic and beautiful, lifted high toward the heavens their clusters of rich, rustling verdure. Conspicuous in the midst of the eternal green were seen the white trunks of cecropias, and the branchless stems of the papaw-tree, crowned with its immense leaves and gourd-like fruit. The milky juice of the tree is said to have the efficacy of making meat tender when boiled in it for a few minutes; and even animals and fowls, when fed upon the leaves, will have tender flesh, however tough it might have been otherwise. We could not refrain from wishing that this tree, upon the strength of the reputation of its lacteal fluid, might be widely introduced in countries outside of the tropics.

But the most interesting form of vegetation which flourishes in the greatest abundance through these rugged mountain-wilds is the famous *palo de vaca*, or "cow-tree," from which is obtained, when incisions are made in the trunk, a milky juice, sweet and agreeable to the taste, and which is considerably used by the natives, to whom it furnishes an exceedingly nutritious food. The tree attains a great height; the coriaceous leaves are from six to ten inches in length. The wood is red, very hard and durable. Mr. Wallace, in enumerating the various uses to which the fluid is put at Pará upon the Amazons, where it grows in great abundance, says that, applied fresh from the tree as a glue, it is more durable than that used by carpenters; it also makes good custard. "Amid the great number of curious phenomena," says Humboldt, "which I have observed in the course of my travels, I confess there are few that have made so powerful an impression on me as the aspect of the cow-tree." There is, indeed, something peculiarly impressive in this remarkable tree, which will not be obliterated from the mind of the traveller by the many other wonders of the equatorial regions that may come under his observation. That there should be a tree mysteriously elaborating a substance devoid of all acidity, bitterness, and the deleterious qualities usually belonging to lactescent plants, and which is, moreover, a delicious and wholesome aliment, is no less a remarkable fact than a beneficent provision for the inhabitants of a country who rely mainly upon the natural resources of the land for the supplying of their wants.

At eight A. M. we reached Trinchera, the place of our

exit from the mountains when upon our memorable tiger-hunt. Here we halted for coffee, and visited the thermal springs which have given such a world-wide celebrity to this place. They are situated a short distance from the road, in a deep hollow, through which flows a rivulet, from whose surface rose hot vapors, giving forth a strong odor of sulphuretted hydrogen. The springs, which issue from a coarse-grained granite, possess a temperature of 196° Fahrenheit, and, according to Humboldt, are, next to the fountain of Urijino in Japan, the hottest in the world. The vapor of the water deposits carbonate of lime, which forms incrustations upon the plants and stones in the vicinity of the stream. If exposed in an open vessel until the gas has escaped, it becomes in a short time as pure as distilled water.

It was not a little surprising to behold how luxuriant was the vegetation along this hot-water river. Giant trees reared high their heads, and stretched their spreading branches over this Stygian stream, as if delighting in the hot, sulphurous exhalations that rose from the surface, while other plants sprung up in the very midst of the rivulet and flourished where we could not for a moment endure to hold our hand. It is also a singular phenomenon that, at less than fifteen yards from the thermal springs, there gush others from the granitic rock, whose waters are perfectly pure and cold.

Resuming our journey from Trinchera, in four leagues more, accomplished in as many hours, we came to the wretched little village of Cambure, comprising about thirty huts situated in a pestilential swamp. Having rested a couple of hours, we proceeded on our way, the valley widening as we neared the coast, and the stream called *Rio Agua Caliente*, Hot-water River, that flowed at the bottom of the ravine, swelling into a considerable torrent. At 4 P. M., at a sudden turn in the road, we were brought in full view of the ocean. We recalled the time when, from the heights of Silla, we took our farewell look of the Atlantic, but little expecting to see it again until we should behold it three thousand miles away, upon the eastern shore of the continent.

At the point where the road reaches the coast and turns eastward is Palito, a settlement of a dozen hovels, a wretched posada for travellers, and three or four pulperias. Reaching here before sunset, we enjoyed a refreshing bath in the sea, which breaks upon this unprotected coast in heavy surges. We then sauntered through the town and along the line of railway which is building from Puerto Cabello to San Felipe, fifty miles to the westward. This heathenish place of Palito is to be the first station, and also the junction with a branch road that is to diverge over the mountains to Valencia. But it is extremely doubtful whether the lines will ever be completed; operations upon them have been suspended, owing to the inability of the government to fulfil its contract with the company.

Sabbath was spent at Palito, and Monday morning, long before day, we left for Puerto Cabello, following the line of the coast to the eastward over a sandy plain a league in breadth. We forded the Rio Caliente and a number of other streams, which, by their overflow, form stagnant, malarious pools, and sedgy, serpent-abounding jungles— real Stygian marshes. As we approached the city, the plain became more fertile and cultivated, and we passed broad fields of maize, plantations of the broad-leaved banana, and extensive groves of cocoa-nut palms. Within two miles of Puerto Cabello we stopped at a hacienda, where we spent a few days. At night we swung our hammocks in the front corridor; and here we slept—no, contended with *sancudos* (mosquitoes) and fleas, and chafed under the exciting effects of poison-ivy, aggravated by an almost unendurable heat. The plant referred to is the

Rhus toxicodendron, so well known with us; it is the bane of these lowlands of the coast. In such abundance does it grow that it is almost impossible to avoid coming in contact with it, and suffering thereby the usual penalty. We here discovered also another of our northern shrubs, *Sambucus Canadensis*, or common elder. This last we found upon the high table-lands and also far in the interior of the country. These were the only familiar indigenous plants that we met with in our rambles in South America; so different is equatorial vegetation from our northern.

One of the marked features of this hot coast is the groves of cocoa-nut palms which here find a genial home. Not often does Nature produce a tree that is so variously useful to man. The leaves are employed for thatching, their fibres for manufacturing many articles, while their ashes produce potash in abundance. The fruit is eaten raw, and in many ways prepared for food; the nut yields an oil which is an important article of commerce; the hard, woody shell answers for cups; the milk of the fruit is a cooling beverage; the saccharine juice of the tree also affords an excellent drink, either before or after fermentation; while from the young stems is obtained a farinaceous substance similar to that of the sago, or bread-palm.* In the cocoa-nut palm, and the same can be said of palm-trees generally, Nature admirably unites the useful and ornamental. There is no other tree which contributes so largely to supply the wants of the inhabitants of

---

* The bread-palm must not be confounded with the bread-fruit tree (*Carolinea princeps*), which is not indigenous to Venezuela, although common in the country. The last is a majestic exogenous tree with immense, shining leaves two and a half feet in length and two in breadth. The fruit is as large as a cocoa-nut, and contains many chestnut-like seeds, which, cooked, have a taste somewhat resembling that of the potato.

the tropics. It is one of the numerous causes which in southern climes tend to encourage the careless indolence of the people. We can imagine but few more beautiful sights, or a more inviting retreat upon a sultry day, than that of a grove of cocoa-nut palms, and, as we recall the many hours of "luxurious ease" spent beneath their cooling shades, we cannot but exclaim with the poet:

> "Oh stretched amid these orchards of the sun,
> Give me to drain the cocoa's milky bowl,
> And from the palm to draw refreshing wine!"

Distant from our hacienda not over half a mile was the sea, whither we frequently resorted. Fringing the shore was a belt of mangrove-trees, whose aërial roots interlacing form an impenetrable thicket, that is submerged at every rise of the tide. This submarine lattice-work is covered with shell-fish, clinging to its branches, and with sea-weeds, drifted thither by the waves, while crabs and mollusks in infinite numbers here shelter themselves from the violence of an open sea. Thus mangrove-forests, by deposits from the waves among their tangled net-work of roots, cause a gradual encroachment of the land upon the ocean; but this increase of territory results in their own destruction; for, as the shore recedes, and their roots are no longer washed by the tides, the trees perish, and mark by their partially-buried trunks the ancients limits of the ocean. The deleterious properties possessed by this submarine vegetation, accompanied with the noxious exhalations that usually arise from marshy ground covered with forest, especially in a heated climate, render these regions along the coast exceedingly unhealthy. The stifling heat of these arid plains seemed to us almost insupportable, after having enjoyed the cool and delightful atmosphere of the valleys among the Cordilleras. The amount of rain that falls annually is much less than at Valencia, and irrigation is necessary to preserve verdure and promote fertility.

At the expiration of a week spent upon this burning and pestilential plain, we took up our abode in Puerto Cabello, the port of entry to Valencia. Affording good commercial facilities, it has become a town of considerable importance, containing a population of ten thousand, among which are many foreigners, in whose hands is much of the business of the place. We see here more indications of thrift and enterprise than we have observed elsewhere in the country. The trade is chiefly in exports, of which coffee, cacao, cotton, hides, and indigo, form the greater part. The harbor, unlike the roadstead of La Guaira, is well sheltered, there being but a narrow entrance upon the west, which is also protected by islands, and by the natural curvature of the main-land; so that vessels can ride at anchor within, secure from the sea which breaks so heavily upon the outer coast. The bay swarms with voracious sharks, so that only at the peril of life can the water be entered; while at La Guaira these cetaceous monsters are harmless creatures, and there the sea is continually filled with bathers, and with natives engaged in transferring freight from shipboard to land. The defences of the town are a battery, which guards the entrance to the harbor; another that stands to the east of the city; with a castle which crowns a rocky eminence five hundred feet high, overlooking the place. There is, however, but little danger to be apprehended from foreign invasion, the security of the city being threatened only by the political convulsions to which this country is subject.

Our stay at Puerto Cabello, which was necessarily short, now drew to a close, and with it terminated our rambles in Northern Venezuela.

CHAPTER VI

OVER THE MOUNTAINS TO THE LLANOS.—AFLOAT IN THE FOREST.

Water-system of South America.—Our Route.—Leave Puerto Cabello.—
Last Visit to Valencia.—A South American Road.—Fording a River.—
Wild Scenery.—Night at a Posada.—First View of Llanos.—Their Extent and General Features.—Town of Pao.—Embarked for Baul.—Our
Bongo.—"Very bad" to wash before Breakfast.—Palms.—Bam-
boos.—Alligators.—Howling Monkeys.—Lost in the Forest.—Navigating under Difficulties.—Shooting Rapids.—Night at a Llano Hut.

THE water-system of South America is a remarkable
one, not only in the vastness of its majestic rivers, but also
in the curious anastomosing of its great streams. The
Orinoco, Rio Negro, and Amazons, with their extended and
united arms, reach around and island the northeastern
portion of the continent, embracing Guiana, with a large
part of Venezuela, and a considerable portion of Brazil.
You might circumnavigate this tract with a canoe. No
continent affords better commercial facilities. Steamers
may pass up the Amazons, by its Peruvian waters, to the
foot of the Andes. The continent is thus not only
traversable its entire breadth, but also length, by means
of its water-courses. A canoe starting in at the delta of
the Orinoco can be paddled lengthwise of the continent to
the mouth of the Rio de la Plata, the paddling being
exchanged for short towages around the rapids of the
Upper Orinoco and Madeira Rivers.

But we must forego these general remarks, and, anticipating the expectations of our readers, recount some of the experiences and incidents which make up the history of our voyages upon these rivers. Let us first briefly designate the route pursued across the continent. From Puerto Cabello, we made the passage of the Cordilleras to the head-waters of the Pao, a tributary of the Apure, and passed down that river to its confluence with the latter, and then down the Apure to the Orinoco. Then we ascended that river, dragging our canoes around the cataracts encountered near its middle waters, and crossed by a portage of ten miles to the Rio Negro.* Down the black waters of the Rio Negro we floated to the Amazons, and then, exchanging our little craft for a steamer, passed down that majestic river to the sea. The distance traversed was over three thousand miles, with obstacles to overcome that can only be conceived of by those who have penetrated into the trackless wilds of these almost unfrequented regions. Much of the journey was performed by canoe across inundated plains, where the sun is the only guide to the traveller; through flooded forest, penetrable only as a path is opened with the axe; and upon impetuous and rock-obstructed rivers. Our bed at night was often the bank of some stream, or in the deep gloom of the forest, with the roaring of crocodiles, the plaintive cry of monkeys, and the howl of tigers to lull us to sleep. Moreover, the climate of the interior was exceedingly hot and malarious, and means of transportation were so limited that scarcely sufficient could be carried to meet our most urgent necessities during our protracted voyage of four months.

Our first care was to dispatch to the States every thing excepting what would be absolutely indispensable to us

---

* This portage might have been avoided by following the Cassiquiare, a circuitous water-channel, which unites the waters of the two rivers.

upon our journey. For the sake of the curious, we will incidentally remark that, aside from the suit worn, which was woollen throughout, the extra clothing of each, to which were added a few other necessary articles, was packed in an ordinary army haversack. Each one was furthermore supplied with a *cobija*, or *poncho*, and hammock, and a gun with its accompanying paraphernalia. A few simple instruments that were also added to our stock, with a botanical box and press, completed our outfit, the entire weight of which did not exceed one hundred and twenty-five pounds, or an average of about forty pounds to a man.

Preparations for our journey being completed, we left Puerto Cabello upon the afternoon of the 17th of September, reaching Valencia upon the evening of the following day, where we spent one day in concluding arrangements for the journey of eighteen leagues over the Cordilleras to Pao—the head of canoe-navigation upon Pao River. A donkey, which we afterward gave away, was purchased for ten pesos, for the transportation of our baggage, and by 5 P. M. we were ready for starting. It was not without many misgivings that we left the genial and salubrious climate of the mountain valleys for the submerged and malarious regions of the Llanos, and the wild, unexplored forests of the Orinoco. We parted, too, with many regrets from the friends formed during our brief stay at Valencia, whose kindness will not soon be forgotten. Especially are we indebted to Señor E. Staal, a letter of introduction from whom to a gentleman in Pao was the commencement of a series which extended from place to place across the continent, and which proved of invaluable service to us. After many a hearty shake of the hand, accompanied with endless "*buenas viajes*," and "*Dios guardes*," we separated, turning our faces toward the sierras of Nigua, with its long lines of shadowy hills stretching away in the distance. As we wended our way through the narrow streets, every window, door, and veranda, was filled with heads, some drawn thither from idle curiosity to see " Los Americanos," others to give us a parting *adios*.

The sun was lingering above the western hills when we made our exit from the city, shedding its golden beams over mountains, plains, and forests, as if to give us one more glorious view of this lovely valley. We shall not soon forget either the beauties of that sunset eve, or the many scenes and associations of Valencia. It was after dark when we halted for the night at the same miserable posada which had sheltered us upon a previous occasion, when overtaken by night, and lost upon the plains. In a small room, shared with a man and boy, benches, tables, boxes, saddles, boards, poles, hoes, water-jars, barrels, green cornstalks, sancudos, and fleas, we managed to pass the night. It was scarcely dawn when we were again on our journey, our road leading across a grassy plain toward the range of hills which separates the valley of Valencia from the Llanos beyond.

One who has travelled only over the finely-built highways of our country, can have but a faint conception of what is analogous to such in the tropics. A road here means simply a beaten path, with branches diverging in every direction, to the utter bewilderment of the traveller. Some of the roads consist of a number of parallel paths, worn by the tread of animals into deep gullies, which, upon the mountain-slopes, in the season of rains, constitute water-channels, through which torrents flow down, rendering travelling not only exceedingly difficult but dangerous. No bridges span the streams, which must be crossed by fording or swimming, while exposed to voracious caimans, or alligators, and other dangerous pests of these tropical waters.

It was along one of these trails that we were now directing our course. We found the streams greatly swollen, and the road nearly impassable, for the rainy season had not yet drawn to a close; but we met with no serious obstacle until some three leagues on our journey, when a river, larger than any we had yet encountered, threw itself across our path. We sat down upon the bank of the swollen torrent to discuss the probabilities of a safe transit, and to watch a party of natives who were making the passage. The animals were forced to swim, while their cargoes were carried over upon the heads of the men. We watched the novel spectacle until sufficiently acquainted with the *modus operandi*, when we commenced the crossing, taking our packages upon our heads, *à la creole*. We reached the opposite shore safely; but our little donkey, unable to stem the current, was swept down the stream; but, fortunately, the precaution had been taken to attach a long rope to his neck, and by this poor *burro* was dragged to land. After some time consumed in these ferrying operations, we continued on over the plain a league farther, when we commenced the gradual ascent of the mountains, and, toward the close of the day, we stood upon the summit of the first range of the Cordillera crossed in going to Pao from Valencia, where we enjoyed a wide sweep of wild mountain scenery. Southward rugged and barren ranges were piled one upon another, and at their bases lay picturesque valleys, slightly wooded, and sprinkled over with little huts, surrounded with patches of maize and bananas, which presented charming spots in the midst of the mountain ruggedness. Wending our way down along the edge of a precipitous cliff into one of the beautiful glens stretched out beneath us, we stopped for the night at a mud posada, a way-side inn, glorying in total darkness within.

The sun had not yet risen when we were again mak-

ing our way over a wild, barren region, either winding
through rugged defiles, or mounting by circuitous paths
the ranges of the Cordilleras. The trail at one time
would lead down abrupt descents into deep and almost
inextricable ravines, not unfrequently between cliffs nearly closing above us, over ranges, furrowed deeply by
torrents, and so precipitous and slippery that our animal
could mount them only as he was lifted almost bodily up
the heights. After a day of wearisome climbing we
reached by 5 P. M. a posada, whose inviting appearance,
added to the uncertainty of finding another stopping-
place within a convenient distance, induced us to make
this the terminus of our day's journey. Dinner being immediately called for, was promised *pronto* (quickly), which
meant any time before next morning. A familiar cry,
heard soon after, prognosticating evil to a feathered
gamester, was suggestive of good things coming. For
three mortal hours, however, we waited for further developments, when at length came the summons, *Venga á
comer.* Turning to the farther corner of the apartment,
where we had been reclining in our hammocks, the faint
glimmering of a light from a bit of rag burning in a cup
of fat revealed to us, upon a table spread with a dirty
cloth, the disjointed members of a half-cooked fowl,
which, judging from its toughness, must have enjoyed
the walks of life for a much longer period of years than
usually falls to the lot of his race. In addition, there
were three calabashes of soup to be eaten by means of
pieces of broken crockery used as spoons.

In the morning, after the customary calabash of coffee,
we resumed our journey, winding along giddy heights,
where a traveller's sense of insecurity is not lessened by
the momentary prospect of meeting, at any turn of his
path, scarcely wide enough for his beast to tread, loaded
animals going in the opposite direction, which, rushing

down, threaten to hurl every opposing obstacle over the
frightful cliff.   Trains of animals crossing the Cordilleras
have a bell attached to the neck of the leader, or are preceded by a drover with a conch-shell that is blown to
give notice of the approaching line, but which does not always prevent a collision that sometimes results most disas-
trously.   We frequently encountered troops of pack-mules
and donkeys going to Valencia; but, being always on the
qui vive, we were spared any of these unpleasant episodes.
We at length descended into a heavily-timbered valley,
and, rising from this to the summit of the last range of
the Cordillera, we beheld for the first time the Llanos of
Venezuela.   One can scarcely imagine the pleasure afforded us, as, after travelling amid the wildest of mountain scenery, we looked down upon this great sea of verdure which, joined with the sylvas of Brazil and the
pampas of Buenos Ayres, stretched far away thousands
of miles into the regions of southern frost.

The Llanos of Venezuela are separated from the great
forest of the Amazons by the mountains of Guiana, or, as
sometimes termed, the sierras of Parima, and bounded
upon the north by the littoral range of the coast, bearing
different local names, as the mountains of Puerto Cabello,
Caracas, and Cumana.   The plains thus have a width of
about four hundred miles, while in length they stretch
from the great delta of the Orinoco more than a thousand
miles westward to the Andes of Colombia.   By far the
greater portion of this immense plain is covered with
luxuriant grass, but often broken by tracts of forest, and
belted by the heavily-wooded courses of the many rivers.
Draining these savannas is the Orinoco, the second river
in size of South America, which is swollen by the thousand streams from the mountains of Guiana upon the south,
and from the Andes of Colombia, and the coast-chain of
Venezuela, upon the west and north.   The swelling of

these rivers during the season of rains causes the inundation of large portions of the country, so that it can be traversed only by canoes. When the waters subside, the grass, which has been parched under the cloudless sky of the dry season preceding the overflow, quickly springs up, and in a short time the earth is again clothed with beautiful verdure. That part of the Llanos situated north of the Orinoco and Apure is divided into tracts known as the plains of Maturin, Barcelona, and Guarico, while the more southern portions are known as the savannas of the Apure, Meta, and Guaviare. The general slope of the Llanos is toward the northeast; or, rather, they describe a quadrant, the upper portion of the basin sloping toward the north, the lower toward the east, which gives direction to the waters of the Orinoco. The slight elevation of these great plains, as well as that of the basin of the Amazons, is one of the striking features in their physical aspect. "If," says Humboldt, "from the effects of some peculiar attraction, the waters of the Atlantic were to rise fifty toises * at the mouth of the Orinoco, and two hundred toises at the mouth of the Amazons, the floods would submerge more than the half of South America. The entire eastern declivity, or the foot of the Andes, now six hundred leagues distant from the coast of Brazil, would become a shore beaten by the waves."

One of the most significant of the streams that flow into the basin of the Llanos of Venezuela from the northern Cordilleras is the Rio Pao, which, taking its rise among the mountains of the littoral chain, winds over the plains in a southerly direction, assuming the name of Portuguesa before its confluence with the Apure. Distant one and a half leagues from the summit of the sierras, where we first came in view of the Llanos, is situated the town of Pao, upon the bank of the stream whose name it bears.

* A toise is a French measure, containing about 6.4 English feet.

It was after sunset when we entered the place, which comprises about five thousand inhabitants.

Through the assistance of Mr. E. Rodriguez, a German resident, we secured a canoe and crew for our journey to Baul, the first town reached in descending the Pao, and about half the distance to San Fernando de Apure. Supplies for a week's voyage were requisite, and these we set about procuring. First was fresh beef, brought to us in leathery strips and gristly sheets, which, after it was thoroughly salted, we dried, and then, with the Venezuelians, called it *carne seca*. To our meat were added cassava, goats' cheese, salt, papelon, or the consolidated sugar of the country, bottles of manteca, or butter, with a liberal quantity of green plantains. Then there were culinary utensils—two iron pots, one for coffee, the other for general purposes—and the indispensable machete, which answered for axe and carving-knife.

The morning of the 25th of October, after three days' delay at El Pao, we were ready to embark upon our voyage. Our craft was long—to uneducated American minds, like ours, too long—but was not at all successful as to width, but then it is in canoes as little as in mortals to command success in every particular, and we can say for our boat that length covered a multitude of sins as well as feet. For a picture of it, scoop out forty feet of a tree, with the largest diameter less than two feet, and the average hardly more than one, build a thatch, or *carroza*, over the middle half, just filling out the original contour of the log, tie a rough steering-oar to the stern, and call the whole a *bongo*, and you have it complete. As at that time we were modest and unpretending, our crew was small. First, Viviano, generalissimo of the *palanca*, armed with a long pole, occupied the bow. His duty was to walk toward the stern as far as the carroza would permit, leaning heavily on his palanca, placed on the bottom of the river, or any neighboring rock or limb, as was most convenient, then, using his pole as a balancer, to walk, *à la Blondin*, up the inclined plane formed by the rise in the bow, and repeat the operation. From his head to his knees, Viviano differed not essentially from the generality of mortals, but below that was somewhat unique. At his knees his legs dispersed, choosing paths of life as diverging as possible. Whether Nature intended Viviano for a palancasist, *par excellence*, is doubtful, but his form was undoubtedly of great advantage to him, for, where more commonplace men would walk with fear and uncertainty, he, his feet just fitting nicely to the sides of the bongo, walked with unconcern. Ever hungry and ever eating, Viviano was yet the leanest of men; but that fact was easily accounted for from his always talking when compatible with eating. Our *patron*, Alvino by name, who handled the clumsy steering-oar, was an old man of eighty-two summers, if it is possible to say " summers " in reference to that country, and was the father of Viviano and the small boy, who was perched on " airy nothing," behind his father. To the words of the patron, his sons and every one whom we met paid the greatest deference, and indeed the respect paid always to old age was very marked; rarely did a young person salute an old man without kneeling. El Patron's knowledge of geography was not extensive, but at least patriotic; his enumeration of the countries of the world ended with Venezuela, uttered triumphantly as the incontrovertible acme of grandeur. Under the carroza were stowed our supplies, utensils, arms, and baggage; and there was also, as Alvino gravely informed us, to be our place of refuge from the storms, although it was difficult for us to conceive how, when every thing was in, there would be space left for more than one at either end, and for only half the length of the body at that.

At length we were under way, floating down the swift-rolling waters of the Pao, adding the strength of the palanca to the progressive force of the current. Picture to yourself a narrow, many-folded river—to which Tiber in its turbidest was, undoubtedly, as a clear and sparkling fountain—a stream so opaque that the idea suggested itself to one of the party that perhaps " Afric's sunny fountain " had got lost, and by mistake had " rolled down its golden sand " into El Dorado, which was successful in damping it a little. However, so long as our gallant craft was floated, we could not complain, and, as for drink, it went further and gave us meat which, if not as nutritious, was at least not tougher than the strips of *toro* which ornamented our carroza. The wooded banks were low, but a few feet above high water, with now and then a hut, just visible through the thick foliage of banana-leaves.

Our first day's voyage was short, as the hour was late when we started, and nearly three hours were consumed in obtaining a meal, which an untimely rain greatly impeded in preparation. The extended acquaintance of our patron, and the respect his whitened head everywhere commanded, readily gained us admission for the night at the house of a friend, the occupants retiring to a neighbor's hut, giving us entire possession. Aroused by the patron at the first appearance of day, we reëmbarked, and were soon shooting swiftly down the current beneath the shadows of the dark forest which rose from either bank. From the depths of those solitudes no sound was heard, and naught broke the death-like stillness of the early morning save the stroke of the oar as it cleaved the waves, and the plunge of the alligator, as, startled from his rest, he glided off the slimy bank, and disappeared in the turbid waters.

Reaching, soon after sunrise, the base of a low, rocky hill, we drew ashore for breakfast. At once we betook ourselves to our morning ablutions, when the chiding voice of Alvino, our ever-watchful guardian, was heard, assuring us it was "*muy malo*" (very bad) to wash before breakfast, as it brought on the *calenture*, or fever. This superstitious notion we found very prevalent among the people of the Llanos; but, notwithstanding the warning of our patron, who was evidently neither a Pharisee nor a holder of their traditions, we went on with our bath. Unfortunately for our side of the question, two of the party eventually were prostrated with the *calenture*, when the old sage shook his hoary head in confirmed conviction of the fulfilment of his predictions. Generally we landed but once during the day for a meal, and that for breakfast, about nine or ten o'clock; our dinner—if the hour will allow the name—being taken when we bivouacked for the night.

Upon the morning referred to above, we delayed several hours, while our boatmen gathered smooth, silicious stones of an oval shape, and large blocks of sandstone. The latter, when hollowed upon one side, together with one of the smaller stones, form primitive mills, such as are seen in every Venezuelian hut. Upon the Llanos, where nothing more compact than sand can be obtained, these stones command a good price; the larger size, in weight about fifteen pounds, bringing from two to three pesos each, and the smaller ones, of two pounds, twenty-five cents apiece. As the remuneration received from us by our patron was not large, we willingly acceded to his wish to collect the stones; and, after our arrival at Baul, we had the satisfaction of knowing that he realized a good compensation for his labors.

With our extra ballast we again got under way, gliding down through the forest channel, now no longer silent, but awakened by Nature's gay-plumaged vocalists, loquacious parrots and paroquets. Aquatic birds covered the water and stalked the shore; while alligators, with opened jaws, lay basking in the bright sun upon the shelving borders of the stream. Not more strange and varied were the forms of animated life than were the beauty and exuberance of vegetation, which rose above us in walls of eternal green, variegated with flowers that decked richly the trees, and filled the air with their fragrance. The small, slender, and delicately-pinnated foliage of mimosas and tamarinds contrasted pleasingly with the many large, coriaceous-leaved species that filled the forest. The arum, that giant of aërial plants, trumpet-flowered bignonias, banisterias, and passion-flowers, with thousands of orchidaceous plants of exquisite beauty, covered the branches and embowered the trees. Palms rose in forms and numbers unknown in the higher altitudes of the Cordilleras. Here was the *palma de cobija* (*Corypha tectorum*) or roofing palm, its palmate leaves few in number, with the lower ones withered and drooping, giving the tree a gloomy and mournful aspect. The stem, twenty to thirty feet in height, like that of the palmetto so abundant along our Southern seaboard, is remarkable for maintaining a constant diameter of eight or ten inches in all individuals of the species. The wood is hard and durable, making excellent building-timber where exposure to the weather is necessary, nor is it subject to the ravages of ants, which are such wood-destroyers in the tropics. The leaves are employed by the natives of the Llanos for covering roofs.

But a far more beautiful palm growing here than the one just described, and one more generally useful, is the Moriche (*Mauritia flexuosa*), or what is known as the sago or bread-tree of the country. It resembles the above in the form of its leaves, which are folded like a fan; but these are much larger than are those of the former species, as is also the trunk, which attains a height of fifty and even eighty feet. It is a tree of wide distribution and very abundant, and with it is intimately connected the existence of the Warauns, a tribe of Indians who inhabit the delta, or submerged lands of the mouth of the Orinoco. Their habitations are hung between the trees, above the reach of wild beast and inundating floods. The farinaceous pith of the stem, its fruit, and saccharine juice, supply the dwellers of these aërial homes with food and drink, while from the fibres of the leaves they weave for themselves mats and hammocks. "It is curious to observe," says Humboldt, "in the lowest degree of human civilization, the existence of a whole tribe depending on one single species of palm-tree, similar to those insects which feed on one and the same flower, or on one and the same part of a plant." This veritable "Tree of Life," with its large, shining leaves, preserves a beautiful verdure through the season of greatest drought, and rises above the summer-parched and barren soil of the Llanos, a guide to the traveller and a grateful shelter from the heat of the noonday sun. The tree thrives only in moist ground, and at its base may generally be found a fountain of refreshing water; or such can be obtained by a slight excavation. The fact that this palm-tree is always found in the vicinity of water has given rise to the belief, among the natives, that the tree attracts moisture from the earth; but in this, as well as in many other cases, they have confounded cause and effect. The sweet and grateful juice of the Moriche palm, either fresh or fermented; the unexpanded young leaves, or what is called cabbage, a most excellent vegetable; the sago, from the farinaceous pith of the trunk; the fruit, which, like the plantain, can be eaten raw when mature, or prepared by cooking in an almost endless variety of ways; the spathe of the fruit, resembling coarsely-woven cloth, and useful for bags, mats, and the scanty apparel sometimes worn by the native, the value of the leaves for thatching, and their fibres for cordage, bowstrings, fish-nets, lines, sails, baskets, cloth, and hammocks—all these from a single tree, supplying the people in abundance with all the necessaries of existence, is only another instance of the wonderful profuseness and adaptation of Nature, in this rude and uncultivated land, for supplying the wants of its inhabitants.

But of the many and varied forms of vegetation that shoot up in such rich luxuriance along the banks of the Pao, and adorn the forests and the plains of this humid clime, forming such a distinctive feature in the landscape, none, perhaps, impresses the traveller from northern latitudes more than the group of grasses. Among these the gudua or bamboo (*Bambusa gudua*) is by far the most majestic and picturesque. It is also a most useful plant to the natives, furnishing them material for building, their hollow stems serving for posts and rafters; and, when split and laid open, they form boards for enclosing their huts; and their joints, which are filled with a refreshing drink for the thirsty traveller, answer for cups, vessels, and various other purposes. This arborescent grass loves a humid soil, and is found abundant along the borders of streams, where the stems shoot up in thick clumps to the height of forty and even fifty feet, with a diameter of from four to six inches.* Masses of long, slender leaves crown the summit of these pliant trunks, bending them downward by their weight into graceful curves, which, by their union over streams that they line, form long, beautiful arcades of evergreen verdure, through which the voyager floats in his canoe, his pathway gleaming with myriads of insects, that rival in the brilliancy of their coloring the richest gems. "Their slender forms are susceptible to the slightest breeze, and, when the gale of the hurri-

---

* Fletcher makes mention of this giant grass being found, on the Organ Mountains of Brazil, from eighty to one hundred feet in height and eighteen inches in diameter.

cane comes, these groves of bamboo exchange an aspect of beauty for that of grandeur. They are heaved and tossed like the billows of the sea, and their rich foliage, driven in every direction, appears like surges breaking on the rocks." *

We can convey to our readers but a faint conception of the richness and exuberance of the vegetation which forms a belt of varying width along the banks of the Llanos. So interested had we been in the countless objects of attraction which were continually coming before us as we moved down the stream, that we were scarcely conscious of the flight of time. The sun had already disappeared behind the deep-green wall of verdure before we hauled up our canoe upon a stony beach for the night. A fire was soon blazing from the drift-wood which lined the shore, and the odor of stewing beef and plantains foretold the evening meal. The impenetrability of the matted woods obliged us to sleep upon the rocky bank of the stream, where we spread our blankets as far as possible from the water, that we might lessen the chances of our furnishing a banquet to the various caimans which filled the river, and at night sought the shore. Truly not a comforting reflection to haunt our dreams, that we were momentarily liable to be aroused from our slumbers just in time to find ourselves within the capacious jaws of one of these cannibalistic monsters, the next moment to be crushed out of existence. The scaly saurians must have bent their steps that night in quest of other game, for were mained undisturbed by them, but fell a prey to a not much less dreaded enemy—sancudos—which swarmed the river-banks.

Responding to the call of our patron at the earliest dawn, we reëmbarked. So, floating down, the half-wake-

* "Adventures in South and Central America." Paez.

4

fulness, half-sleep of the dusky morning, hushing even Viviano, we left our camp behind. Now and then we would pass beneath rustling, sighing banana-groves, which, waving like great fields of corn at evening, brought to our half-sleeping minds blended pictures of home and southern scenes. To one who has never seen tropical forests, no word-painting can convey any idea how grand and weird and graceful they are—they stand so unutterably mysterious and dark, as if—a race chained ages ago by a conquering will—they, grown old and hoary, are waiting a release to being.

By the time that we were fairly awake, we reached a spot where the banks, breaking, extended a muddy flat on the left side. Here we landed for breakfast, and, while this was preparing, we wandered into the forest with our rifles, proceeding in the direction whence was heard the plaintive cry of *araguatoes*, apparently near at hand. But we were as yet unenlightened as to how deceiving is the distance these howling monkeys can be heard, and so were enticed farther and farther into the tangled jungle. At length we came to the object of our search—a group of large monkeys, walking leisurely along the branches of a tree, casting down suspicious glances upon the intruders on their realms. Selecting the finest-looking fellow, he was brought wounded to the ground; when the whole band, that had ceased their noise at our approach, set up again a most terrific howling. As we stood a little exultant over the bleeding animal, he turned up his large eyes, filled with tears, and, casting upon us a look that we shall ever remember, uttered a mournful cry, which was answered by the wails of his companions in the trees.

The araguatoes, which are the largest monkeys of the New World, are represented by several species. According to measurement, we found one of these animals (*Myce-*

FLOODED LLANOS.

les ursinus) four feet from tip to tip, or about three feet
when in an erect posture. This species is the most common, has thick fur of a reddish-brown color, and a long,
prehensile tail, which answers as a third hand. The features of its face have a grave and melancholy expression ;
its beard is long, and its movements like the slow and
measured gait of an old man. It generally seems perfectly indifferent as to what is transpiring about it ; but, when
aroused, its whole aspect changes, and it will perform evo-
lutions through the trees with surprising agility. As
Humboldt observes, "monkeys are melancholy in proportion as they have more resemblance to man. Their
sprightliness diminishes as their intellectual faculties appear to increase." In disposition the araguato is mis-
chievous and savage, and will, when wounded, attack
man in a most ferocious manner. It cannot be tamed,
and shows none of that affection for human beings which
some of the smaller species of the monkey-tribe exhibit.
It is gregarious in its habits, and delights in the solitary
forest, feeding upon nuts and fruits. One peculiarity
that distinguishes the howlers from other members of
the monkey group is, the remarkable development of the
larynx, by which it is enabled to produce those tremendous noises that are heard at so great a distance. When
the causes were favorable for the propagation of sounds,
we heard the yelling of these creatures over half a league.
Frequently during the darkness of the night they break
forth with their terrible howls, such as deeply impress the
traveller who hears them for the first time, and "leads
him to suppose," as truthfully observes Waterton, "that
half the wild beasts of the forest were collecting for the
work of carnage: now it is the tremendous roar of the
jaguar, as he springs on his prey ; now it changes to his
deep-toned growlings, as he is pressed on all sides by su-

perior force; and now you hear his last dying moan beneath a mortal wound."

There is, perhaps, no animal that possesses a greater interest than the monkey. It has been the subject of countless nursery-tales, and a fruitless source of fiction, arising from that inherent propensity so characteristic of human nature for making what is marvellous appear still more so. The oft-repeated story, familiar to every boy, and which finds credence among so many, of monkeys crossing streams on aërial bridges, constructed from their own bodies, exists only in fancy. Travellers to South America have often referred to it as one of the astonishing feats of these animals. In the course of our travels in the tropics, during which we saw multitudes of these creatures, our observations convinced us that there was no foundation for the truth of the tale of the bridge-building monkeys; and in this belief we were, moreover, further confirmed by the statement of the natives, who testified to their having never witnessed such a novel performance. Humboldt also says that five years' observations of these animals led him to place no confidence in the statements respecting these monkey-bridges.

Returning to our canoe from our ramble in the forest, we found in waiting a smoking breakfast of *sancocho*, the national dish of the Venezuelian—a concoction of beef, yuca, bananas, peppers, garlics, and annatto* for a coloring principle. Our energetic Viviano had also been on a foraging expedition with Angel, the small boy, to a house upon the opposite bank, and returned with plenty of milk,

---

* Annatto is the product of a shrub (*Bixa orellana*) ten or twelve feet in height, with a foliage resembling our common lilac. The bush bears a prickly bur, like the chestnut, only smaller, that contains the seeds from which the coloring substance is obtained. It grows wild throughout Venezuela, and is extensively cultivated in Brazil, constituting one of the exports from that country.

enabling us to enjoy the luxury of *café con leche*. We were amused to see our patron pound the tough, leathery, jerked meat between two stones; but it was not long before we learned to follow his example, and even then, with our full quota of molars, experienced no slight difficulty, and much hard work, in making an impression on the nearest approach to leather that ever went by the honorable name of meat.

On again, all the morning, till toward noon the banks began to sink, and finally were not to be distinguished from the river, save by the lines of forest that marked their limits. Then we knew that we had reached the delta country of El Pao, and, coming to an *igarapé*, or canoe-path, we turned in and deserted a river that soon would have deserted us. But our igarapé soon lost all individuality, and we floated in a flooded, tangled forest, with no path but what we might cut ourselves. The difficulty of this can only be apparent to those who have undergone a like experience. Our bongo, long beyond all proportion, and as cranky as is natural to a log, could make no short turns, and continually suggested the possibility of our becoming food for the caimans. Then the matted and snake-like curtains of vines, aërial roots and branches, hard as southern wood only can be, presented an obstacle almost insurmountable, had it continued long. Often, after having cut a way in one direction, we would be brought to a stand-still by a fallen tree, or the necessity of a short turn, and be obliged to back out and try again. Occasionally Viviano would utter a low hush, and, gathering himself into the smallest possible compass, push silently back. That meant, usually, an immense nest of bees, or perhaps a long, green, velvet spotted snake stretched out along the branches. Sometimes the water would be shallow, and we would float on a slimy mass of black mud, requiring all of Viviano's strength and skill to continue our journey and keep us right side up. On one of these occasions, when the mixture was a little denser than usual, Viviano, bracing his palanca against a tree, bent all his might to cleave the flood, but unfortunately his pole slipped, and, his very form aiding the catastrophe, by holding his feet firmly in the boat, he disappeared headlong into the chocolate-colored paste. Both El Patron and Angel screamed out simultaneously, "Look out for the caiman!" but Viviano needed no warning to hasten his return to the boat, and so great was his nervous hurry that, had it not been for a friendly tree to steady us, we should have upset. The wrath in the face of our muchacho warned us not to laugh, but his mud-lorn features were too much for us; and we were forced to grin audibly. As a consequence, Viviano was grandly silent the rest of the day. Providentially for us, the forest along the river-banks never extends very far back from the stream, and late in the afternoon we emerged from our toiling labyrinth into the wide Llanos. But Llanos no longer—rather a great sea, illimitable in extent, but very limitable in depth; lacking the ceaseless motion of the ocean, it was ten times more lonely and waste. Silence does not necessarily enhance loneliness. The forest through which we passed was at mid-day as silent as the grave; the few birds flitted about noiselessly without a note of song, yet the forest even then was as a company of friends, compared to the loneliness of the Llanos, which, however, were flooded with a multitude of noises. Numberless *guacharacas*, whose name itself means ever-moaning, myriads of ducks, geese, and water-birds of every kind, filled the air with strange cries, till finally, as the sun went down, they disappeared and left us still. For a short distance out from the forest stood isolated trunks of trees, which, covered deep under luxuriant masses of vines, were shaped into many graceful and often grotesque forms. Sometimes in the rapidly-gathering dusk we would seem to see a thatched hut rise up friendly before us, but, on approaching it, some disturbed bird would fly out with a scream and dispel the illusion.

For some time before we reached the open water, we perceived that our crew were in doubt as to the direction, and just as the sun went down we were brought to a stand-still on a little spot of land rising out of the water, with no idea where to turn. El Patron and Viviano left the boat to have a reconnoitre and consultation, while we waited for them in a dubious frame of mind. "Angel, we are lost, are we not?" "Yes, sir." A pleasant idea, that of spending the night in the boat, no possibility of lying down, the air full of the deadliest miasma, while the low humming song from millions of tiny pipers, gradually growing louder and louder, told us of a night of torture worse than the mere loss of sleep.

But our journey for the day was not yet at an end. As we sat meditating in the dark, there came to us faintly a roar as of distant water. "El cañon," said our patron, and we immediately started in the direction of the sound. Soon we entered a little narrow stream, barely wide enough for our canoe, but running with considerable swiftness, which rapidly increased, till we were hurrying along like a race-horse. Viviano stood up in the bow, using his palanca like a madman, now on one side, now on the other, to keep us free from the banks, but suddenly his pole was torn from his grasp, scraping along the carroza to the imminent danger of our heads, while at the same moment, the river making a quick bend, our bongo far too long to turn, stuck fast in the bend, keeling over till the water rushed in at the lower side. Disembarking with our available crew, we righted our craft and then dug away the bank till there was room enough for us to turn. Galloping on, the stream grew wider, and the current

suddenly so swift, that we endeavored to fasten to the
bank, but it was too late; we could no more stop our
courser than the stream itself, and as we turned a bend
we were greeted by a roar that sent our hearts into our
mouths. But a moment longer, and we were swept into
a seething, boiling *raudal*,* nothing visible but the leaping, white foam on which our log was tossed like a feather.
Viviano dropped down helpless with a stifled *caramba*,
while we speculated on the chances of the rapid ending
in a fall. El Patron clung to his steering-oar like a hero,
and kept the bongo head on, which was our only chance.
By the rocks we dashed like lightning, for what seemed
an interminable length of time. But the caimans were
cheated of their prey for once. We escaped the rocks,
with no more damage than a large amount of water
shipped, and floated quietly on deep water once again.
Our zest for adventure for that day, however, was gone,
and the sooner we were on dry land again the better. Our
patron now knowing his whereabouts, we travelled on,
sleepy and tired, till the faint glimmer of a light ahead revived us, and soon we were watching our supper cooking
over the fire, and slinging our hammock within the walls
of a Llano farm-house. Great slabs of leathery meat disappeared like snow in summer, washed down by numberless calabashes of coffee and milk, before we desisted, and
then we turned into our hammocks, while El Patron, in a
low, monotonous tone which came from a cloud of tobacco-
smoke, like the voice of some ancient bard, sang the day's
story, till the song, blended with a hum of mosquito-music,
turned a lullaby, and the day was finished.

* A rapid.

CHAPTER VII.

THE sun was many degrees in the heavens when a
voice summoned us from blissful slumber to partake of
the good fare so bountifully provided by the kind people
of the Llanos. The fragrant *café*, the hot corn-cake, *carne
frita*, or fried beef, with the oft-replenished calabash of
delicious milk, were luxuries fully appreciated. Departing from our hospitable friends and their island-like home,
lifted above the spreading waters, we pushed on over the
inundated country—through tangled forest, thick jungles,
and open reaches, the abodes of millions of aquatic birds,
which displayed the greatest variety of species. Great
white herons, some as tall as a man, were perched aloft
on the leafless branches of giant trees, standing erect in
couples upon their nest, like ghostly sentinels, guarding
the watery realms. Files of ducks stood stretched along
outspreading boughs,* and thousands more rustling up

---

* Many species of ducks on the Llanos, contrary to the habit of those
birds with us, the wood-duck (*Anas sponsa*) excepted, perch with apparent
ease upon trees, which we have often seen loaded with them.

from the turbid element, floated in clouds over our heads. Guacharacas, parrots, paroquets, and guacamayas, filled the heavens with their piercing cries, mingled with the wild notes of countless numbers of flamingoes and spoon-bills, while bright-colored birds of untold species winged their way over the waters. Monstrous caimans floated in the slimy floods, groups of chattering and yelling monkeys gambolled through the forest, and *iguanas*, alligators in miniature, lay basking upon every fallen trunk, and darkened the trees with their ugly forms, occasionally dropping from their aërial perches into the water with a startling plunge. These repulsive saurians, from three to six feet in length, answer well to the description given by one who probably was not particularly charmed with their beauty of form, as being " very ugly snakes, which Nature, after forming the head and tail, had neglected, until too late, to roll into shape, giving them afterward four legs, by way of compensation for her oversight." These large lizards are of a variety of species and color, with a comb-like crest running along the back, which the animal elevates when frightened, giving it a most hideous aspect. They pass a great part of their existence in trees, and may be seen clinging to the branches which project over the streams, into which they let themselves drop, upon the approach of danger. Their flesh is esteemed a great delicacy and is eagerly sought by the inhabitants.

Finding no land whereon to build a fire, that we might cook some of the game which strewed the bottom of our canoe, we hauled up at mid-day beneath the shade of a tree, and relieved our hunger with cassava and *guarepo*, a favorite beverage of the natives, taken both hot and cold, made by dissolving papelon in water. Again we floated on, the banks beginning to rise, and the waters to collect themselves in a single channel, until, at length, they were once more united in a large and impetuous stream, which

carried us rapidly down its course. Large patches of
grass, sometimes acres in extent, torn from the banks, or
brought from the flooded plains, were borne along like
floating meadows. Our bivouac for the night was in a low,
pestilential jungle, where an untimely rain cut short our
evening meal, and sancudos disturbed our slumbers. We
quitted the inhospitable place at early light, and committed ourselves once more to the swift current of the Trinaco, as the lower Pao is called. The scenery was less
varied than upon the previous days of our voyage, and a
stillness pervaded the forest that now fringed the banks,
that was profound as compared with the confused din
of the inundated plain. Here and there a hut was seen
through the woods, surrounded with plantains and yucas—
feeble exponents of civilization in this strange land.

At 3 p. m. we encountered one of those severe storms
which the traveller so often experiences in the tropics.
The heavens opened, and the floods came in torrents that
threatened shipwreck to our frail bark. In vain we endeavored to protect ourselves from the fury of the storm.
There was only room for one at either end of the carroza;
and here two forlorn beings might have been seen, with
their heads stowed away among the kettles and provisions,
and with their legs protruding, as convenient conductors
to convey the water which the projecting members might
collect, trickling down the back toward the head, whenever the canoe gave a favorable lurch; and, at an adverse
plunge of the unstable craft, coursing back into their boots
at the opposite extremity. The strength of the tempest
was at length exhausted, when, dripping with wet, and
shivering from cold, we drew up to the shore, where a
small hut told of food and shelter. Our ever-loquacious
Alvino, revived by hot coffee and *sandcoche* to an uncommon flow of eloquence, rehearsed the tale of our journey and adventures, drawing forth the frequent exclama-

tion "*Caramba!*" from his admiring listeners. Reclining in our hammocks, closely wrapped in our blankets as a protection against sancudos, we dropped into sweet oblivion, with the tongue of Alvino still "flowing rapidly." How long it may have continued we cannot say.

From the time of leaving Pao, one of the party, Mr. Gilbert, had shown symptoms of the dreaded *calenture* which is so prevalent at this season, upon these submerged and malarious regions. We at first supposed it only a slight attack, which need occasion no apprehension, but the discomforts and exposures of the voyage caused the fever to assume a more malignant form. We were in no condition to do much for our companion, and could only hasten forward to Baul, where was promise of medical attention and better accommodations. On the afternoon of the following day, the sixth from our embarkation at Pao, we reached Baul. In a few days Mr. Gilbert became convalescent; but it was, however, too evident that the fever still lurked in a latent state, and only waited for favorable circumstances to again develop itself. For him to remain longer upon these pestilential plains, could not be done with impunity, and a return to the north seemed imperatively demanded. It was with feelings of regret that we contemplated separating from a member of our small party, just as we were starting upon our long, overland journey. But there seemed no alternative, and accordingly preparations were made by which he accompanied our boatmen back to Pao; from there he made his way across the Cordilleras to Puerto Cabello, whence he sailed for home.

Two days after this event, the time fixed for our departure from Baul, the calenture again invaded the party and prostrated my only remaining companion. For three days we watched, with no little anxiety, the progress of the fever, as it continued to increase in severity. These

were, indeed, dark days to us. We recalled the admonition so frequently given us not to venture upon the mias-
matic rivers, and lowlands of the interior, especially at
this season. We were even now persistently urged to
turn back. But a brighter day soon dawned, and hope
began to take the place of momentary despair. The fever
having spent its strength, the patient rapidly recovered;
and we again sought opportunity to resume our journey.
We may here state that, notwithstanding predictions,
which were far from being comforting to us, this was our
only detention from sickness during our four months'
voyage upon the rivers of the interior, although we were
continually meeting with natives, oftentimes entire families, who were sufferers from the intermittent fever of the
country.

Our delay of two weeks at Baul gave us an opportunity to become acquainted with the place and its environs.
There was, however, not much that had special interest
either to the naturalist or casual visitor. Baul stands at
the junction of the Trinaco and Cojede Rivers, stretching
mostly along the latter, between its right bank and the
hills which rise directly back of the town upon the south.
These isolated hills were the last elevations we saw, until
reaching the Orinoco. The town claims ten thousand inhabitants, but probably has less than two-thirds that estimate. The botany of this region is not extensive, and
the zoölogy still less varied, but it has some fine representative species; tigers, pumas, deer, and several species
of monkeys, abound upon the savannas and in the forest
tracts. Morning and evening we heard from the corridor
of our posada the howls of the araguato; while deer
would frequently be seen taking their lookout from the
brow of the hills in rear of the town.

Our protracted stay at Baul was at length terminated.
Through the assistance of Dr. E. Landaeta, a gentleman

who had been a warm friend to us through all our sickness, we procured passage to San Fernando de Apure in a bongo which was bound thither with a cargo of maize and fruits. The 14th of October had been agreed upon for our departure; but, as it was late in the day before the captain, or patron, could complete preparations, it was determined by him to defer sailing until the second day following, although ready to go upon the morrow, but that was Tuesday, the "unlucky day" of the Spaniard. The matter was, however, finally readjusted: we were to go that day a short distance down the river, when we would draw up for the night, thus commencing our journey; then the following morning we could proceed, without being subject to the evils which would befall us for starting upon such an unpropitious day as Tuesday. Our feelings of pleasure, in being able to resume our journey, were mingled with those of regret at parting from friends who had been so attentive to our wants, and who, upon our departure, gave us kind tokens of remembrance, and comforts for our voyage. We could see the tears glisten in the eyes of the good old lady, our hostess, as she gave the farewell shake of the hand, saying, "*Cuidado que los sancudos ne se le coma*" (take care that the sancudos do not eat you up). How much there was to heed in this injunction will appear hereafter.

Our resting-place for the night was, as we have intimated, but a short distance below the town, where we were tendered the hospitalities of a hut in the midst of a banana-grove; some swinging their hammocks inside the dwelling, others under the trees, both places alike so infested with sancudos that self-preservation was our only thought.* Were we so soon to realize the import of the last

---

* There are several species of culices, or sancudos, in South America; the one most common on the Portuguesa and Apure being of a blue color, with a bite more irritating than that of our northern mosquito.

words from our hostess at Baul? Was this the region of insect torments of which we had so often heard? Poor innocents, we little knew the capabilities of Venezuela, or dread would have possessed our souls. This was but a paradise to where our journeyings were yet to lead us. We battled with sancudos until the hour of midnight, when the moon, appearing above the forest level, suggested the practicability of navigating by its light; and, as any thing was preferable to remaining in such an infested place, we reëmbarked, and, pushing out into the middle of the stream, floated slowly down the dark waters, the dull thud of our heavy oars alone breaking the silence, so profound as to be almost painful. We were now less annoyed by insects, the few there were being swept astern by the gentle breeze produced by the motion of the boat.

Our four days' journey down the Portuguesa, from Baul to San Fernando, was not a very stirring or eventful one. The scenery was the most monotonous we had witnessed, not even a hill, or the slightest elevation, rising upon the view for a relief; but we were shut in by forests that lined the shores, with no escape for the eye except as it gazed heavenward, toward a dazzling, burning sun. Owing to the sancudos which so densely populated the riverbanks, our voyage was interrupted at night only by a short rest, we leaving our bivouac as soon as the moon arose, and dispelled the darkness that settled in the forest channel. Rains were frequent; and when they came we sometimes sought the shelter of our carroza, which, in this bongo, was sufficiently high to admit of a sitting posture; but, as it was a perfect paradise for sancudos, besides being as hot as an oven, we often preferred a wetting to remaining in such a place of torture.

At noon of our third day from Baul, we came to the small town of San Jaime upon the right bank, and by dark we arrived at Camaguan, a town upon the left bank of the Portuguesa, of some three or four thousand inhabitants, the most considerable place upon the river between Baul and San Fernando. In the morning, having discharged a portion of the cargo from the bongo, we departed. There was the same monotonous aspect of the scenery as had characterized the landscape from Baul; the banks, nowhere of any considerable elevation above the river, were generally covered with forest varying in width from a hundred yards to upward of a mile, with the plain beyond, an open savanna, submerged by the water. The Portuguesa is quite a formidable river, and of sufficient depth to float the largest vessels up to Baul. Since our return from Venezuela, we have been gratified to know that there has been established, by an American company, a line of steamers which pass up the Orinoco and Apure to San Fernando, thus opening up a vast and important region to the commerce of the world. A similar line was in operation some years ago, but political dissensions occasioned its discontinuance. We hope for better success to the new enterprise.*

The morning of the fifth day of our voyage from Baul had not fully dawned, when our canoe, gliding into the waters of the Apure, brought us soon in sight of San Fernando. Having had our imaginations highly wrought by exaggerated reports—a prevailing weakness characteristic of this people—it was a feeling of disappointment that accompanied our first view of the narrow town with its long row of low, white buildings, stretched along the scarcely-elevated margin of the river, and backed by a monotonous forest. What most attracted our attention

---

* Since writing the above, we learn that steamers have ceased running up the Apure, going only as far as Ciudad Bolivar, or Angostura, as more commonly called by Venezuelians, a town about three hundred miles up the Orinoco.

was a small steamer, that had come up from Angostura, with a party of Venezuelian officials, and was lying at anchor in the river. A shrill whistle from the craft as we approached, breaking the stillness of the morning, as it resounded through the half-wakeful town and the deep forest, was a strange sound to hear in these wild regions of the Llanos. The position of San Fernando, at the junction of two great rivers, whose tributaries, taking their rise in the littoral chain upon the north, and among the snowy peaks of Colombia upon the west, traverse so large a territory, and its easy communication with the coast by a water-course that is navigable for the largest vessels, afford to the town unusual commercial facilities.

San Fernando, far removed from the centre of volcanic action, has rested secure from the devastating shock of convulsive Nature, but has witnessed other scenes scarcely less dreadful than those of the earthquake. During the season of 1855–'56 it was visited by that terrible scourge, cholera, which, confining its ravages almost exclusively to those whose mode of life and sanitary habits are so conducive to contagious diseases everywhere, swept off nearly all the lower and laboring portion of the inhabitants. Buildings stood partially erected; the forge was abandoned; shops were closed; and work of all kind ceased on account of an unanswered call for labor. Sewing-machines were introduced, and even then it was with the greatest difficulty that the people could be supplied with clothing. Although more than a decade of years has since passed, still the equilibrium of the labor and capital elements has not yet been restored. The population is, however, slowly increasing, and at present is estimated at about four thousand. In 1859, during one of the political convulsions we have so often had occasion to refer to, the town again suffered a serious calamity, in being sacked and one-half of it being destroyed by fire. It has again been rebuilt in a more substantial manner. The introduction of brick a few years since, for architectural purposes, is one stride forward in Venezuelian reform—the clay of the Llanos furnishing the requisite material for their manufacture.

During the season of greatest floods, the country around San Fernando is submerged, thus islanding the town, when the canoe is the only means of maintaining communication with other places. The heat throughout the year is excessive, attaining its maximum in July and August, the months of heaviest rains, when it reaches a height of about 100° in the shade. In the dry season the temperature is about ten degrees lower. In October, the time of our visit at San Fernando, the rainy period of the year was rapidly closing; but the Llanos were, for the most part, still inundated. The subsiding of the waters marks the time when intermittent fevers rage the worst, and insects swarm the thickest. The fearful accounts we had received of sancudos upon the Apure, and our own experience with them upon the Portuguesa, led us to procure netting of fine cloth, which we made into *mosquiteros* of such form and dimensions that they would cover our hammocks entire when suspended. Beneath this protection, we could lie secure, and smile at sancudos as they hovered in clouds without.

Through our letter of introduction, we made the acquaintance of Señor L. Diaz, an intelligent and gentlemanly physician, highly esteemed in San Fernando, who cordially invited us to partake of the hospitalities of his house. The doctor was a great lover of pets, and lived surrounded by a perfect menagerie of the inhabitants of the savannas and forest. Birds, large and small, of singular species and beautiful plumage, filled his house and court-yard; among them a great noisy guacamaya, which had the run of the premises, and was as loquacious and as great a gormandizer as Viviano, our Pao boatman; for he was, seemingly, never happy unless calling for "El doctor," who would comply with his peremptory demands for bread, fruits, and the long list of edibles, which he would roll off in Spanish, like some old veteran in the language. Among his larger fondlings was a young jaguar, or tiger, which, although quite large, evinced none of the unpleasant traits ascribed to that species. This animal the doctor desired us to accept and take to our country; but lack of transportation privileges, with the thought of a jaguar in the same bongo with ourselves, for a voyage of two thousand miles, led us reluctantly to decline the proffered gift. What contributed still more to the pleasure of our visit in San Fernando, was our further acquaintance with General E. Esté, who was unremitting in his attentions, and who could, withal, converse in our native tongue, a treat we always richly enjoyed, and which was not again afforded us until we reached the Amazons.

Three days had been spent at San Fernando, when, an opportunity presenting itself whereby we could proceed on our journey to the Orinoco, we determined to embrace it. Two large bongos, freighted with maize, papelon, and aguardiente, and accompanied by a small canoe, were on their return down the Apure, and were ready to start within two hours from the time we first received intimation of their intended departure. As the large boats were heavily loaded, the little craft was to convey us to Asaiba, a hacienda upon Rio Clarito, where we could exchange for one of the bongos, which, with a reduced cargo, from that place was destined for Urbana on the Orinoco. Having been promised letters of recommendation from the president of the province of Apure, we sought the chief executive at his private residence. Reaching the house designated to us, rather an inferior one even for San Fernando, we passed through the open arcade, and, crossing the court-

yard, came to a low, dirty room, black with soot and blinding with smoke, where we beheld a large, swarthy negro,
with coat off and sleeves rolled up, engaged in the culinary operations of the kitchen. To this gentleman we
were introduced as the official in question. He proved
eminently successful in inditing a grandiloquent recommendation.

Having hastily secured our supplies for the voyage, we
were at the landing by 5 P. M., the hour designated for
starting, and found the two bongos just pushing off; but
our own crew were nowhere to be found. Waiting until
dark, without any signs of their appearing, we started
upon a hunt for them through the town, returning, after
an hour or more of fruitless search, to find one of the
rascals, the best part of whom was Indian, sitting with
great complacency upon his haunches, on the beach,
smoking his evening regalia. In course of another hour
the patron, a great shambling son of Afric, made his appearance, and, doubling his lower extremities under him,
also squatted very coolly upon the ground to discuss " the
situation." We brought the conference to a hasty close,
when they very deliberately collected the provisions,
kettles, and luggage, into the canoe, and stationing themselves, one in the stern to steer, and the other at the bow
to paddle, we were finally moving along, more by the force
of the current than by any exertions of our boatmen.

CHAPTER VIII.

Aspect of the Inundated Plains.—Wild Horses and Cattle.—Crocodiles.—
Anacondas.—Electric Eels.—Cannibal-Fish.—Experiences upon the
Payara.—Myriads of Aquatic Birds.—A Breakfast and Cock-fight.—
Manati, or "Sea-cow."—Upon the Arauca.—Over Flooded Savannas.—At Asaiba.—Niguas.—Jaguar.—Abnormal Butchering.—Embarked for the Orinoco.—Navigating Submerged Forest.—Lost upon
the Llanos.—An Uncomfortable Night.—Arrival upon the Orinoco.

Our first experiences upon the Apure were terminated
at a late hour, by our hauling up in the immediate vicinity
of a sugar-mill in operation, where all night long the
tramp of animals, as they turned the rude grinding-ma-
chine, kept time to the hum of sancudos that filled the air.
The next morning, early, we recommenced our voyage.
The banks became lower as we proceeded, until they finally sank beneath the floods, when we pushed out of the
river-channel over the inundated savannas. During the
season of rains, the Apure, Arauca, Conaviche, and Ca-
panaparo Rivers, with their labyrinth of branches, by their
overflow submerge a vast territory, which presents the aspect of an inland sea. The hamlets and huts which are
scattered here and there over the savannas scarcely rise
above the surface of the water. Crocodiles and anacondas, with other reptilian monsters, which lie buried in the
dry mud of the Llanos during the months of drought,

now hold high carnival in their flooded realms. The wild horses and cattle, which feed in such immense numbers upon the plains, seek the mountains and elevated lands until the waters subside, and the renewed verdure of spring invites them again to their favorite haunts. Thousands are oftentimes overtaken by the periodical deluge, and perish by drowning, or fall prey to crocodiles, water-serpents, and other inhabitants of the element.

When we reflect upon the many influences that are continually at work for the diminution of these animals, it is not a little surprising that they should maintain their races against the great devastation which would seem to threaten almost their annihilation. Those that escape the perils of the water are continually in danger from the wild beasts which are crowded with them upon the uplands of the savannas. Pestilential diseases often sweep them away by thousands, while man is ever waging against them a war of destruction. Nor are they free from annoying insects, which torment them by day and night, and bats that drain their blood, while lulling them with the breath of their noiseless wings, leaving wounds that become dreadful by reason of poisonous flies which infest them. The wild cattle are far more numerous than the horses, and are mostly owned by herdsmen, whose mark they bear. At certain seasons a grand hunt is organized, the cattle are gathered, and all unmarked ones branded, when those not wanted are released to again roam at freedom upon the savannas. The *llanero* is as little able to tell the number of his cattle, as he is to bound the limits of his vast possessions. Humboldt estimated that 1,200,000 cattle and 180,000 horses graze upon the plains of Venezuela; while there exist upon the Pampas of Buenos Ayres 12,000,000 cattle and 3,000,000 horses.

There are several species of scaly saurians, to which we

have alluded, that inhabit the waters of the Llanos. The largest is the true crocodile, like those of the Nile and Ganges. It differs from the alligator, also common here, and which resembles the species of that name found in our Southern States, in having a longer and narrower head, as well as in dentition. The alligator and crocodile, especially the latter, are the most crafty and dangerous pests of all the lagoons and rivers of the Llanos. Both species are known to the natives by the name of caiman. They are oviparous animals, laying eggs, small in proportion to their size, with a hard, rough shell. Their laterally compressed tail is the great instrument of progression when in water, and possesses such strength that a crocodile can easily overthrow with it the canoe of the Indians, when the hapless voyagers fall an easy prey to the voracious monster. The wearied traveller, sleeping at night upon the bank of the stream, is liable to a stroke from this powerful appendage, which will send him reeling into the water—and into the jaws of waiting crocodiles. They seem to have an antipathy to attacking any thing upon land, but in the water they are masters of the situation. They delight in basking upon the shelving bank of the stream, where they lie with gaping jaws, and motionless as a log, as disgusting and horrible looking objects as can well be imagined. Like the colossal anaconda, and most of the serpent-tribe of the Llanos, the caiman buries itself in the mud, when the falling waters leave bare the savannas, and spends the long, dry season in a state of hibernal lethargy. Upon the return of rains, the moistened soil gives up its living dead, and the plains again swarm with reptilian life. The Llanero hut, which has been deserted by its occupants during the months of inundation, is sometimes said to become the hibernal quarters of these inhabitants of the deluge, which, bursting their prison walls with the vivifying showers of spring, come forth to the astonishment and horror of the inmates of the dwelling. In the equinoctial zone it is the increase of humidity that recalls these animals to life, while, in temperate latitudes, it is the increase of heat that rouses them from their lethargy. "It is a curious physiological phenomenon," remarks Humboldt, in his "Travels," "to observe the alligators of North America plunged into a winter-sleep by excess of cold, at the same period when the crocodiles of the Llanos begin their siesta or summer-sleep. If it were probable that these animals of the same family had heretofore inhabited the same northern country, we might suppose that, in advancing toward the equator, they feel the want of repose after having exercised their muscles for seven or eight months, and that they retain under a new sky the habits which appear to be essentially linked with their organization."

We have referred to the ophidian monsters which tenant these submerged regions, and are such a terror to the animal kingdom over which they hold universal sway; even the large and fierce jaguar yielding superiority to these reptilian monsters. The species most common upon the Llanos of Venezuela is the anaconda (*Eunectes murinus*), called by the natives *culebra de agua*, a larger and more voracious serpent than the boa-constrictor, and less terrestrial in its habits. The anaconda is from twenty to thirty feet in length, and instances are not uncommon of its attaining the enormous length of forty feet. Its capability of swallowing prey so many times its own bulk is truly astonishing; not even the pride of the herd, the llano bull, says Paez, escaping its deadly embrace. It does not attempt to swallow the horns of stags, but, as is asserted by the writer above quoted, these indigestible appendages are left protruding from its mouth, until time removes them by the natural process of decay. The anaconda is able to survive a long period without food, even when not gorged; and we have seen them decline a live creature, introduced into their cage, when they had been confined for months without any thing to sustain life. The skin is converted into leather for straps, which are remarkable for their toughness and durability. This, together with the thick hide of the caiman, which makes excellent saddles, furnishes the native with his outfit for travel and the chase.

The caiman and serpents are not the only terrors of these Stygian floods. The lagoons and marshy waters are inhabited by innumerable gymnoti, or electric eels, which are able to communicate an electrical shock sufficiently strong to overpower a man, and paralyze for hours the limb that comes in immediate contact. In experimenting with some of these "animal electrical machines," which had been secured by the Indians, we received discharges that caused, for some time afterward, a most painful sensation in the member with which we grasped them. Humboldt, in his "Views of Nature," gives the following graphic description of the mode of capturing the gymnotus by the natives: "A number of mules and horses are driven into a swamp, which is closely surrounded by Indians, until the unusual noise excites the daring fish to venture on an attack. Serpent-like they are seen swimming along the surface of the water, striving cunningly to glide under the bellies of the horses. By the force of their invisible blows numbers of the poor animals are suddenly prostrated; others, snorting and panting, their manes erect, their eyes wildly flashing with terror, rush madly from the raging storm; but the Indians, armed with long bamboo staves, drive them back into the midst of the pool. By degrees the fury of this unequal contest begins to slacken. Like clouds that have discharged their electricity, the wearied eels disperse. They require long rest and nourishing food to repair the galvanic force which they have so lavishly expended. Their shocks gradually become weaker

and weaker. Terrified by the noise of the trampling
horses, they timidly approach the brink of the morass,
where they are wounded by harpoons, and drawn on shore
by non-conducting poles of dry wood."

But what is dreaded even more than the jaws of the
crocodile, the coils of the anaconda, or the powerful battery of the electrical eel, is the caribe, or cannibal-fish,
which literally swarms the rivers of the Llanos, rendering
it exceedingly dangerous to enter the water. The ferocity
of this bold and ravenous little pest is terrible; and at
the scent of blood they are attracted in such myriads,
that the largest animal will quickly be consumed by them.
The largest caribe is four or five inches in length, with
fierce eyes, large mouth, and teeth so exceedingly sharp
as to be able to sever ordinary hooks as if they were but
slender threads. The Waraun Indians, alluded to in a
preceding chapter, who inhabit the submerged lands at
the mouth of the Orinoco, and live in trees, without even
a spot of ground in which to deposit their mortal remains,
avail themselves of the ravenous proclivities of the caribe-
fish to dispose of the flesh of their deceased relatives.
" For this purpose they tie the corpse with a strong rope,
and plunge it into the water, securing the other end of the
rope to one of the pillars upon which their dwellings rest:
in less than twenty-four hours the skeleton is hauled out of
the water perfectly clean, for the teeth of the caribe have
stripped it of flesh, arteries, tendons, etc. Now all that
the mourners have to do is, to separate the bones, which
they arrange with much care and nicety in baskets made
for the purpose, gaudily ornamented with beads of various
colors; and so well have they calculated beforehand the
space the bones will occupy in the funereal urn, that the
skull, tightly adjusted against the sides of the basket at
the top, comes to be the lid of it." *

* Paez, " Adventures in South and Central America."

But, to return from this zoölogical digression. In the season of inundation, the native who wishes to cross the Llanos, instead of following the sinuosities of the rivers, whose boundaries are generally marked by wooded banks, themselves often submerged, turns his canoe in the direction of his destination, and, by known land-marks that rise above the spreading waters, or, when these are wanting, by the sun in the heavens, guides his bark across the country. While distance is thus generally saved, difficulties are not unfrequently encountered—shallow water and tangled thickets, which impede the progress of the voyager. The traveller from San Fernando to Urbana, by traversing the flooded lands of the Apure and Arauca, escapes stemming some twenty leagues of the strong current of the Orinoco. Although the waters had considerably subsided, our natives chose the shorter route, as it would lead them more direct to their llano home. Over this wide expanse of water we now pushed; at times following the channel of a stream, again threading our way across broad plains, covered with grasses, the tops just rising above the surface of the floods. The aspect of the country was dreary in the extreme; a flat, monotonous waste upon every side, sweeping to the horizon; the eye finding relief only now and then as it rested upon a clump of palms, lifting themselves above the waters, or a line of trees, marking the course of some river. Vast herds of wild cattle were seen, which, at our approach, would go plunging and swimming through the water. The amphibious life these animals lead at the season of inundation is a remarkable feature in their existence. The flora of this region presented nothing striking, and but few species of flowering plants were found. This is characteristic of the Llanos, which produce little, aside from sedges and grasses, upon their level expanse.

Toward the close of our first day's adventures upon

the flooded plains constituting the great delta of the Apure, we emerged from a creek, that we had for some little time been following, into the Payara, one of the large branches of this net-work of rivers. Discovering upon its elevated banks a habitation, half-concealed in a banana-grove, we pulled up for the night. For want of room within the dirty, gloomy hovel, we stretched our hammocks between banana-trunks—herbs of a year's growth, eight and ten inches in diameter, and ten to twelve feet in height. We were not yet initiated in the use of mosquiteros, and many sancudos secured admission at the same time with ourselves, much to our discomfort. Turning and shaking our nets, we made another trial for solitary companionship, which proved even more unsuccessful than our first. Again and again, the reversing and shaking process was repeated, but after each operation the number of sancudos within multiplied, until they seemed to be more numerous within than without. As a last resort we rolled ourselves in our blankets, from head to foot; but the stifling heat soon rendered this unsupportable, when, in despair, we abandoned our hammocks, and passed the long hours of the night in walking to and fro along the river-bank, crouching occasionally, when wearied in batting with our unseen foe, in the smoke of our smouldering fire. Morning came, when we wreaked vengeance on our persecutors, by gathering up our nets, and crushing by wholesale the imprisoned sancudos.

Our bongos, having gone some distance to an estate to discharge a portion of their cargo, were detained through the day, and, having with them the supplies for the entire party, we were forced to wait for their return, and pass another night in this infested place, to which Egypt, in the days of its plagues, must have been a perfect paradise. Of all the annoyances to which the traveller on these rivers is subjected, the insects are the most to be dreaded.

For supper we obtained a fine ichthyological specimen from the river, and invited the sole occupant of the hut to share with us, which act we had ample occasion to seriously regret. That, like ourselves, he had eaten little or nothing since the day previous was more than probable, although a banana-grove stood at his door, loaded with fruit, and a stream filled with fish flowed by his hut. His mud hovel, where, in his hammock, he spent the greater part of his existence, was a den of filth and darkness. At intervals, when the stings of sancudos were no longer endurable, he would gather an armful of weeds and sticks with which to build a smudge for expelling the insects from his hut, which being secured, he would remove the heap of burning rubbish just outside the entrance, and place a stiff ox-hide against the only aperture to render the exclusion of the pest doubly effectual, and then settle himself back into his hammock for another siesta.

After another wretched night among the sancudos of Payara, we were joined by our bongos and gladly pushed on our journey. The banks again gradually lowering, we once more found entrance upon the submerged land. In some places the waters were collected into channels of great depth, in others they spread out over the plain, repeating again the scenes of the Pao. The air was literally filled with dense flocks of cranes, herons, flamingoes, spoonbills, and other aquatic birds, while thousands more whitened the half-submerged plain. Where the banks were visible they were lined with caimans, alongside which stalked with martial air great *soldados*,* while toninas, fresh-water porpoises, sported in the water, spouting jets of water, like the larger cetaceans of the ocean, and, frequently rising near the boat, would salute us with a start-

---

* The soldado, or soldier-bird, is a species of heron; one we secured measured eight feet and seven inches between the tips of its wings, and stood about five feet in height.

ling explosion. At 11 A. M. we drew up to an elevated island-spot for breakfast, where we shot a wild-boar, such as wander in herds over the savannas. Removing the head, and dividing the body lengthwise into halves, the hair was singed, and the meat sufficiently roasted over a huge fire to preserve it until we should bivouac for the night. The wild-hog of the Llanos is the common species, escaped from domestication, and, like the wild horses and cattle which feed upon the plains in such numbers, is not indigenous, but was introduced by Europeans upon the first settlement of the country.

Having spent the night upon a wooded bank, at three o'clock the following morning all things were again towed on board, and we were once more in motion up the Ata-maica. At 10 A. M. we stopped for breakfast and a cock-fight. A feathered gamester constitutes an essential accompaniment of the Llanero voyager, and, on every opportunity that presented itself, our patron trotted out his bird for a contest.

We saw here the manati, or *vaca marina* (sea-cow), called by the Brazilians *peixeboi*, or cow-fish, which had been captured by the natives. This seal-like mammal belongs to the cetaceous family, is from eight to fifteen feet in length, and sometimes exceeds one thousand pounds in weight. The head is small, with thick, fleshy lips and a large mouth. Its eyes and auricular organs are very small, yet the senses of both these organs are exceedingly acute. The body is covered with a smooth, thick skin; the flesh, something between pork and beef, is held in high estimation by the inhabitants. The fat of the animal, called *manteca de manati*, manati-butter, is void of that odor peculiar to cetaceous oil generally, and is used for illumination and cooking; while the strong skin, cut into strips, supplies the natives with cords and ropes. This herbaceous cetacea inhabits the waters of the Lower Orinoco and most of its tributaries below the Great Cataracts, being especially abundant in the lagoons and marshes of the Llanos, where prodigious numbers are annually caught. One mode of capturing it is by building stockades across the outlets of fords and lakes, up which the animals have passed during the time of high water, and when the floods subside they are easily taken. Another method is by harpooning them when they rise to the surface to breathe, which they are frequently obliged to do. When exhausted by its mad flight, dragging after it in wild speed the canoe to which it is attached by a long cord, fastened to the missile that has penetrated its body, it at length yields itself a victim, and its body floats upon the water. It is then dispatched by its pursuers, who, springing overboard, immerse the canoe and slip it under the huge monster. They then bale out the water, and, seating themselves upon their captive, row to land with their cargo.

Before noon we entered upon the broad, muddy current of the Arauca. The banks were elevated and heavily wooded; and groups of monkeys (araguatos and monos), gambolled through the branches and upon the thick cordage of lianas, that embraced the giant trunks, and interlaced their boughs. Conspicuous amid this luxuriant growth of vegetation was the saman, that species of mimosa which attains to such magnificent proportions in the valley of Aragua. Its umbrella-shaped crown of delicate, feathery leaves, with each tree almost a forest in itself, presents one of the striking features in the vegetation of the Llanos of the Apure. The *Bombax ceiba*, or wild cotton-tree, is also abundant here, and is one of the most useful, as it is one of the most imposing, of the forest monarchs. The immense size of its trunk, and the softness of its wood, render it extremely valuable for large canoes. Our two bongos were hollowed out from this tree, and would measure forty feet in length and over six between the sides, with scarcely any perceptible difference in size between the two extremities. The ceiba produces a pod, containing a fine, silky cotton, which is used by the Indians for the *flechetes*, or light arrows, of their blow-guns, besides being useful for a variety of purposes where the ordinary cotton would be too coarse and heavy. We occasionally got sight of a *perro de agua*, or water-dog; but their extreme shyness seldom afforded us an opportunity for a close acquaintance with these somewhat singular animals. They resemble in their general aspect a beaver, are three and four feet in length, and have a very fine fur. Another strange denizen of these rivers, which we frequently saw, is the *chiguire*,* or water-hog, but in no way is it allied to the land-quadruped of that name. It is the largest known rodent, measuring at least three feet in length, is exceedingly bulky, and without a tail. It is found in great numbers in the districts of the Apure and Orinoco, roaming over land and water for its subsistence, delighting particularly in the sweet stalks of the sugar-cane. It possesses a most offensive odor, with a fishy flavor to its flesh; notwithstanding, the jaguars feed ravenously upon them, while the Indians regard them as excellent eating.

After several unsuccessful attempts to reach the submerged plain which stretched out to the southward, by passing through breaks in the low banks of the Arauca, we at last succeeded. The water was nowhere of any great depth, and often our heavily-laden bongos ran aground; when the natives, jumping overboard and applying their shoulders to the crafts, would push them along to where the water was of sufficient depth to again float them. We soon entered a lagoon, the source of the Rio Clarito, but its boundaries it was impossible to determine, as the banks were nowhere visible above the water

---

* Hydrochærus capybara.

which inundated the country in every direction to the horizon. Garsons, and the many species of white aquatic birds which had become so familiar to us, had left these domains almost exclusively to ducks and geese, which were here in thousands, and filled the air with their cries. Now and then was seen a brace of noisy gnacamayas, or a flock of parrots, winging their way over the watery waste toward more promising realms. Unable to find dry land upon which we could bivouac, we contented ourselves with some bits of cassava we had remaining on board, and continued our voyage, reaching, by 10 P. M., Asaiba, the island estate of the commander of our log fleet.

Here we had our first experience with jiggers, or *niguas* (*Pulex penetrans*), which, as we discovered in the morning, filled the sand beneath our hammocks. We had heard much, and seen not a little, of the effects resulting from the burrowing of these minute insects beneath the skin, but had never ourselves before been made the object of their attentions. This microscopic insect generally buries itself in some part of the feet, but no portion of the body is exempted from them. Having found for itself a home, it deposits a cluster of eggs, enclosed in a sack, which, upon developing, colonize the limb in which they are established. The first indication of the presence of the insect is a peculiar itching sensation, which is followed in a few days, if the removal of the nigua be neglected, by swelling, that in time becomes exceedingly painful. It is not uncommon to see among the natives jiggered feet distended to frightful proportions; the affected member retaining permanently its unnatural size. Not unfrequently they render amputation necessary, and sometimes occasion death. Foreigners are especially subject to their attacks; and the effects resulting therefrom upon such are also worse than upon the natives of the country. For mothers to search the feet of their children for niguas, is as much a part of their daily task as to furnish the household with food ; while their own extremities are to them a source of ceaseless care.

We were shown at this hacienda a huge jaguar, or tiger, as it is called by the natives, which had been shot upon the day previous. This animal, the *Felis onça* of naturalists, is abundant in the Llanos, as well as in most parts of South America. It is nearly equal in size to the royal tiger of the East, and possesses much of the ferocity and daring of that animal, but differs from it in the marking of its skin, which, instead of being striped, is mottled. Another characteristic peculiar to the jaguar is, unlike the Bengal tiger, its ability to climb trees with ease, however smooth the trunk. It moves with the greatest agility among the branches, making birds and sometimes monkeys its prey. It is a frequent visitor, at night, to the encampment of the traveller, but is kept at a respectful distance by a fire. Turtles, with their impenetrable covering, often fall a prey to the jaguar, which secures the flesh, asserts Humboldt, by first turning them upon their backs, when, insinuating his paw between the shells, he empties them of their contents. He is also a good fisher, confining his operations to the margins of streams, hurling his prey upon the land with his paw. Allied to the jaguar is the puma, or South American lion (*Felis concolor*), the same as our panther, but much larger, and more predaceous in its habits. It is of a tawny and nearly uniform color, possessing most of the traits of its spotted congener. It is frequently met in the mountains of Venezuela, and is not uncommon upon the lowlands of the interior. Besides the jaguar and puma, there is a black tiger, which is larger and more ferocious than either of the others, but is not common upon the Llanos, the forests of the Orinoco and Amazons being its more favorite haunts.

We delayed half a day at Asaiba to procure supplies

for the remainder of our voyage to the Orinoco. An ox was slaughtered, and the meat rolled in salt and thrown upon the hide which covered the cargo of the boat, there to bake in the hot sun. The manner of killing a beef on the Llanos is not one of the least novel sights beheld by the traveller in that country. If the herd be in a corral, the animal is easily captured, but, if upon the savanna, the lassoing and bringing of a victim to the place of execution generally afford an exciting time. The bullock being secured, the matador cautiously approaches with a knife, and, by a dexterous thrust just back of the horns, brings the animal to the ground. The flesh is stripped from the carcass, without any special regard to anatomy, or the "cuts" of the butcher, leaving the skeleton whole as if picked by vultures. Sitting in a circle around the slaughtered beast are a dozen or more half-starved, wolfish dogs, while the trees about are dark with *zamuros*, or black vultures,* waiting for their portion of the spoils. Almost before the way is clear, there is a general rushing, tearing, and pulling, and not always does the best harmony prevail among the hairy and feathered scavengers. The gristly sheets of meat are salted and hung over poles out of the reach of birds and dogs, to cure and toughen. The more flies, dirt, and smoke that can get to it, the better; for thereby is secured that odor so peculiar to South American jerked beef.

By noon we were ready to embark. One of the large bongos, freighted with maize and papelon for Urbana market, together with supplies for our voyage thither, received us aboard. Our crew consisted of two rowers, and a patron, Celestino Gomez, who bore the title of captain, from having served in that capacity in one of the political wars of the republic. Our craft was uncovered, thus exposing us to the excessive heat of the sun. Upon

* Cathartes atratus.

the savannas of the Apure, the temperature of the day, as we have before stated, often rises above 100° Fahr., and this is but little lessened by the shades of night. When the sun was obscured by clouds which overcast the heavens, thus impeding radiation from the earth, the heat became even more oppressive.

The Rio Clarito, down whose course we were floating, has its waters, as the name of the river signifies, beautifully clear; yet the stream appears of an inky color, reflecting light so admirably that we could see our image as in a mirror. Notwithstanding the presence of a coloring principle, imparted to the waters by percolation through the thick masses of vegetable matter which cover the earth, these *aguas negras*, or black waters, as they are called, had to us an agreeable, although a peculiar, taste, and were preferable to the white, muddy mixtures of the Pao, Apure, and Orinoco, such as we were compelled to use for so long a time. It must be borne in mind that springs in the interior are of rare occurrence; we travelled from Valencia to Pará, a distance of over three thousand miles, without as much as once quenching our thirst with a more refreshing beverage than the impure and tepid water obtained from the rivers we navigated. It is a remarkable phenomenon that the same district of country should give rise to streams, some of whose waters are white and thick with sediment, while others are black, yet admirably clear. The explanation must, doubtless, be sought in the different nature of the soil over which the rivers flow, and the varied tinctorial qualities of the vegetation along the courses of the streams.

Two hours of steady rowing from Asaiba brought us to Rio Claro, also a black-water river, where the banks again disappeared, and the stream lost itself in the *Laguna de los Indios*, a section of country partially covered with forest, in places so intricate as to make navigation exceedingly difficult and laborious. No longer guided in this trackless maze by a regular channel, we frequently would be brought to a stand by an impenetrable thicket, and obliged to retrace our course, and try another, with, perhaps, like success. Our bongo was forced through dense bushes, oftentimes grounding, then floating high among the trees, which barely lifted their spreading summits above the waters. Our toilsome windings at length terminated in our becoming entangled in the labyrinth of forests and waters, from which there seemed no escape. The thought of going supperless was by no means a comforting reflection, but that was easily to be foregone, compared with the torture of sancudos, the busy hum of whose marshalling legions was already heard. Night came on apace, and settled round us black and cheerless; when, unable to proceed in the thick darkness, we moored to a tree which rose above the black waters, to wait for the morning. Weary and hopeless, we threw ourselves in the bottom of the boat and tried to sleep; but myriads of insects swarmed the air, with which we contested until conquered, and then in despair yielded ourselves their prey. The long-wished-for daylight brought us relief, when, casting loose from our aërial anchorage, we resumed our efforts to extricate ourselves from the flooded forests. Pressed by hunger, we devised means of relief by taking the larger of our two iron kettles, and, with the simple modification of putting the fire inside instead of out, the fuel for which was dry branches procured from trees, we soon had coffee made in our reserved pot, and this, with meat roasted on spits, furnished us a meal to which our appetites were prepared to do ample justice.

Again pushing on, rowing where the depth of water and absence of forest allowed, elsewhere poling or hauling ourselves along by the branches of the trees, we slowly made way through the gloomy labyrinth, from which the compass furnished the only clew by which to extricate ourselves. After many hours of wearisome efforts, we emerged into the Arauca; only known to be a river by the forest walls which formed a narrow channel. So floating down, we came, by 2 P. M., where dry land appeared, and here we disembarked for food and rest After a couple of hours spent upon the slightly-elevated bank, we continued our voyage, shut in by interminable lines of verdure which bordered the stream. Just before night shrouded all, a sudden turn in the river revealed to our view in the distance the hills of Guiana, beyond the Orinoco. After our long voyage over an inundated country, where not the slightest elevation breaks the sameness of the landscape, it was with a feeling of relief, mingled with inexpressible joy, at the near prospect of a more propitious land, that we beheld the range of hills, which stretched in distinct outline against the rich background of the evening sky.

It was after dark when we floated into the waters of the Orinoco, and moored our canoe upon the western shore of that majestic river, whose floods, gathered by the countless tributaries which drain the vast regions of Venezuela, together with much of Colombia, bringing down the melting snows from the Andean summits, rolled onward in one mighty, impetuous torrent until lost in the Atlantic. No river in the world possesses such grand and sublime scenery, varied by such picturesque mountains, plains, rapids, lovely islands, forests, and life in so many thousand and attractive forms. This was the stream upon which we were now to sail, and these the scenes that were to delight us. Upon the sandy bank of the river we threw ourselves for the night, with the mountain glimpses calling to our dreams the hills of our own distant home.

CHAPTER IX.

EARLY on the morning of the 28th of October, we
crossed the Orinoco—which, at this point, is a league in
breadth—to Urbana, located directly opposite the mouth
of the Arauca. The river had fallen to its medium height,
from the annual rise, which lifts the Orinoco, at Urbana,
from thirty to thirty-five feet above its lowest water-mark;
a change of level much less than occurs higher up, where
the stream is forced through narrow passes, as at the
Straits of Baraguan and the Great Cataracts. Landing
a short distance above the town, beneath the shelter of a
projecting promontory of granitic rocks, we proceeded to
make ourselves look as respectable as circumstances would
permit, before encountering civilization. A small wooden
trunk was hauled out from the bongo, and Celestino, our
patron, soon underwent a transformation that gave him a
decidedly picturesque appearance. His habiliment, the
usual dress suit of the llanero, consisted of a pair of light-
brown pants extending to the knees, whence each leg was
prolonged into two points, reaching to the feet. Beneath

these flowing appendages were fastened separate pieces of white linen, serving for extensions of the abbreviated trousers. A blue-flannel camisa, ornamented with white trimmings, was worn outside of his pantaloons in lieu of a coat. Two hats, the inner wool, the outer straw, constituted his head-gear, supplemented at the other end by white stockings and shining patent-leather shoes. Our boatmen were less grotesquely but neatly attired, being barefooted, and encumbered with only one hat each. We confess that "Los Nortes," when "fixed" in their best, did not loom up very high in their own estimation; and, we apprehend, did not cut very impressive figures in the eyes of their natives. The probabilities that we should be taken by the Urbanians as attendants of our crew were rather mortifying. But what could we further do to improve our appearance? Our soiled and rusty garments had been whipped and our panamas washed; our coarse flannel shirts, with collars of the same, were as clean as muddy water would make them, and as smooth as they could be stretched; neck-ties, which were reserved for special occasions like the present, had been drawn from our overloaded pockets, and now graced our sunburnt necks. A glance around upon the motley-arrayed group told that all were ready, when *vamos* was given, and we were off for the town.

Reaching Urbana, we were met upon the beach by the president of the village and other officials, with many of the citizens, who received us with the hearty welcome so characteristic of the Spaniard, and which was extended us wherever we went. We had arrived upon one of their numerous fiesta-days, and the people were luxuriating in the festivities of the occasion. A grand banquet was to be given to all the celebrities of the town at the *casa*, or house of the chief executive, and to this we accepted an invitation. At 10 A. M., the designated hour, we made our way to the president's dwelling, where, in his main apartment, we found a cockfight in full blast as a prelude to the dinner. One of the gamesters belonged to the chief executive, who, with much gusto, was personally attending upon his feathered representative in the contest. This affair at length terminated, the bloody arena was cleared, and the crowd for a while dispersed. Assembling again at the expiration of another hour, the guests, about thirty in number, at the announcement of dinner, with a rush like a pack of half-famished wolves, surrounded the festive board. Had it been desirable to seat the guests, the table would not have accommodated over a third of the number present. Such inconveniences as chairs were therefore dispensed with, excepting a couple which were provided for *Los Americanos.* The dishes displayed were many in number, but seemed, for the most part, to have originated from one individual of the swine species. The head of the victim was upon one platter, its ribs upon another, the legs projected over a third, while the other portions, fried, roasted, boiled, and hashed, had been served up for the occasion. There were, furthermore, a single bowl of soup, and another of boiled beans, of which only those could partake who were favored with plates and spoons; while piles of broken cassava lay scattered in every direction. Coffee was not wanting, neither claret, nor aguardiente, of which latter many were tempted to imbibe too freely. Every man was his own waiter; filling his fist with a great piece of meat, and then falling back from the table to give another the opportunity to secure a portion. Toasts and *vivas* followed each other in quick alternation from the feasting guests. Finally, with *vivas* for " Los Estados Unidos," and " Los Americanos del Norte," they betook themselves to the street, where a procession was formed, at the head of which was borne, by two girls dressed in white, the Venezuelan flag and our own star-spangled banner side by side. Music and dancing in the evening closed the celebration and festivities of the day.

We now turned toward our temporary home, the best that the place afforded, an abandoned pulperia, and, upon opening the doors, were greeted by a swarm of hideous, screeching bats, as they made their exit from the building. A war of extermination was at once inaugurated; but we soon discovered our enemy had the better of the game; for, when we made an attack with poles, they clustered up beneath the high palm-leaf roof, whose loose meshes seemed to be fairly alive with the creatures, and whence they poured out reënforcements unlimited. Smoking was then resorted to, which, we inferred, would bring them to a realizing sense of the undesirableness of their presence; but they very quietly secreted themselves in the thatched roof during the operation, while we were compelled to seek refuge without. Failing to expel the creatures, we in despair composed ourselves in our hammocks. We cannot say that the bats proved themselves such undesirable night-companions as our imaginations had pictured them to be, for the oppressive heat of our ill-ventilated room was greatly mitigated by their winging their way to and fro, fanning the air to a constant breeze.

Urbana, which has a Spanish population of about five hundred, comprises a church, three pulperias, and about sixty dwellings, which are mostly on two streets parallel to the river. A portion of the houses are made of mud; while the others are constructed wholly of palm-leaves that are twenty-five to thirty feet in length, a dozen making an ordinary load for a yoke of oxen to drag in from the plains where they are procured. For convenience in building, the houses are made the length of a leaf, which is fastened on with lianas, or vines. Aside from a small patch of maize, we saw nothing growing in this district of country for the support of the people. They depend for subsistence upon the fish and turtles of the river, cassava and maize from the Apure and other sections, and upon their herds, which find abundant pasturage on the savannas among the broken sierras of Guiana. Other necessaries of life are brought up from Angostura; with which town there is carried on a considerable trade in hides, large numbers of which are exported annually from Urbana.

The village of Urbana is beautifully situated at the foot of semi-isolated hills, whose granitic rocks, under the effects of decomposition, exhibit upon their summit grotesque columns which appear like the remains of ancient ruins. We were desirous of visiting these curious formations of Nature; so one morning, accompanied by some natives, we made the ascent of the cerros. Their sides are exceedingly precipitous, and covered with matted woods, which were difficult to penetrate. At length, after an hour's hard climbing, we stood upon the rocky crest, and clambered up to the cross that had been planted by devotees of the Catholic faith, upon the top of the natural tower which rises high above the forest. From here we had a most lovely view of savannas, mountains, and the broad expanse of the Orinoco, which here spreads out like a vast lake. The little village of Urbana lay quietly nestled at our feet, and beyond, across the broad river, a boundless forest of eternal green, while in other directions rose range after range of the broken sierras of Guiana. We saw few landscapes in the tropics so varied and extended. These hills seemed to be a perfect den for *casca-bels*, or rattlesnakes. Of no other section, visited in our equatorial wanderings, could we more truthfully speak as being a place

> "Where at each step the stranger fears to wake
> The rattling terrors of the vengeful snake."

Occasionally they found their way into the town. Seated

one evening with some natives upon the ground in front of a dwelling, the head of one of these serpents, which had lain concealed in the grass, suddenly appeared in our midst, causing a hasty dispersion of our group.

At this village we came across some stray books and papers that had found their way up from Angostura, among which were several numbers of *Harper's Week-ly*, and a copy of "Smith's Primary Geography" in Spanish print, but with the same illustrations that adorn the English edition of that work. It is doubtful if ever, in our school-boy days, we thumbed over with greater interest this little volume for the sake of its pictures, than we leaved it for a similar purpose upon this occasion. Any thing that awakens in the memory of the traveller in distant lands thoughts of home and country, seems to possess a peculiar charm, which, under other circumstances, might be passed unnoticed.

Our rambles about Urbana were productive of much that was new and interesting. Among the many beautiful insects were the blue Monphos, those giants of the insect-world, which were abundant in the forest of the sierras. There was also a species of white butterfly, with black-tipped wings, the same as we have observed in the tropical clime of southern Florida. But what especially interested us were the wonders of the formicariæ, or ant family, many species of which abound here ; some building in hollow trees, others suspending their nests from the branches, while still others construct their homes underground. A large black species, an inch or more in length, is the most numerous, as it is also the most voracious and destructive to vegetation; stripping the foliage from trees with a rapidity truly astonishing. Diverging in every direction through the forest and across the savannas, are their broad and well-beaten trails, resembling sheep-paths. We have often, in our rambles, followed for long distances deserted ant-roads, as affording an easy path to travel. Branches of these *caminos reales*, or royal roads, may be traced to favorite species of trees, along whose trunks will be found two dark lines of these industrious workers; in one they are ascending, in the other descending, each ant in the latter line hid beneath a piece of leaf, which he carries vertically, as he hurries onward to his home. It is evident that they perform their journey, not by sight, but by the sense of smell; for we have often broken their lines by sweeping away the surface of the earth, when they would become confused, until in their wild ramblings the connection was discovered, when they would rush on again in heavy phalanx. When they wish to cross a stream, they seek a fallen trunk which spans the same, or ascend a tree whose boughs form a union with others upon the opposite side. To test their instinct we have removed their bridges, taking the precaution to place ourselves out of harm's way. Satisfying themselves that their connection with the opposite bank was severed, they sought a crossing above or below, which being found, they made good their lines, and business went on as before. Some Indian tribes esteem certain species of these large ants as excellent food. Humboldt informs us that he saw, upon the headwaters of the Orinoco and Rio Negro, natives who subsisted during a portion of the year mainly upon these insects, which, being dried and smoked, were mixed as seasoning into a sort of paste. At Quito, in Ecuador, we have ourselves observed the Indians to eat a species of coleoptera collected in quantities and roasted. With less preparation, the natives pick certain hemipterous insects from one another's heads and eat them with peculiar satisfaction.

So infested are some districts with ants, and so great their destructive proclivities, that it is almost impossible to secure the growth of tender and succulent plants, which

are almost sure to be attacked by them. Upon the Orinoco and Rio Negro we frequently observed the hanging
gardens of the natives, who, when they wish to cultivate
a few vegetables, suspend from the trees, or lift upon
poles, a canoe filled with earth, and in this plant their
seed with some hopes of a harvest. Should some formic
forager discover this aërial garden, immediately it is filled
with voracious insects, and, before the planter is aware of
their presence, his little crop has vanished. We found
them exceedingly annoying, depredating upon every thing
within their reach—and nothing can be placed beyond it.
Especially did they seem to delight in feasting upon the
insects collected by us with so great labor. We mention
these facts to show some of the obstacles that entomolo-
gists in the tropics have to contend with, and how the
very superabundance of insects renders it extremely difficult to secure any for the purposes of science. We see,
furthermore, what a strife for existence man, in these tropical regions, has to maintain. The soil is unsurpassed in
fertility, yet devastating insects prevent him from receiving therefrom his food, while others inflict upon him
venomous stings, or, burrowing themselves in his flesh,
cause festering limbs. Even the elements combine in
making life one unwearied struggle for prolongation.
Driven by swelling rivers which submerge the land, he
is forced, like the wild beasts, to seek refuge in the mountains and on the island-like elevations, or even compelled
to fix his habitation in the trees, there to subsist upon the
products of his arboreal home.

The ornithology of this district is not remarkable;
troupials, parrots, and a species allied to our common
meadow-lark, being among the most noticeable birds.
The first-mentioned suspends its nests in colonies from
branches of the trees; many stately monarchs on the
skirts of the forest, or upon the open savannas—for

these birds seem to love the sunshine—hang with hundreds of their long, sack-like homes, with flocks of the brilliant-colored inhabitants hovering about them, presenting a beautiful sight. Among the many peculiar sounds of animated Nature we recognized the familiar one "Whip-poor-will," recalling pleasant memories of our northern home.

Although Urbana is situated three hundred miles from the gold-regions of Venezuelian Guiana—the veritable "El Dorado," whose fabulous wealth is just being made known to the world—still the Urbanians were suffering from the "gold-fever," so prevalent throughout Venezuela. The story of the "Gilded King," which inflamed such a spirit of wild adventure among the *conquistadores*, had, indeed, a more substantial foundation than we may have thought—it was not wholly chimerical, but had such a basis in facts that we can easily excuse the introduction of the gold-bespangled monarch. The gold-regions embrace the broken mountain-ranges lying about one hundred miles south of the Orinoco, in the eastern portion of Venezuela, between the rivers Essequibo and Caroni. The auriferous quartz is found not only in immense veins, but also in ledges or mountain-like masses, all of a richness which is said to far exceed the gold-bearing quartz of California. These gold-districts are easily accessible from the coast, being situated inland scarcely two hundred miles. Thus far the greater portion of the gold obtained from these rich fields has been the result of unsystematized labor, but already several companies are formed in England, Germany, France, and the States, for the opening of mines and the scientific working of the auriferous quartz. The limits of our own work will not enable us to speak at length upon the wonderful developments that have been made in this incredibly rich yet (until recently) comparatively unexplored field; but we must refer our readers to the excellent work, "Adventures in South and Central America," by Don Ramon Paez, where will be found, in the chapter, "The Land of El Dorado," a full account of these regions.

The temperature of Urbana, although hot, is not so oppressive as that which we experienced elsewhere. This lower temperature is due to the trade-winds, which are constant from east to west, but are felt with diminishing force as you ascend the Orinoco, until reaching the Great Cataracts, beyond which no breeze is ever felt. The winds generally rise at 8 or 9 A. M., continuing until about 4 P. M., and then are felt again from 10 P. M. till three o'clock in the morning. These uniform winds are of great service to vessels navigating the Lower Orinoco. The largest craft that are employed on the river above Angostura are *lanchas*, which consist of a canoe for the hull, its capacity being increased by planks raised upon the sides, with a carroza covering about half its length. To ascend the rapids of the river, smaller boats are necessary.

Our stay at Urbana had been protracted much beyond our first intentions, and we now watched the earliest opportunity to continue our journey. The padre and gobierno of San Fernando de Atabapo, a town above the cataracts of the Orinoco, were daily expected upon their return from Angostura, whither they had gone, and we determined to accompany them up the river. One day the village was thrown into a state of the greatest excitement by a sail heaving in sight, which was supposed to be the governor's. The artillery of Urbana, which consisted of a single brass piece that a boy could easily have carried, was dragged from the arsenal—some back kitchen—and salute after salute pealed forth over the water to greet the approaching vessel, the enthusiasm of the crowd increasing as it neared the land. At length, amid deafening *vivas*, the boat pushed to its anchorage, when, much to the chagrin of the inhabitants and our disappointment, it proved only a loaded lancha bound for the Rio Meta. But, what was still more depressing to us was, the intelligence that neither the governor nor the padre would leave Angostura for several weeks yet to come. Urbana seemed destined to be the highest point upon the Orinoco we were likely to reach. Neither craft nor crew could be secured, nor a single guide be found to accompany us who was acquainted with the passage of the Great Cataracts.

While thus despairingly discussing the probabilities of "going through," our Apure boatmen, who had returned to Asaiba, again appeared at Urbana with a *buco*, or small lancha, which seemed just the thing for ascending the rapids. Negotiations were at once opened with Celestino, the patron, which resulted in his agreeing to take us to San Fernando de Atabapo, for the sum of eighty pesos; he furnishing the crew and supplies for the voyage. A guide alone was all that was lacking. At this juncture of affairs an Indian fortunately wandered into the town, who, with the bribe of a cotton camisa, which we thought his advent into civilization rendered desirable, was induced to accompany us in the capacity of pilot to San Fernando, a distance which it would require nearly a month to accomplish. Our craft measured thirty feet in length, with its greatest breadth about six, and was furnished with a sail that could be hoisted when the wind was favorable. In front of the carroza, which covered about eight feet of the middle of the boat, and was sufficiently high to admit of a sitting posture, were seats for the rowers, while the patron, as steersman, occupied the stern. A stock of provisions sufficient for the long voyage, excepting meat, of which we were able to obtain but little, was put aboard. The wanting substantial we expected to be able to sup-

ply ourselves with by the way. In addition to our staples,
cassava, coffee, papelon, and salt, we added a few bunches
of green plantains, with several armfuls of sugar-canes to
eat when our appetites inclined. Thus we were prepared
for our voyage up the Orinoco.

CHAPTER X.

UP THE ORINOCO.

UPON the afternoon of the 9th of November, with sails
set and flag floating, we took our departure from Urbana,
amid the vivas of the inhabitants who lined the shore,
and were borne swiftly along by the breeze which swept
up the river. To avoid the strong current and catch the
wind, we hugged the southern bank, drawing up at sunset to a *playa*, or sandy beach, some two hundred yards in
breadth, left dry by the falling of the waters. Here we
spread our blankets and stretched our mosquiteros over
us, by fastening them to the palancas of the boat, stuck
in the ground; but this precaution was unnecessary, for
all insectile pests are swept by the winds from these barren
sand-stretches. Wild ducks and geese stalked the playa,
casting suspicious glances toward our encampment; but
they were shy, and we were unsuccessful in our attempts
to secure some for breakfast.

It was scarcely light when we were again breasting
the strong current, propelled by the paddles of our swarthy
trio. At 9 A. M., the wind rising, the sail was hoisted,
and the men rested upon their benches. About noon we

entered the Strait of Baraguan, where the Orinoco narrows to a mile in width, with a current so strong that we were compelled to land and pull up by towage. Having made the passage, we halted at the base of the picturesque granitic hills of Baraguan, which stretch along the eastern shore, and give their name to the strait. The huge masses of rocks, often disposed in columnar form, seemed as if piled up by art; but only the agencies of Nature have here been at work. By the process of decomposition, always rapid in the tropics, the softer parts of the rock are removed, while the harder portions, worn away more slowly, are left standing above the general rock-surface. Upon the Upper Orinoco we frequently observed stones, nicely poised one upon another, forming tall pillars like some ancient ruins, which have been produced in the manner above described. On the mountain-slope at Atures we saw a stone wall—the remains of a dike—over three feet in height and two in thickness, which, left bare by the crumbling and removal of the softer rock by which it was enclosed, appeared as if erected by the hand of man.

Upon the western side of the river, opposite the mountains of Baraguan, was a large playa, upon which was an Indian encampment, to which we crossed. It consisted of a dozen umbrella-shaped huts, about four feet high, constructed from poles stuck in the sand in a circle some eight feet in diameter, with the upper ends brought together, and the whole covered with a few palm-leaves, scarcely sufficient to ward off the sun, and offering no protection against the rains; but, as there was nothing to get wet, aside from iron pots and calabashes, with their own naked persons, we imagined that a shower on this hot shore could be considered no special inconvenience. . Unlike the Guaicas and Guainares of the Upper Orinoco, who are remarkable for their diminutive size, these Ottomac Indians were large, their skin of a brownish-red color, their hair thick and long, hanging over their shoulders, but cut square off just above the eyebrows, giving them a very grotesque appearance. They were unpainted, and without clothing or ornaments of any kind; excepting some of the women, who had their lower lips punctured, and sticks two inches long inserted. Upon inquiry for the *gobierno* of the settlement, who was a Spaniard, we were directed to one of the contracted habitations, where we found that dignitary seated upon the ground, outside of his apology for a dwelling. His wife was squatted inside, a sufficient reason why he must remain excluded. Two or three royal offspring lay rolling naked in the sand. Where the camp were to get their next meal was difficult to tell, as they possessed not a morsel of food among them. Perhaps they were intending to make a very satisfactory one of the clay of the river banks; for these Ottomacs were the veritable dirt-eating Indians mentioned by Humboldt. There is always a great scarcity of food in the wet season, and during that period these Indians eat incredible quantities of clay, taking at the same time only an extremely small amount of other aliment. Humboldt has spoken at some length of this strange habit of dirt-eating, so common among many of the natives of tropical regions. He failed to find, upon analysis, any nutritious elements in the clay, and refers its tendency to appease the sensation of hunger to the secretion of the gastric fluids of the stomach, excited to powerful action by the presence of the earthy substance. The same authority also refers the remarkable preservation of health and strength during protracted periods, when earth constitutes the principal aliment taken by the Indians, to habit, prolonged through successive generations. "Man can accustom himself to an extraordinary abstinence, and find it but little painful, if he employ tonic or stimulating substances (various drugs, small quantities of opium, betel, tobacco, or leaves of coca); or if he supply his stomach, from time to time, with earthy insipid substances, that are not in themselves fit for nutrition."* This habit of eating dirt is prevalent among the Indians of Brazil, and we learned from foreign residents upon the Marañon that their children evinced a morbid appetite for earths, that they sought gratification in swallowing large lumps of innutritious clay.

Departing from this Indian encampment, we poled to the upper end of the playa, which was a league in length, and one-third that in width, and there encamped. The heat of the sun was most intense, and the plain was undulating, like the surface of disturbed water, from the effects of mirage, and every object about us appeared to be elevated and dancing in the air. This singular atmospheric phenomenon, occasioned by the refraction and reflection of light in traversing the strata of rarefied air next the surface of the earth, is common upon the arid playas of the Orinoco. We sometimes saw the long line of barren coast apparently in greater agitation than the river upon which we were sailing; but, approaching, instead of floating into rougher water, we would land upon a sandy, burning shore.

We roamed the playa in search of turtles' eggs, but found only a few, which were those of the *terecai;* it unfortunately not being the season for the great harvest of eggs, which occurs in the months of April and May. From the natives, however, we gathered many interesting facts respecting the "egg-harvest," and by them were made acquainted with the habits of this reptile, which is found in such prodigious numbers upon the Orinoco, between the cataracts and the mouth of the Apure. To Paez, and other travellers on the Orinoco, we are also indebted for much valuable information concerning this animal. The great turtle, called by the Spaniards *tortuga,* and by the

* "Humboldt's Travels," vol. ii., p. 502.

Indians *arrau*, the largest and by far the most abundant of the tortoises inhabiting the Orinoco, is about two feet in length, and weighs fifty pounds. It commences to deposit its eggs in the month of February, when the river has fallen to its lowest level, leaving dry the playas, or sand-bars. Nights are selected for the laying, when the tortuga crawls upon the beach, excavating with its hind-flappers a hole in which from sixty to one hundred and fifty eggs are deposited. It then refills the pit with sand, and smooths it over so as to obliterate all traces of its work. The parent then retires to the water, leaving her eggs to the fostering influence of the sun. During the height of the laying season, the gathering of turtles is so great, says Father Gumilla, "that the multitudes already out prevent the passage of still greater numbers, which, with heads above water, are waiting a chance to pass on."

Scarcely has the laying commenced before the Indians begin their preparations for gathering the eggs. To determine the limits of a stratum of eggs, or to discover scattering nests in the playas, the Indian uses a pole, on thrusting which into the sand, a sudden yielding denotes the presence of the sought-for treasure. Where the tortugas have frequented the most, the beach is one vast layer of eggs; for the turtles, in their zeal to make their deposits, are regardless of the rights of others, one destroying the nest of another, and scattering its contents in every direction, until the sand becomes literally filled with eggs to the average depth, according to Humboldt, of three feet. The eggs are spherical, about one and a quarter inch in diameter, with a calcareous shell, that is soft and coriaceous. The yolk floats in oil instead of in albumen, which gives the eggs their value. The manner of procuring the oil is to place the eggs in canoes or large wooden troughs, where they are broken by sticks, or trodden by children, when water is added, and the whole left exposed to the sun. The oleaginous portion, rising to the surface, is removed and clarified by boiling, forming the article so well known in the country as *manteca de tortuga*, or turtle-butter. Angostura is the principal market for this animal product, and traders are upon the ground at the season of the harvest, to purchase from the Indians the results of their labors.

It is not easy to conceive how great is the destruction of these useful creatures by their various enemies. Even thousands of those that hatch are destroyed before reaching their natural element, falling a prey to vultures and other carnivorous birds, jaguars, and the Indians, who esteem them a delicious morsel, eating them shell and all. Nor are they free from capture when they have entered the water; for caimans and ravenous fishes there await them; still, they perpetuate their race in such untold thousands, that, as Father Gumilla has observed, " it would be as difficult to count the sands of the extensive banks of the Orinoco as to compute the immense number of turtles which it harbors on its borders, and in the depths of its current. . . . Notwithstanding the size of the Orinoco River, it is the opinion of the experts of that country that, were it not for this extraordinary consumption of turtles and their eggs, the increase of these animals in the river would be such as to render it unnavigable; for boats would find it impossible to make way through the immense number of turtles which would appear, were all these eggs to be hatched." What is also an astonishing fact in connection with these reptiles is, the number of years' eggs each contains. There are the eggs fully formed for deposit, then those still smaller for the next year, and so on, diminishing in size for each succeeding issue; and, says the pious Father Gumilla, " God only knows for how many years these creatures are endowed with similar receptacles of life in embryo."

Besides the tortuga, there are several other species of tortoises inhabiting the Orinoco and its tributaries, the largest of which is the terecai, weighing about twenty-five pounds. *Gobesonas, galapagos,* and the little *chipirics,* scarcely five pounds in weight, also abound, especially in the upper waters of the Orinoco and Rio Negro. The large tortuga is not found above the cataracts of those rivers; not that these would be barriers to its ascent, but probably because of the absence of extensive beaches, the favorite and essential haunts for the deposit of its eggs. Turtles are, ecclesiastically, classed the same as fishes, being cold-blooded animals, and their flesh is allowed to be eaten during Lent and on other fast-days of the Church.

The second night from Urbana, spent upon a playa, we experienced a severe storm, which nearly caused us the loss of our buco. It shipped the water to such a degree, that we were obliged to land every thing from the boat. The tempest subsiding, about three o'clock in the morning, we reëmbarked, that we might have the benefit of the favorable breeze then blowing. As daylight came, the wind died away, and the men took to their paddles. During the forenoon we passed upon our right Sinaruco, a stream of considerable dimensions; and the outlets of Suapure and Caripo to our left. To avoid the strong current we kept close in to shore, which afforded us frequent views of groups of audacious monkeys that sat among the branches of the trees, seemingly indifferent to our passing.

It was late in the evening when we stopped at a playa upon which was a camp of Indians similar to those before mentioned. The women were huddled in the small, Hottentot huts, with their heads and feet protruding from all sides, while their naked lords lay stretched in the sand without. Their language, like that of Indian tribes generally, we found to be exceedingly simple and curious, consisting more in signs than verbal utterances. We observed that in conversation, even among themselves, they designated the time of day at which any event would occur by simply pointing toward the heavens; to denote noon, the finger was directed toward the zenith; to express three o'clock in the afternoon, the hand would be inclined toward the west at an angle of forty-five degrees. The dispersion of gathered clouds threatening rain was indicated by a broad sweep of the hand from the mouth outward, the movement being accompanied with an expulsion of the breath. From this was to be understood that a wind would arise, the force of which was to be inferred from the strength of the breath; and the direction in which the clouds would be driven was shown by the movement of the arm.

In the morning, some time before day, we departed from these children of the forest, envying them not their simple and untoilsome life. Toward noon we came upon another small company of the same tribe, who were roasting whole, with simply the entrails removed, two large chiquires, or water-hogs, the stench of which kept us at a respectful distance. The Indians were armed with bows and arrows, and the faces of their naked persons were painted red with the coloring matter extracted from the crushed seeds of annotto (*Bixa orellana*). Bargaining with them for tortugas, which were to be brought us at Santa Barbara, where we proposed remaining a few days, we hastened from the spot, glad to escape from the odor of their savory chiquires.

At 1 P. M. we reached the above-mentioned town, where, upon the beach, we partook of our first meal for the day; regaling ourselves on monkey-steak, which we had secured with our guns by the way. This Spanish *pueblo*, or town, was a collection of a dozen houses scattered along the river for three-quarters of a mile. A strip of land, fifty yards in breadth, had been cleared from the virgin forest, and was waving with banana* trees—the most useful plant to the inhabitants of the tropics. Like the cereals of northern latitudes, it has accompanied man at every step of his progress in these southern climes, and every cottage rests beneath the shade of its banana-trees. It is a herbaceous plant, growing almost spontaneously, with a stem that attains a height of ten to twelve feet, crowned by a cluster of silky, shining leaves, six to eight feet long, and a foot in width. These are extremely delicate and easily torn transversely by the winds, so as to hang in narrow strips from the midvein, resembling pinnate leaves. The plant, which comes to maturity in about twelve months, produces a single cluster of fruit, when the stem dies and new shoots start from its base, several of which are allowed to grow, so that banana-trees are generally in clusters, upon some of which fruit may always be found. No other plant yields so great an amount of nutriment from the same extent of soil, producing, according to the estimate of Humboldt, twenty times as much as corn, forty-four that of potatoes, and one hundred and thirty-three times more than wheat.

At Santa Barbara we received our first introduction to gnats (*simulium*), which were afterward such a source of annoyance as we ascended the cataracts of the Orinoco. They are known to the Spaniards by the name of mosquitoes (diminutive flies), while our insects of that name (*culex*) are called by them sancudos, signifying long-legged. The sting of these minute insects is painful, and leaves a dark spot, caused by the coagulation of blood beneath the skin where the proboscis pierces. These marks are exceedingly lasting: we retained traces of them for

---

* We use the word banana popularly as a generic term including several species: the plantain (*Musa paradisiaca*), dominico (*M. regia*), camburi (*M. rosacea*), are the species most generally cultivated.

months after we had left the regions infested by these insects.

On our second day at this pueblo, the Indians we had met down the river, accompanied by many others of their tribe, arrived, bringing with them the promised turtles. Their chief, who was among the number, and who was distinguished by no outer adornment, observing us for a while very intently, as we were engaged in removing, for preservation, the beautiful plumage of a guacamaya, innocently asked for the long red tail, which seemed particularly to have taken his fancy. Without doubt it would have afforded him no little gratification to have possessed it for his pow-wow embellishments; but, as its removal was incompatible with the object for which we desired the specimen, we felt compelled to refuse the request, as harsh as it might seem to the old chief, who turned away like a disappointed child denied some cherished plaything. There is something impressive in the infantine expression and primitive simplicity of the wild Indians of the Orinoco and Amazons. Their lives are passed with no higher aim than simply maintaining an existence. They seem to entertain no system of belief that can be called religion, and appear to have no knowledge of a Supreme Being. Most of the tribes are tractable, peaceful, and quietly disposed; and, where civilization, so called, has made no encroachments among them, instances of gross vice and immorality are unfrequent.

After three days' delay at Santa Barbara, we resumed our voyage. Some two hundred pounds of jerked beef, which we had the good fortune to secure, had been added to our supplies, and lay piled in a heap in the bow of the boat, covered with banana-leaves to keep off the sun, and the feet of the natives, who were continually treading over it. Our crew had also been strengthened by two additional men for ascending the cataracts. To our left were-broken ranges, which in places approached the river, and in others receded to a distance ; they were not wholly lost sight of until we passed the upper rapids of Maypures ; the western shore was bordered with forest nowhere of any great depth, beyond which spread out the grass-covered plains of the Rio Meta. Occasionally we landed to procure some beautiful bird we saw through the branches of the trees, or to secure game for our commissary department ; but it was not good hunting-ground, at least, so we thought, after having crossed the plains of Apure swarming with animated life. Evidences of deer were to be seen in the piles of horns around every hut. They were abundant on the savannas, but lack of time prevented our making any extended expedition for them. We missed our noisy friends, the guacamayas ; and the shrill cries of herons, flamingoes, and other water-birds, were seldom heard. Pheasants and wild-turkeys were more abundant, but difficult to obtain, from their extreme shyness. The height of the trees rendered our shot-guns useless, and only with the rifle-ball could an object be reached in the top of the forest giants.

At mid-day we landed at a deserted hut, where a sugar-cane grove had fallen beneath the tread of ravenous chiquires and prowling jaguars ; but from banana-trees, which had been undisturbed, we gathered some fine bunches of fruit to carry with us. Opposite us, upon the eastern shore of the river, rose a granitic mountain, whose naked declivity descended to the water's edge. Upon its bald top a fort was erected by the Jesuits, and occupied by them as a military post ; during the war for independence it served as a fortress to the Spaniards, who were compelled to evacuate it, after a siege of four days, by the Venezuelian forces. The place, although nothing is now seen but the rock, still bears the name, " El Castillo de los Españoles "—the castle of the Spaniards. In the face of an adjoining cliff, near its summit, we had pointed out to us the entrance of a dark cavern; its height up the rocky wall renders it inaccessible, but, according to a legend, as given us by our patron, a passage to it was discovered by a padre, who was accustomed to resort thither. He died without divulging the mystic way to the gloomy recess; and it is said that his spirit now frequents the place. The forbidding aspect of the jagged cliff and its wild surroundings make it appear as though it might, indeed, be a favorite haunt for wandering spirits.

Not far from here a violent tempest struck our vessel, and produced a heavy sea that nearly shipwrecked us before we could gain the shore, which being reached, we hastily unloaded our stores, for our buco seemed destined to be dashed to pieces, the high bank preventing us from drawing it upon land. The peaks of the granitic hills were wrapped in one vivid sheet of flame, while peals of thunder, of a nature well calculated to disturb the rest of the good padre, rattled along the cliffs.

Upon the following day we passed without difficulty the *Raudal de Marimara*. Here upon the east bank rises a solid mountain of granite, called *Piedra de Marimara*, its river-front abrupt and without a trace of soil. Separated from this huge rock by a beautiful little inlet upon the south is another granitic pile, which bears the name of *La Piedra del Zamuro*, the rock of the zamuro.* Upon its walls we could distinctly trace the high-water marks, showing that the river had fallen sixteen feet, about half its usual rise. Upon the opposite side of the river was the immense rock, *Piedra del Tigre*, which, sloping up gradually from the stream, presented a favorable place for refection and rest, and accordingly we drew to shore. There is a singular phenomenon connected with these rocks of *Piedra del Tigre*, which is also peculiar to others upon

* Cathartes atratus.

the Middle Orinoco. By putting our ears close to their surface we were able to detect low, musical tones, which our guides observed were more audible in the early morning. The granite is split with deep crevices, that seem to give emission to these mysterious sounds. Humboldt says that he never himself heard these musical tones, but, relying upon trustworthy information as to the reality of this phenomenon, gives the following explanation of the cause : " It may easily be conceived that the difference of temperature between the subterranean and external air attains its maximum about sunrise, or at that moment which is at the same time farthest from the period of the maximum of the heat of the preceding day. May not these organ-like sounds, which are heard when a person lays his ear in contact with the stone, be the effect of a current of air that issues out through the crevices ? Does not the impulse of the air, against the elastic spangles of mica that intercept the crevices, contribute to modify the sounds ? "

By noon of the 18th we reached the *Raudal de Cariben*, where we encountered cataracts that could not be passed with the paddle. The river was blocked with great masses of granite, while huge bowlders strewed the shore, some resting far back from the stream, and often nicely poised one upon another. Traces of ancient water-levels high up on the walls, which in places enclose the river, point unmistakably to the time when the Orinoco was a mighty stream, rolling its volume across the continent like an ocean, but now reduced to the comparatively little rivulet that courses through the bed of the former channel. In those periods of greater floods these bowlder-like masses, now at a distance from the river, were separated by destroying forces from the rock upon which they rest, and by the erosive agency of the waters were worn and left in their present isolated and often strange positions. In

the stream and along its borders, which are submerged
during the annual swelling of the river, we often saw what
might be termed the progressive formation of these granitic bowlders. The upper stratum, several feet in thickness, of a flat rock, would be separated into huge fragments by decomposition. Frequently the blocks would
be arranged in a row, longitudinally with the stream, with
the upper one, from being most exposed to the action of
the current, worn into a perfect bowlder; the next in order
exhibiting not so much the effects of the erosive element;
the third still less; and so on diminishing until, before the
last was reached, no change was perceptible, the rock
being simply divided into sections. Should all but the
first be removed, it would scarcely be conceived that the
isolated bowlder was hewn from the rock upon which it
stands, but rather that it had been deposited there by
some external force.

We ascended the *Raudal de Cariben* by towing; the
current making with violence through the narrow channels
found by the rocks that filled the bed of the stream. A
mile or more to the west of the river, across a treeless and
sunburnt plain, is the little village which bears the name
of the rapids. At 5 P. M. we were in front of the mouth
of the Rio Meta, next to the Guaviare, the largest tributary of the Orinoco. Canoes and lanchas ascend this
stream, penetrating as far as the base of the Andes, and
by an overland journey of about twenty leagues the traveller reaches Bogotá, the capital of Colombia. Its banks
are infested with the Guahibos, a warlike race of savages,
who are a constant source of terror to the voyager on
those waters. They also inhabit the west bank of the
Orinoco as far as the Great Cataracts. Unlike most of
the Indian tribes of the Orinoco, who are peaceably inclined, and follow the tillage of the soil, cultivating the
banana, yuca, and sugar-cane, the Guahibos lead a no-

madic life, deriving their means of subsistence from the chase and depredatory excursions upon the neighboring agricultural tribes.

Opposite the mouth of the Meta, and near the eastern shore of the Orinoco, rises a large rock called *Piedra de la Paciencia*, the stone of patience, from the difficulty boats experience in making its passage. The height and steepness of the cliffs, upon either side of the channel that must be made, prevent towing, and render it necessary to stem the powerful current with the paddles. We found occasion to call into requisition an unusual amount of "paciencia," but, after a severe pull, being swept back each moment almost as much as we ascended, we at length moored safely above. We spent the night upon the rocks, spreading our blankets beneath us, which relieved in a degree their hardness, but not their heat, which they receive during the day and retain with apparently little loss through a large portion of the night.

Three hours before daylight we embarked, in order to pass the *Raudal de Tabaja* before night. The wind rising by 9 A. M., we were enabled to use our sail for the first time in many days. At noon we halted upon the right bank, where a narrow belt of woodland bordered the river. The country to the eastward presented a rocky and desert waste, filled with jungles—fit haunts for jaguars and venomous serpents. A wilder scene we found nowhere in our wanderings; and with no little apprehension we roamed over the place in search of the few plants which clung to the jagged cliffs, or sprang up in the deep morasses. We observed with interest the melo cactus, which found a genial home upon these burning rocks. It is of a globular shape, from eight to twelve inches in diameter, and covered with thorns that make it dangerous to disturb. The juice contained within its prickly shell tempts the thirsty animal of the sun-parched plains, which, it is said, carefully penetrates with his hoof to the hidden beverage. Thus Nature in times of rain stores up within this humble plant the nourishment it needs for itself during the long period of drought, and which also serves to quench the thirst of the herds that roam the savannas.

A short distance farther on and we came to the *Raudal de Atabuja*, where, half an hour was consumed in the passage, when we turned into a small creek to seek shelter from the heat of the mid-day sun. Our boat had scarcely touched the bank before the ominous cry of " El tigre! el tigre!" rose from our natives, who were rushing frantically about. With our rifles we hastened upon the shore, but looked in vain for some huge jaguar among the tree-tops, whither our attention was directed. The creature responsible for the disturbance proved to be a venomous serpent whose long, slim body was as spotted as the animal whose name it bore.

The night of the 19th was passed upon a rock, where bats took the place of sancudos in disturbing our slumbers. These filled the crevices and lay in scores beneath every bowlder. As soon as darkness invited them from their hiding-places, they poured out in hundreds, and made night hideous with their screeching. We had scarcely composed ourselves, before a cry from our Indian guide told that he had been made a victim by one of these creatures, which had taken a large mouthful at the expense of one of the poor fellow's toes. Presently another, and soon a third one of our natives received similar visits, when we deemed it advisable to protect our own pedal appendages, which were exposed, as we had other use for them than feeding ugly bats. The nose seems also to offer them particular attractions; but we, being especially opposed to molestation at that point, rolled ourselves in our blankets *cap-a-pie;* but the heat of the atmosphere, and the still hotter rocks beneath, led us to abandon the experiment, and very resignedly to offer ourselves as their prey. But, while exhibiting a strong predilection for our natives, they left us unmolested. These carnivorous and sanguineous creatures seem to show a great partiality for some persons, paying them their nightly respects, while others are entirely free from their molestations. With the great vampire-bat, which has been so often referred to by travellers in the tropics as such a formidable enemy, we never had any personal experience. They, however, abound, to the terror of both man and beast. Differing from some of the smaller species we have mentioned, they are contented with simply taking the blood of their victim, which they extract in such profuse quantities that it is hazardous to sleep in the open air where one is exposed to their attacks. The danger to be apprehended from these winged demons is the greater, because they inflict so little pain in their operations that the person or animal is not aroused from slumber. Making a minute puncture, they drain by suction the blood from their victim, while lulling him into sounder repose with the noiseless fanning of their wings. It is a disputed point as to the manner in which the bat makes the incision; whether with its tongue, with the sharp nail of its thumb, or by boring with one of its long canine teeth by flying around in a circle. The wound, although exceedingly small, bleeds profusely; and the person, upon awakening, will find himself covered with the flowing blood.

Above the *Raudal de Atabapa*, the river, which below is contracted and encumbered with rocks, again broadens, and is filled with sandy shoals and picturesque islands. The wooded banks, the lowest we had seen on the Orinoco, were often overflowed, leaving dry immense playas, which, when connected with the shore, obliged us to go far out into the stream. Not unfrequently our buco ran aground, when our natives, springing into the water, would push us off into deeper sailing ; often they towed the boat along for miles over the shallow places, as a relief to constant rowing. The heat was most intense, and the mosquitoes increased as we neared the Great Cataracts. We tried covering our hands and faces with gloves and veils, but the heat was insupportable. Expelling, by means of smoke, the torments from beneath our carroza, and spreading a blanket over the entrance, we could enjoy a few minutes' repose; but the vertical rays of the sun upon our palm-leaf thatch would soon drive us to the external air. The little caribe fish that filled the river, and huge caimans which showed their scaly backs everywhere above the surface of the water, prohibited bathing, that would have afforded so refreshing a relief.

The night of the 20th was passed upon an island plaia in the middle of the river, whither we carried wood in our boat for a fire. Roving bands of Guahibos had been seen during the day along the western shore, and jaguars were also unpleasantly abundant on this portion of the Orinoco. Having no particular desire to encounter either, we selected a camping-ground where surprise by them would be more difficult than upon the main-land. The following night we passed upon a rock, and early upon the morning of the 22d of November we arrived at the far-famed cataracts of the Atures.

RAPIDS OF MAYPURUS, ORINOCO.

CHAPTER XI.

THE GREAT CATARACTS OF THE ORINOCO.

THE Orinoco, eight hundred miles from the sea, forcing
its way through a granitic range of the Guiana Mountains,
forms the cataracts of Atures.   To obtain a view of these
rapids, let the traveller place himself on the summit of
overlooking hills which rise just to the east of the river,
and he has before him a scene that is stupendously grand.
Other landscapes may be viewed and forgotten; but the
majestic appearance of the rapids of the Atures leaves an
impression that will never fade from the memory.   For
more than a league the river is broken by rapids and filled
with huge granitic masses, piled on one another in endless
confusion; while islands, clothed with crested palm-trees
and beautiful vegetation, rise above the whitened waters.
The river is divided by these enchanting islets into numerous channels, through which the waters, lashed into foam,
tumble with frightful violence, breaking with deafening
roar upon the rocks.   At the season of the greatest rise of
the Orinoco, when these stones and crags which fill the

bed of the channel are submerged by the floods that pour their impetuous volumes down this inclined plain, the aspect of the river must be grand in the extreme. The mountains upon the west of the cataracts are rugged and barren, and closely follow the river; while in the distance the lofty peak of Uniana, three thousand feet in height, rises like a huge column in the midst of the plain. East of the Atures the hills are wooded, and bound a plain a league or more in breadth, strewed with great bowlders, sometimes heaped in huge, irregular masses, with here and there a verdant ravine and clump of trees that meet the eye as it wanders over this wild and desolate tract. Upon the isolated peak, from whose crest we take our view of the rapids, are the remains of a dike, referred to in a previous chapter, which runs like a wall up the steep slope of the sierra. The summit of the hill is also mounted by huge bowlders of granite, twenty to thirty feet in diameter, some of them so nicely poised and resting upon each other two and three in height, that it seems as though they might easily be pushed down into the river-channel.

In the afternoon we started with our natives for the village of Atures, to procure a *practico* to aid us in passing the cataracts. A league over the rocky and burning plain brought us to the river Cataniapo, which we were unable to cross; but our Indian guide, swimming the stream, succeeded in reaching the settlement, returning soon with the promise of assistance on the morrow. Retracing our steps, we observed fresh tracks of tigers, which are exceedingly numerous in the wild districts about the Cataracts of the Orinoco. That we were unarmed, with the prospect of darkness overtaking us before we could reach camp, was by no means a comforting reflection. In the morning, footprints of tigers, within a few yards of where we had slept in our hammocks under the trees, gave evidence of their visits during the night, our fires having been suffered to expire.

Our practico, or pilot, arriving from the village by sunrise, we commenced the passage of the rapids. The river, a third of a mile in breadth, emerged from the first line of obstructions in two main channels, along each of which rolled a tremendous flood over the stony blocks that filled their beds, while between these were numerous small openings in the islands and rocks, through which the waters poured in whirling eddies and dangerous whirl-pools. Lanchas, or large canoes, descending in time of high water—for at no other season can they descend the rapids—choose the large channel upon the west; but no craft can ever ascend against the powerful current and heavy breakers of this river-torrent. Plunging into the swift stream, we pulled over to one of the small channels, and then upon an island landed our stores, which were carried over a short portage to where, if successful, we would again embark. Now, entering the rapids, we clamber over the huge granitic bowlders, springing from rock to rock, pulling our boat along through the whirling waters : sometimes a projecting point must be reached; when, with rope in hand, a native plunges into the river, but often the bold adventurer is borne down by the impetuous torrent. At length, after several unsuccessful attempts, the crag is reached; he is joined by others, and the boat is hauled up past the obstruction. But now another obstacle, perhaps more difficult and dangerous still, presents itself. Some climb the rocks, while others swim the breakers, and thus from crag to crag, with pushing, pulling, and poling, we slowly make our way up the cataracts. At length a cliff lifts its bold front directly in our pathway, beneath whose stony masses the roaring waters flow in subterranean caverns. Over the granitic pile we with difficulty drag our canoe, when the first line of barriers is overcome, and we float into smoother water. Reloading our craft, we pull up, through verdant and picturesque islands, to the second rocky dike that spans the river. Our baggage and supplies are to be carried from here over a portage of a league to the upper limit of the rapids, and the boat to be dragged up through the rocky obstructions.

The village of Atures, whither we now directed our course, is two miles distant upon the plain, or one below the upper terminus of the portage. The heat of the atmosphere, augmented by reflection from the stony soil and granitic masses, was excessive in the extreme. Upon arriving at the village, our Indian guide, who had carried our papelon in a banana-leaf basket upon his head, presented a unique appearance. His head had perforated the mass, which, under the influence of the hot sun, flowed in streams down his naked person. The village consisted of six inhabited mud huts, a little chapel, now used as a dormitory for cows, and two abandoned, dilapidated hovels, in one of which we established ourselves for the time we might remain at the Atures.

Here we saw, for the first time, that curious weapon, the *cerbatana*, or blow-gun, in the use of which the natives of the country are so skilful. It is made of a light, hollow reed, which grows in abundance in the forests of the Upper Orinoco. As these are slender, two, and sometimes three, of different sizes are taken, so that they can be inserted one into the other.* These are then wound with smooth, black, shining bark, which gives it a tasteful appearance. At one end is fitted a mouth-piece of horn, and a short distance from it a projection of the same for a sight. The whole, when completed, is ten or twelve feet long. The arrow, generally made from the leaf of a palm,

---

* The blow-gun of the Upper Amazonian Indians is constructed of two pieces of hard wood, generally chonta-palm, each of which is hollowed out, then the two united, wound with bark, and coated with a resinous substance.

is the size of a common straw, and a foot in length. One end is nicely wound with the light cotton of the ceiba-tree so as to fill exactly the tube of the gun, and the other extremity is pointed and dipped in *curare*, a poison distilled from a vine of the forest. So powerful is this venomous juice that it will kill a bird almost instantly, and the large jaguar succumbs to its effects in a space of ten or fifteen minutes. The flechetes, as the little missiles are called, can be propelled, with a single puff of breath, through the cerbatana one hundred or one hundred and fifty feet with the greatest accuracy. The quiver is twelve or fourteen inches long, beautifully woven from fibres of the palm-leaf, the lower part coated with a resinaceous substance obtained from a forest-tree.

Equipped with his cerbatana and quiver of poisoned arrows, the Indian goes in quest of game. "Silent as midnight," quaintly writes Waterton, "he steals under them, and so cautiously does he tread the ground, that the fallen leaves rustle not beneath his feet. His ears are open to the least sound, while his eye, keen as that of the lynx, is employed in finding out the game in the thickest shade. Often he imitates their cry, and decoys them from tree to tree, till they are within range of his tube. Then taking a poison arrow from his quiver, he puts it in the blow-pipe, and collects his breath for the fatal puff. Silent and swift the arrow flies, and seldom fails to pierce the object at which it is sent." The flesh of game thus shot is in no wise injured for eating, as the poison can be taken internally with impunity. In its preparation the Indians test its strength by tasting; but care must be observed that the skin of the lips or mouth be not fractured so as to bring the substance into contact with the blood. Salt is an antidote for the poison, and, if timely employed, will neutralize its deleterious effects. When the Indian desires to capture a monkey or bird alive, he uses a flechete anointed with diluted curare, and instantly upon the fall of his prize fills its mouth with salt, which soon restores the animal unharmed.

The manufacture of curare is known to but comparatively few, the Indians of the Cassiquiare and Upper Rio Negro being the principal producers for all the neighboring regions. The virulent principle it contains is extracted from the bark of *benjuco de mavacure* (*Strychnos toxifera*), a vine abundant in the forests of the districts where the curare is made. When prepared, it has the color and consistence of tar, and is sold in small calabashes at an exorbitant price. It is an interesting fact that this concentrated juice of the *mavacure*, which is so deadly when introduced into the circulation, has been found to be a specific for that other powerful poison, strychnine, whose pernicious effects are so difficult to counteract.

The other weapons of the natives, besides the cerbatana, are bows and arrows, in the construction of which they exhibit no little taste and ingenuity. The bow is generally from five to six feet long, and made from a hard, black, elastic wood, with a string woven from the fibres of the palm-leaf. The arrows, from five to seven feet in length, consist of a light reed, in one extremity of which is inserted a head about a foot long, made of hard wood, with the point dipped in curare; the other extremity is winged with feathers arranged spirally so as to produce a rotary motion, thus exhibiting an acquaintance with principles applied among civilized nations. The question is naturally suggested, Is this contrivance, for giving directness and effectiveness to missiles, an invention of civilization, or must it be recorded as an achievement of barbarism, developed and improved by modern genius? The arrow employed for the capture of turtles, during the season when they do not appear upon the playas, differs from the above-described in having a barbed iron point fitting loosely in the shaft, to which it is attached by a long cord. The smooth, hard shell of the turtle, if struck obliquely, would ward off the arrow; the hunter, therefore, calculates his distance, and, with an unerring aim, sends his missile into the air, when, describing a parabola, it descends with force and pierces the back of the victim Immediately the animal dives, carrying with him the iron point fastened in his coat of mail, unreeving the string that connects it to the shaft, which floats upon the water, and enables the Indian to regain the cord and secure the turtle. We have often been astonished in observing at how great a distance the keen eye of the Indian will detect an object, and the precision with which he will send an arrow, apparently drawn at a venture.

Nowhere as at Atures had we suffered so severely from insects, and yet we were told that the climax would not be reached until we arrived at the Maypures. At early dawn the mosquitoes made their appearance, nor did they disappear till the shades of evening invited forth the larger insects, the sancudos, which fortunately are not so abundant in this season at Atures as they are during the rainy months, when they swarm in clouds. The mosquitoes seem to be constant throughout the year, filling the atmosphere in numbers sufficient to dim the vision. We could not breathe or speak, without taking in these noxious insects; they gathered in our eyes, and pierced every exposed part of our persons. Humboldt, in speaking of these districts, says: "The lower strata of air, from the surface of the ground to the height of fifteen or twenty feet, are absolutely filled with venomous insects. If, in an obscure spot, for instance in the grottoes of the cataracts formed by superincumbent blocks of granite, you direct your eyes toward the opening enlightened by the sun, you see clouds of mosquitoes more or less thick. At the mission of San Borja, the suffering from mosquitoes is greater than at Carichana; but in the Raudales, at Atures, and, above all, at Maypures, this suffering may be said to attain its maximum. I doubt whether there be a country upon earth where man is exposed to more cruel torments in the rainy season."

On our second evening at the village of Atures, we walked to the river to see how our boat advanced up the cataracts. Nine men had been employed in the work, and had succeeded in bringing it through the rapids to where it became necessary to drag it some distance overland, by putting it upon rollers, as at this point obstructions completely filled the eastern channel of the river—the one we were ascending. The rocks exhibited those peculiar erosions, called "pot-holes," twenty or more feet in depth, and from three to five feet in diameter; while at their bottom were small stones and quartz-gravel, which, given a revolving motion by the action of the water, had slowly drilled themselves through the solid rock. The primitive rock of the Great Cataracts is a coarse-grained granite, often containing hornblende; yet it does not constitute true syenite. We observed traces of black coating upon the stones wherever they are washed by the water, such as excited the interest of Humboldt; yet they did not exhibit that glistening, metallic appearance which that traveller mentions as giving such a singular aspect to this wild river-scenery.

North of the village of Atures, and nearly two leagues distant, is a settlement of a few houses, called Pueblo Viejo, the old town, which, like the one upon the line of portage, was at one time quite a flourishing village; but the plague of insects, with the insalubrity of the climate in these misty and heated districts, caused its depopulation, and it has fallen nearly into decay. It is surprising that any persons should so persistently remain; but the attachment which inhabitants of frozen regions entertain for their homes, amid inhospitable snows, seems to possess these people of the burning, pestilential plains of the Orinoco, fraught with so many causes of annoyances and death.

On the morning of the 26th of November, after over three days spent in making the passage of the cataracts of Atures, we renewed our voyage, leaving behind one of our natives, sick with the calenture, so prevalent in the malarious districts of the Great Cataracts. The Orinoco, at this point where it enters the *Raudales*, is two-thirds of a mile in width, or twice that where it issues from the rapids below. Of the several channels into which the stream divides, the western is the largest, and, as we have remarked, the one through which vessels pass in making the descent of the falls. The other channels are, for the most part, beds of granitic rocks, which are covered only during the annual swelling of the river. Black bands and erosions upon the stones indicated that the waters had already fallen twenty feet below their highest level. To our left, at a short distance from the river, were the mountains which contain the cave of Ataruipe, the sepulchre of the destroyed nation of the Atures. We regretted that we were unable to visit this cemetery of a departed race, which Humboldt saw and describes as a place of so great interest. That traveller counted nearly six hundred skeletons within the cave, all well preserved, each being placed in a basket wrought of palm-leaves. " A tradition circulates among the Guahibos, that the warlike Atures, pursued by the Caribs, escaped to the rocks that rise in the middle of the Great Cataracts; and there that nation, heretofore so numerous, became gradually extinct, as well as its language. The last families of the Atures still existed in 1767, in the time of the missionary Gili. At the period of our voyage an old parrot was shown at Maypures, of which the inhabitants said, and the fact is worthy of observation, that 'they did not understand what it said, because it spoke the language of the Atures.'"*

At noon we arrived at the *Raudal de Garcita*, which we passed by towing. To the southeast, in the distance, we beheld the truncated peak of Calitamini, nearly four thousand feet high, towering far above the surrounding hills. Its peculiar outline and lofty height attract from afar the attention of the traveller on the Upper Orinoco. The vegetation along the river displayed that luxuriance, beauty of form, and freshness of color, peculiar to the rich and humid regions of the tropics. The white trunks of Yagrumas, or Cecropias (*Cecropia peltata*), the home of the sloth, with their large palmate leaves, were abundantly intermingled with statelier trees, which towered up to a height we had seen nowhere surpassed, while vines hung in beautiful festoons from the borders of the forest. Palm-trees were especially a striking feature in this tropical landscape; the fan-leaved Mauritia, the lofty Cucurito, and spiny-trunked Macanella, rose in marked conspicuousness amid the endless variety of arboreal forms. The Jagua, the most majestic of palms, whose stately trunk attains a height of seventy to eighty feet, especially invites the attention of the traveller. Its immense plume-like leaves, twenty-five to thirty feet in length, and nearly vertical, with their extremities gently curving, form a coronal of verdure of exceeding grandeur. Of the many and varied forms of vegetation we beheld under the tropics, none impressed us more with its beauty and gracefulness than the Jagua-palm. The Jagua of the Orinoco must not be confounded with the *palma de Yagua* of other parts of Venezuela, the vernacular name of which is the Corozo Colorado, from which the inhabitants obtain their supply of palm-oil, in the same manner as the African

* "Humboldt's Travels," vol. ii., p. 484.

negroes obtain theirs from an allied species, viz., by boiling the fruit in water, and crushing it in a wooden mortar, until the sarcocarp is separated from the seed, and the oil floats on the surface of the liquid mass thus produced.

Discovering smoke curling upward from the trees of a forest-island, we landed and found a large palm-hut, inhabited by several families of Piaroas, who were living in a patriarchal community. Hearing us disembark, the naked inmates came swarming out from their wretched dwelling. The women were unornamented; but the men, imitating Nature, who adorns the male in the gayest robes, were decorated in a most fantastic manner. A necklace of tiger or crocodile teeth was worn around the neck, with bands of the same on the wrists. Upon the head was a wreath, made by weaving in a circular band the variegated plumage of the bright-colored macaw; while down the back hung a bunch of feathers, tails of animals, beautiful humming-birds, and trinkets of various kinds. We were to them objects of the greatest curiosity; they examining our persons, clothes, and things, with the utmost delight and childish admiration. Our watches especially excited their attention; but their utility, besides subserving the purpose of ornamentation, they could not comprehend. From these Indians we supplied ourselves with a number of *candalas*, or torches, which consisted of a strip of bark a yard long, rolled into a tube three inches in diameter, filled with a resinous substance, which in burning gives out more smoke than light. The natives of the Orinoco often make use of phosphorescent insects (*pyrophorus noctilucus*), as a substitute for artificial light. A number of these natural lamps placed in a calabash, and shaken when wanted for use, will emit light sufficient to make visible all objects within the hut.

Late in the afternoon of the 27th, gathering clouds indicating a heavy storm, we hastened to a large rock and made fast. Our natives, undressing, tucked their clothes away in the boat under shelter, and then sat quietly down upon the bank to await the coming rain, while we crept beneath our carroza. Soon the heavens opened, and the floods came. Darkness also coming before the tempest was over, we were obliged to remain here during the night, sleeping upon our arms from fear of jaguars and Guahibos. Leaving our anchorage early in the morning, we soon came to the *Raudal de los Guahibos*, which is a single ledge of rocks stretching across the river. Our natives plunged into the water, and, by swimming from rock to rock, they managed, after much difficulty and danger, to pull the boat through the rapids. A league farther, and upon a sudden turn in the river, we came directly in front of the *Raudales de Maypures*. We gazed with emotions of strange awe up the long vista of water, as, lashed into foam, it came plunging down over the rock-masses and through palm-covered islands that studded the river. We landed in a cove upon the west bank, at the lower terminus of the portage, near the confluence of the Orinoco and Guahibo Rivers. Here we took our Thanksgiving-dinner. Kindling a fire, we boiled some strips of tough beef and a few remaining bananas, which, together with cassava and guarapo, constituted our meal. Pacing backward and forward along the hot beach, our feet burning from contact with the heated earth, with food in one hand, and the other in rapid motion with a large leaf to disperse the thick clouds of mosquitoes which darkened the air, we succeeded in taking our dinner—we trust, with thankful hearts.

Skirting the rapids upon the west is a low, granitic ridge, partly wooded, from whose summit may be viewed the great cataracts. We wish that we could picture the majestic scenery that we from those heights beheld. For over a mile the river is filled with great blocks of granite, and islands with ledges of rocks stretching between them, or reaching from shore to shore. Through the narrow channels, over the huge bowlders, and long dikes, the waters wildly plunged as if they would whirl the very rocks from their foundations, and sweep them down the rapids. The islands and larger rocks were covered with alluvial deposits, supporting a growth of beautiful palm-trees and tropical vegetation, which rose in luxuriant masses of most vivid green through the vapory clouds which hovered over the waters. The river at the foot of the cataracts is contracted to less than five hundred yards in breadth, opening a short distance below to twice that width. There are three grand dikes, or falls, which form the striking features in the *raudales* of the Maypures. The most remarkable of these is the one terminating the cataracts. Above this is the Cascade of Manimi, formed by the continuation across the river of the granitic ridge upon the west, before alluded to. The most southern, a mile above the base of the *raudales*, is divided by a huge and nearly naked rock some three hundred feet in height, which rises like an immense tower out of the midst of the whitened waters. Above this, the river gradually widens to two miles in breadth, and for nearly a league is filled with rocks and shoals, which render it difficult of navigation.

East of the cataracts is a chain of hills, connected upon the south with the lofty mountains of Cunavami, and the truncated peak of Calitamini. The Suniapo River, taking its rise among these ranges, flows into the Orinoco just above the lowest cascade of the rapids. Upon the west are the hills of Manimi, with isolated cliffs, rocks, and island-like formations, scattered over the partially-wooded plain which stretches out to the horizon. Some distance to the westward of where the Orinoco at present flows is a valley, which indicates itself as having been the ancient bed of an arm of that majestic river. The land between it and the present channel also gives evidence of having been overflowed; so that the rocks and wooded peaks which now rise in this dry tract were formerly islands in the great current that anciently rolled its floods across the continent. It was the opinion of Humboldt—and we see nothing to militate against its probability—that a canal could be cut around the cataracts of Atures and Maypures, and thus this great river rendered navigable a distance of upward of twelve hundred miles, or nearly to its source among the lofty mountains, to the east of its bifurcation. The perpendicular fall which the river makes in its descent of these rapids is not so great as might be supposed from the turbulent appearance of the waters; and the nature of the ground presents excellent facilities for artificial channels around these obstructions to the free navigation of the river. The entire fall of the Maypures scarcely amounts to more than thirty feet, while that of the Atures is still less.

At the upper terminus of the portage, which is a league in length, we found three mud houses; one possessed by a Spanish family, another by some Indians, and the third abandoned. This was the village of Maypures, once a thriving mission-station, containing in the time of the Jesuits about six hundred inhabitants, but now almost deserted, its site overgrown with bushes and forest, with here and there sad traces of past prosperity. As we have before remarked in speaking of Atures, the insalubrity of the climate about the Great Cataracts, together with the intolerable plague of insects, has caused the depopulation of these regions. Night here brings no relief from the annoyances and pains of the day. There is no cooling breeze, as at Atures, upon the approach of evening, to assuage the heat of a burning atmosphere; for at Maypures no wind is ever felt. Time has made no diminution in the number of insects. At the commencement of the present century, it is said that the suffering occasioned by them was so unendurable, that the inhabitants of the village were accustomed to retire to sleep amid the rocks and islands of the cataracts, as there the insects were less numerous. We now see the wretched natives, in order to escape in a degree their torments, build a fire within their huts and suspend their hammocks in the smoke. A few coffee-shrubs and plantains are cultivated, while here and there an orange or cocoa-nut tree is seen growing about the deserted and decayed village; but the chief subsistence of the few inhabitants is the game of the forest, fish and turtles of the river, together with yuca raised by the neighboring Indian tribes. The cultivation of maize on the Upper Orinoco is now entirely neglected; and the herds of cattle, which at one time grazed upon the savannas, have disappeared.

We spent but one day at Maypures, and at noon of the 29th we again embarked, having been fortunate enough to secure a large canoe above the cataracts, which spared us the labor of dragging our own boat through the rapids, and saved us a delay of two or three days. Paddling down a winding *caño* but a few yards in width, that flows through a majestic woodland, we soon emerged upon the Orinoco, which, for more than a league, was divided into two channels by a chain of islands in the middle of the stream. The atmosphere we breathed seemed as if drawn from a furnace. Not the slightest motion in the lower strata of air was perceptible; for, from the Great Cataracts of the Orinoco to the celebrated Falls of the Rio Negro, a perpetual calm prevails. On the Lower Orinoco and Amazons, where the streams take the direction of the trade-winds, which are from east to west, breezes are constant, and the climate more salubrious than where the air is stagnant through the absence of atmospheric currents, as upon the Upper Orinoco and Rio Negro.

In this humid climate, so destructive to whatever moisture can affect, our watches became useless. But what need of such contrivances when the hour of the day can be determined by animated life, which so thickly swarms these districts? Each species of insect alternately comes and disappears at invariable hours. Between the departing of some species, and the appearing of the one which succeeds, there is a short intermission; others overlap each other. Each produces a peculiar sensation by its sting, that cannot be mistaken, so that, even though clouds obscure the sun, or darkness veil the night, one may be assured how far upon its course the day or night has gone. The seasons, too, in sections of this tropical clime where no alternating periods of rains and drought note their passage, but where vegetation is ever green, and falling showers moisten the earth throughout the year, can be known by the migration of birds, as, driven by swelling rivers inundating the land, they seek other sections where food may be found, returning at their appointed time, when the subsiding of the waters invites them back to their favorite haunts. Thus the Indian of these equatorial regions reads from Nature the times and seasons: the opening flowers, the birds and insects, all tell him of the fleeting hours and years.

Early on the second day from Maypures, we passed the *Raudal de Cameji;* farther on, and to our left, the Sipapo River; and a little later we arrived opposite the mouth of Rio Vichada, next to the Guaviare and Meta, the largest of the western tributaries of the Orinoco. The following morning we passed on the west, first the Zema, then the Mataveni—rivers which have *aguas negras,* or black waters. Our progress was slow against the broad, strong current of the river, although to avoid its force we kept close to the banks, which rose abruptly, in places twenty to thirty feet high. Along these cliffs we observed strata of red, yellow, and white clay; the last equalling in quality that from which porcelain-ware is manufactured in our own country. They all doubtless belong to the great ochraceous formation, known as Tabatinga clay, met with throughout the valleys of the Rio Negro and Amazons. But few islands or rocks here obstructed the river; and often, looking up the broad stream, marked upon either side by a long forest-line, our eyes rested upon a blank horizon—the meeting of the water and sky. On the morning of the 3d of December, we passed a large square rock standing in the river, called *El Castillito*, the little castle. Here was also a *raudal*, through which we hauled our canoe, and two hours after sunset, under the light of a bright moon, we crossed the river for the last time, and, bidding farewell to its waters, entered the mouth of the Guaviare. Thus terminated our long and tedious voyage up the Orinoco. Following up a short distance the Guaviare to its confluence with the Atabapo, we turned into the latter, and soon after landed at the town of San Fernando.

CHAPTER XII.

ATABAPO AND UPPER RIO NEGRO.

San Fernando de Atabapo is one of the most delightfully-situated towns we met with in the interior. It occupies a central position upon the great water-shed of the Orinoco and Amazonian valleys, and lies at the junction of three considerable rivers—the Guaviare, Atabapo, and Orinoco. The town seems scarcely to have felt the influence of Spanish and Portuguese civilization, marching up the Orinoco and Amazons. It contains a population of four or five hundred, chiefly Indians. The mandioca, sugar-cane, cacao, and coffee, are cultivated in sufficient quantities to meet the wants of the people. Cocoa-nut palms, which have accompanied man in his migrations in all lands, thrive here, notwithstanding their distant removal from the coast. Cotton grows spontaneously, as it does throughout the mountainous regions of Guiana. This plant is here a perennial, and attains a height of six to eight feet. Pine-apples grow wild in the greatest abundance, and possess a richness of flavor often deficient in cultivated varieties. Broken savannas roll out from the town, but no cattle roam their grassy stretches. These animals were introduced at San Fernando when the mission was first established, but have long since disappeared.

Ship-building, in rather a primitive way, is quite largely carried on at San Fernando, the forests affording the best of timber for that purpose. Craft upward of a hundred tons burden are constructed with no other tools than the saw, axe, and hammer. Only the hulls are completed, and when the water is highest these are floated down the Orinoco, or taken around by the Cassiquiare to the Amazons. As they cannot ascend the great cataracts of those rivers, they do not return, but new ones are annually built and run down during spring-tide. These hulls are loaded with hammocks, mandioca, piassaba-rope made from the fibres of that palm, and other products of this region. In passing the cataracts of Maypures and Atures, and the great rapids of the Rio Negro, the cargo is removed and carried around the obstructions by portage; while only a pilot remains aboard to run the vessel through the rapids —a perilous feat to the adventurous navigator. Both the vessel and its contents are sold, and the voyagers return in small canoes. These craft, when fitted out with rigging, are used in the coasting-trade, and in navigating the rivers of the lower country.

During our sojourn in San Fernando, we occupied a residence temporarily vacated. Naked timbers stretched across from side to side, one of which, giving way one day, came crashing down, striking the ground where, but a moment before, one of our number had been seated. Ants had eaten off the extremities where it rested upon the mud walls, and caused its falling. One who has never visited the tropics can form no conception of the devastation wrought by voracious insects. Houses are literally consumed by them, and whole villages often rendered a pitiable scene of desertion and ruin.

Until our arrival at San Fernando, we were undecided as to which of the two routes to the Rio Negro we should take; whether to ascend the Atabapo and Temi, and then make the portage of three leagues to the caño Pimichín, or to ascend the Orinoco and make the passage of the Cassiquiare. The former was much shorter, with no serious obstacles to overcome, and could, furthermore, be performed, at this favorable season of low water, in twelve or fifteen days less than would be required to make the other, which necessitated a journey against the current of the Orinoco of nearly fifty leagues through a wild, barren, and uninhabited country. Reaching Esmeralda, near the celebrated bifurcation of the Orinoco, the traveller descends the Cassiquiare, traversing a forest-region infested with insects, which, we were told, were more "ferocious" than those of the Great Cataracts. After navigating that stream sixty leagues, and passing the many rapids that obstruct its course, he emerges upon the black waters of the Rio Negro. After our severe experiences upon the Orinoco, we had no inclination to endure the still greater annoyances attending a voyage upon the Cassiquiare, and therefore determined to ascend the Atabapo.

We encountered no little difficulty in procuring a boat and crew by which to continue our journey. Again we seemed doomed to delay, if not destined to be turned back. Could we but make Javita, we felt that our connection with the Amazons was assured. Once more fortune favored us. Señor Andres Levél, a Spanish trader, from Moróa, on the Rio Negro, arrived at San Fernando, having come by the Cassiquiare, and for the sum of one hundred and ten pesos agreed to take us to Bárra, near the confluence of the above-mentioned river with the Amazons. Our boat, or lancha, as it was called, was similar in construction to the buco by which we ascended the Orinoco, but was a much more commodious craft. It was manned by a crew of four Indians, and provisioned with oranges and mañoca. The latter is a coarse, grated flour, made from the yuca-root (*Manihot utilissima*), the Portuguese substitute for the Venezuelian cassava.

Upon the 6th of December, we set sail up the Atabapo, a stream one-half a mile in breadth, whose low, wooded banks were submerged by the overflow of the river. Its waters were of a brownish color, and yet so transparent that objects could be seen at the depth of three and even four fathoms. The temperature of these *aguas negras* is much lower than that of the white waters of the Orinoco, and afforded a more grateful beverage than the turbid element we had been compelled to use for so long a time. We were now no longer annoyed by the torment of insects, for mosquitoes and sancudos are seldom found on black-water rivers. Neither do crocodiles haunt the limpid stream of the Atabapo, and the splash of the falling iguanas does not startle the voyager. The forest, too, seemed hushed in silence; the plaintive cry of monkeys was no longer heard, and but few birds were seen. Not a leaf rustled, for no breeze ever disturbs the quiet of these deep solitudes—all was silent as the grave. The mountains were also wanting, and our eyes scanned in vain the forest horizon for the slightest elevation to relieve the sameness of the landscape.

The first night upon the Atabapo we passed with our boat anchored to a rock in the middle of the dark stream. When some distance on our way the following morning, we discovered that a little basket belonging to Señor Levél, containing several letters he was conveying to individuals upon the Rio Negro, twenty dollars in gold, and, what he seemed to regret most, his cigarettes, with which he was intending to regale himself upon the journey, had somehow been lost overboard where we had spent the night. Comforting himself with the assurance that his treasures were safe in the bottom of the river, we did not delay to recover them, he intending to secure them upon his next voyage that way. We might here remark, *en passant*, that our money, which was in coin, was often left unguarded in our boat without any apprehensions being entertained for its safety. Honesty is a virtue characteristic of the Indian tribes with which we were thrown in contact. We have seen them, when actually suffering from hunger, decline to molest food discovered in huts temporarily vacated. These natives, with that confidence in their race unknown among civilized communities, leave their homes unprotected, and go on distant excursions, with the assurance that upon their return nothing will be found missing; nor are they ever disappointed, unless some straggling *blanco* chances to wander that way during their absence.

At 10 A. M. we reached Camachina, an Indian pueblo of some thirty houses, upon the left bank of the stream. The inhabitants, like most of those in the towns on the Atabapo, were quite well dressed; their general appearance indicated some degree of intelligence; and their dwellings, which were comfortable abodes, presented some regularity and neatness in their arrangement, as compared with the wretched huts of the tribes on the banks of the Orinoco. We bartered with them for a few chipiries, or small turtles, and plantains—a cambric needle or a fish-hook being an equivalent for a turtle or a bunch of bananas. Two more Indians were here obtained, who accompanied us to assist in passing the rapids of the river. In the afternoon we arrived at another small Indian settlement upon the same bank, and late in the evening reached *Piedra del Tigre*, a granitic rock upon the eastern shore, where we spent the night.

The inundation of the banks of the Atabapo presents no little inconvenience to the traveller; for often, when making the long stretches which separate the villages, he can find a resting-place, or where to build a fire to prepare his food, only upon some solitary rock rising above the water. These spots are known to the Indians; and, in their voyages up and down the stream, they will not pass one unless confident that they can reach another before they have need of fire or rest. A striking feature of the river is the fine, white sand which here and there lifts itself in banks above the water. Its dazzling brightness is almost blinding, and in the distance the long lines of coast present the appearance of drifts of snow glistening in the sun. Another marked peculiarity is the diminutive size of the trees, which constitute the forests of the inundated banks of the river. This is noticed the more in coming from the rich lands of the Orinoco, where stately monarchs tower up with such grand proportions.

On the afternoon of the 8th we were at the *Raudal de Gauriname*, which, next to the Great Cataracts of the Orinoco, seemed the most formidable we had encountered. Our Indians, by entering the water and towing the boat, succeeded, after much hard work, in placing it above the rock-obstructions. All hands then enjoyed a bath, a luxury that crocodiles and caribes no longer rendered a hazardous experiment. Just before sunset we pulled up to the east bank at Baltazar, a neat Indian pueblo of some twenty houses. A single Spaniard, who was both the temporal and spiritual adviser of these people, held absolute sway in his little realm. We were unable to barter with the Indians, excepting as we did it through him, he seeming to sustain a patriarchal relation to the whole village. We spent the night at this place, sleeping in the open air upon a rock in front of the village, leaving before daylight in the morning. Santa Cruz, upon the right bank, a village the size of the last, was reached by 3 P. M. We obtained from the inhabitants some chipiries' eggs, which are oblong in shape, with a hard, calcareous shell, containing oil like those of the tortuga. We found this oleaginous portion extremely delicious, although our Indians discarded it, eating only the yolk.

A short distance above Santa Cruz we left the Atabapo, which turns to the east under the name of Atacavi, and entered the mouth of the Temi, whose waters were also inky black. Passing one night upon this river, the following day we entered the Tuamini, a still narrower stream, equally black; and at 4 P. M. of the same day, the 10th of December, we landed at Javíta, the terminus of our journey up-stream. It was the turning-point in our travels, for from here we were to float down the current of the Rio Negro to the Amazons. Sixty-eight years before, the illustrious Humboldt penetrated these very wilds by the Orinoco and Atabapo, as far as the borders of Brazil, returning by the Cassiquiare. In 1851, the English naturalist Wallace, in his journey upon the Rio Negro, ascended that river as far as this place, retracing his steps as he had come. But no American traveller had before us penetrated to these remote regions; we were the first to unfurl the stars and stripes upon these upper waters of the Orinoco.

The village of Javíta has some thirty houses, with a neat little church, and a great square which is kept scrupulously clean. The inhabitants, about three hundred in number, are all Indians, and speak the Baniwa language, although many of them converse fluently in Spanish. All were well clothed, the men wearing pants and a camisa, and the women gowns which hung loosely about their persons. Some of the young girls were exceedingly beautiful, and when attired in their best, with their black hair neatly plaited, they presented a really attractive appearance. Many among them, not over twelve years of age, were already mothers and owners of chubby, enterprising

followed in the line of march, and, although unencumbered with burdens and walking briskly, making the distance of over three leagues in as many hours, all of the carriers, excepting a couple who were detained by the giving way of their load, reached Pimichin some time before us.

A short distance from the village we entered the dense forest, and were surprised to see the magnificent growth of the trees as compared with the dwarfed vegetation upon the submerged lands of the Temi and Atabapo. Growing along the path was the beautiful Cucurito palm, the Inajá of the Portuguese (*Maximiliana regia*), and hairy stems of the Piassaba (*Leopoldinia Piassaba*) were interspersed throughout the forest. In these humid woods and sombre shades, where scarcely a sunbeam ever penetrates, but two species of flowers were found,* excepting a few that had fallen from stately trees high above our heads; but our herbarium received many curious and interesting ferns and mosses which carpeted the earth, and covered the trunks and branches of the trees. We remember seeing nowhere in such numbers the large, blue Morphos, that gigantic butterfly which so attracts the attention of travellers in the tropics. Other beautiful insects fluttered plentifully about us, for it was now the dry season at Javita, the time when they are the most abundant. The inhabitants of this district enjoy for three or four months an unclouded sky and most delightful weather. This, however, is not true lower down on the Rio Negro, where rains are constant throughout the year, so that often for days and weeks at a time the heavens are obscured with clouds, and falling vapors saturate the earth. We experi-

---

* *Voyria flavescens* and *V. nuda*, little plants from four to six inches high, with yellow and white flowers. They are among the few representative species of the floral kingdom that grow beneath the dense forest of the tropics. We found them upon the mountains of Valencia, and also in the deep woods of the Rio Negro.

enced great difficulty in those humid regions in taking observations; for frequently many days in succession the sun
could not be observed through the thick fogs and clouds
which hovered over the forests.

The road from Javíta to Pimichín, which runs directly
through the forest, is only with much labor kept free from
vegetation, that would soon, in this fostering soil, blockade
the way. At least once a year, the entire population of
the villages near either terminus of the road turn out
en masse, with axes, machetes, and brooms, and the path,
over twenty feet in width along its entire length of three
leagues, is cleared from vegetation and all obstruction,
and the whole swept clean of leaves and rubbish. Logs,
hewn upon the upper surface and roughened so as to offer
a secure footing, are stretched across the marshes and
streams. A cross marks the half-way point between the
termini. As far as this, the inhabitants of Javíta keep the
road repaired; while the villages of the Upper Rio Negro
attend to the other half. No indication of life and enterprise awakened in us such a feeling of surprise as this
truly royal road, cut through the virgin forest, and con-
necting the civilization of the Orinoco with that of the
Rio Negro and Amazons. Some geographers have laid
down a mountain-range as running lengthwise of this
isthmus. On the contrary, this water-shed is low, with
slight elevations, scarcely noticeable as the ground is
walked over. In these marshy grounds and tangled thickets, we were told that venomous serpents were most abundant, and that the black tiger, an animal fiercer and bolder
than the spotted jaguar of the Orinoco, was not unfrequently encountered.

By 11 A. M. we reached Pimichín, a hamlet of two
houses, besides the casa real, a dilapidated building.
Here we delayed only a short time, but, loading our cargo
into a boat the size of the one abandoned at Javíta, in

which we were to go as far as Moróa, we commenced
floating down the meandering Caño Pimichín which leads
to the Rio Negro. The breadth of this black-water rivulet
where we embarked is scarcely thirty yards, and a more
crooked stream it would be difficult to imagine, its windings taking us to every point of the compass. The forest
bordering the river was, like those of the Atabapo and
Temi, inundated, and exhibited but few signs of animated
life. We passed two rapids in the descent of the stream,
at one of which we ran upon a rock, and for a moment
stuck fast, while the current, breaking against our frail
bark, made it quiver like a reed from stem to stern. Five
hours from the time we embarked at the village of Pimichín, we arrived upon the Rio Negro, or Guainia, as the
river is called above Moróa. A long line of huge bowlders,
appearing like the central moraine of an ancient glacier,
stretched down the middle of the stream directly in front
of the mouth of the Caño Pimichín. The Rio Negro
(black river) has been rightly named, for it is inky black,
nor do the many white-water tributaries which it receives, in its course of over twelve hundred miles from its
source among the isolated group of hills in the plains to
the east of Javíta, seem to affect perceptibly its peculiar
colorization. The water itself as it pours from the paddle
appears of a reddish tinge.

A short distance below the mouth of the Pimichín,
upon the left bank, is the village of Moróa, where we soon
landed and took possession of the casa real, while our
Indians dispersed through the place, and Señor Level
sought the domestic retirement of his own cottage. He
had never married, still his family was quite an extensive
one, consisting of a number of Indian women and girls,
together with several youngsters of various complexions
who called him padre. In this country of loose morals,
where social ties are little regarded, such scenes are not

unfrequent. Moróa has a population, which is mostly Indian, of about three hundred. Scarcity of food upon the Rio Negro is so great that the inhabitants often suffer extremely for the want of subsistence. "But hunger never comes to my house," said Señor Levél, "for, in the season when tortoises appear upon the beaches, I provide myself with meat against the time of famine." The Indians, less provident, take no thought for the morrow but obtain their food from the forest and river as their wants require. Scattered through the forest and along the rivers, may be seen small yuca or mandioca plantations, with patches of coffee-trees and the sugar-cane, aside from which but little of any thing is cultivated. Cacao and rice, generally in a wild state, add to the scanty supplies of the inhabitants. So rich is the soil of the Rio Negro, that, with the greatest facility, abundance of every tropical product might be raised; but, rather than clear the forest and till the land, the people prefer to pass a wretched life of constant privation and suffering. The difficulty of securing means of subsistence was a great annoyance to us while we were upon this river.

We found at Moróa three Spanish families, in whose homes were many of the accompaniments and comforts of civilized life. It was a little curious to find, in this remote land, a Yankee clock; but, as is liable to be the case with such inventions, it had long since ceased to be of any practical value to its owner, who, laboring under the delusion that Americans are universal geniuses, proposed to us that we repair his time-piece. After a grave examination of the machine, some pulling to pieces and putting together again of the parts, not less to our astonishment than his delight, the pendulum moved on and the different sections of the contrivance resumed their proper functions. For this artistic achievement we received several preserved specimens of beautiful birds.

8

At Moróa we saw, for the first time, the beautiful bird called *gallo de piedra*, cock of the rock, which is the size of a pigeon, with a bright-orange color, and a large feathered crest of the same brilliant hue upon its head. They are highly prized by the Indians of the Rio Negro, who capture the gorgeously-colored birds of the forests with their cerbatanas and poisoned arrows, for the sake of their beautiful plumage, which they use in adorning their hammocks. These are manufactured from the palm-leaf, the fibres of which are twisted by hand into threads and dyed of various colors, then closely woven on rudely-constructed hand-looms. A border of the same material ten or twelve inches broad is added, ornamented with designs of birds and flowers, beautifully wrought with feathers, constituting an exceedingly rich embroidery. The manner of weaving hammocks, as well as the material which enters into their construction, varies with different tribes. The Indians of the Rio Negro and Upper Orinoco use, as we have observed, the fibres of the palm-trees, and make a coarse cloth-like fabric; those of the Apure and Lower Orinoco generally employ a species of grass of great strength and durability, which is woven with large, net-like meshes.

We could procure, at Moróa, only mañoca with which to provision ourselves for our long voyage to the Amazons, while the towns and *conucos* * along the river, we were told, would be found equally destitute, which our experiences afterward fully corroborated. It was also the wet season, in which we could depend but little upon game or fish, as during the time of high water the forest animals are driven from the inundated plains of the river, and the fishes are less easily taken on account of the deepening waters, from which also many species migrate to the swollen tributaries. Our vessel was one of the roughly-

* The same as *rancho;* a rude hut constructed of palm-leaves for temporary residence.

made sailing-craft of the country, twenty-five feet in length and seven in width. A palm-thatched roof, covering ten feet of the stern, constituted our cabin. In these contracted quarters was stowed a quantity of hammocks, which Señor Levél was sending to Bárra, our baggage, and collections to which we had added largely of Indian curiosities at Moróa. Beneath the floor of our carroza our turtles were kept, when we were so fortunate as to have any. In front of the carroza were placed our baskets of mañoca, which, as we have said, constitutued our sole supply of provisions. Our crew consisted of five Indians; four of whom were paddlers, and the other, a gray-headed patriarch, was our patron. One of the number we had secured with special reference to his knowledge of the river, and familiarity with the peculiar languages of the various Indian tribes which inhabit its banks. None of the others had ever been to any considerable distance down the Rio Negro.

It was sunset on the 13th of December when we left Moróa, descending rapidly with the swift current of the dark stream, one-quarter of a mile in breadth. A few miles down we tarried a short time at Tóma, a village of some three hundred inhabitants, at the mouth of a small stream bearing the same name; and still farther down, upon the opposite bank, we came to San Miguel, where we spent the night. This town is the largest we had seen since leaving San Fernando de Apure, and is the most considerable of any upon the Rio Negro before reaching Bárra. Like the other towns of the Upper Rio Negro, its inhabitants are engaged in ship-building; the vessels, such as we have before alluded to, being taken down to the Amazonian market, or, by the Cassiquiare, to Angostura and the northern coast.

At two o'clock in the morning, after five hours of rest, we reëmbarked. The river, although rapidly falling, was still quite high, and the rocks, which at low water obstruct navigation, were now covered, so that, with a strong current to aid us, we made rapid progress. We stopped during the day at several Indian conucos in hopes of purchasing turtles, but found none until reaching Tiriquín, at 4 p. m., a village of some forty dwellings upon the west shore, at which place we were successful, and partook of our first meal for the day. Coming to anchor, at nine o'clock in the evening, where we observed a deserted hut, we took possession, and rested until two hours after midnight. At sunrise we passed without difficulty the *Raudal de Cocui,* and just below this the mouth of the Cassiquiare, which is about one-third of a mile in breadth. Its white waters, similar to those of the Orinoco, of which they are a part, presented a striking contrast to the black current of the Rio Negro. Three leagues farther, and we were at San Carlos, the frontier town of Venezuela, and the lowest point on the river reached by Humboldt and Bonpland in their passage from the northern coast of Venezuela. A custom-house is established here, from which it was necessary to obtain clearance even for our small craft, before we could pass into the Portuguese country of Brazil. Our passports also required to be viséed, and, for the first time since they were received from our Secretary of State, these interesting documents, requesting that the bearer be permitted " safely and freely to pass, and, in case of need, to give him all lawful and needful protection," were presented to the scrutiny of an official. It was a little amusing to observe the *comandante* curiously scanning the mysterious parchment, such as he had never before seen, and which he was also unable to read, and then very gravely prefixing his signature, certifying that all was right.

The village of San Carlos consists of eighteen or twenty miserable huts, surrounding a great square, whose

principal use was to serve as sleeping-quarters at night
for cattle, the first we saw after leaving the Lower Orinoco. A few hairy sheep were wandering about, grazing
the scanty herbage of the town. These creatures, in the
warm regions of the tropics, when neglected, do not produce wool, as the climate renders such a thick covering
unnecessary. Nature, too, in this land of perpetual summer, forgets to wrap the buds of plants in imbricated
scales and resinous coatings, the winter protection of
northern vegetation. How striking an adaptability do
we observe, of life animate and inanimate, to varying conditions!

Neatness and taste, characteristics of other Indian
villages upon the Upper Rio Negro, are not virtues of
San Carlos—it is too near Portuguese civilization. The
place presents an uninviting aspect. The principal building, formerly occupied by the padres, is now the headquarters of the comandante. Old flint-muskets, accou-
trements, and other paraphernalia of war, covered with
rust from the excessive humidity of these districts, filled
one of the apartments. The remains of an old fort were
opposite the town, upon the high bluff of the western
bank.

Having breakfasted with the Venezuelian official, we
departed from San Carlos, reaching, late in the afternoon
of the following day, Cocoí, a collection of three or four
houses, and the frontier post of Brazil. Here the formal-
ities of the custom-house, and the examining of passports,
require the stopping of boats in their passage. Opposite
the settlement, upon the east side of the river, is the *Piedra de Cocoí*, an enormous, seemingly monolithic rock,
nearly one thousand feet in height, and half that in diameter at its base, which marks the boundary between the
countries of Venezuela and Brazil. Upon one side it rose
almost perpendicularly, allowing no foothold for vegeta-

tion; while upon its remaining sides, that sloped more gently, bushes and dwarfed forest-trees partially clothed the otherwise barren walls. The traveller on the Upper Rio Negro frequently has his attention attracted by these curious, isolated, granitic masses, which often, in tall pillars or gigantic towers, clothed with little or no verdure, rise abruptly from the surrounding forest-level, forming a striking feature in the monotonous landscape.

CHAPTER XIII.

First Glimpse of Portuguese Civilization.—Climate.—Cross the Equator.—
Cataracts of San Gabriel.—Grand Scenery.—Desertion of Guide.—
India-Rubber Manufacture.—Christmas on the Rio Negro.—Floating
at Night.—Beauty of the Southern Firmament.—Lost on the River.—
Barcellos.—Geology of the Rio Negro.—Desolation of the River.—
Reach Maunás.—Tidings from the Quitonian Party of our Expedition.—
Farewell to the Rio Negro.

Soon after leaving the borders of Venezuela, the Rio
Negro widens to half a league in breadth. We were now
floating through another country, yet our surroundings
would scarcely reveal to us that we had passed from a
republic to an empire. Still, some things tell us of a change.
We hear a new language, the Portuguese, and reckon in a
new currency. We no longer estimate in Spanish pesos,
reales, medios, and centavos, but, to our utter bewilderment, must compute in milreis, petacas, vintas, and numberless other denominations which are employed in the
circulatory medium of Brazil. To reduce our new currency into Spanish, and that again into American money,
was a complication of difficulties which not always left us
with a clear conception, when change was returned, as to
how much we had given for the article purchased.

On the morning of the 14th we reached Coána, where
we again delayed, to have our passports examined. The
village, of twenty scattering huts, stands upon quite an
eminence on the left bank. We do not see, in the Indo-

Portuguese settlements of the Rio Negro, the square so characteristic of Spanish towns; and the houses, instead of having their roofs formed with two sides, have the slant upon four, with a short ridge at the top. While the comandante was absorbed in the mysteries of our passports, we were partaking of a cup of chocolate, with which delicious beverage we were always welcomed to the home of the Portuguese. This customary act of hospitality was a new feature in our experiences, and one of which we heartily approved. Supplying ourselves with *cobres*, or coppers, the common currency on the river, we journeyed on a couple of hours, when we halted to breakfast upon a smoked peccary, an animal about the size of a fox-squirrel. In our culinary operations, where spits were required, great caution was requisite in their selection, as some woods possess such virulent properties, that meat roasted upon them will prove fatal when eaten. Before partaking of a meal our Indians were always careful to bathe in the river; or, when this could not be done with impunity, to pour water over their persons with a calabash. The belief of our Pao *savant*, that it was *muy malo* to wash before eating, was no part of the creed of these children of the forest. Soap is unknown among them; but a substitute is found in a shrub, the leaves of which, by simply crushing in the hand, yield a saponaceous substance that answers equally well for cleaning the skin or clothes.

All day our Indians pulled at the paddles, passing several villages and conucos; but nothing could be secured for a meal until evening, when, at a little settlement, we purchased, for a few *cobres*, a large fish-head, from which we made a scanty repast. For three hours longer we pushed on, our Indians keeping time to their paddles with their wild, monotonous chant. At length we moored to a rock in the stream, upon which our men slept, while we kept beneath our palm-leaf covering; for showers were babies. The people employ themselves in collecting the fibrous bark of the Paissaba palm that grows abundantly in the forest, which substance is extensively used for manufacturing ropes and cables. Every thing which crosses the isthmus of Javíta is carried by them, and the loads they are able to transport is truly astonishing. The distance across is three leagues, and the round trip is made in one day, the carriers often taking a burden each day.

In every Indian hamlet and village of these interior districts there is a *casa real*, a house for the use of travellers, itinerant officials, and padres. This beneficent arrangement of these hospitable people furnishes shelter to the stranger, which would often be difficult to secure in their overcrowded huts. In such a place we were quartered at Javíta. Wishing to delay here but a short time, we made arrangements to cross the portage to Pimichín on the day following our arrival at the village. Our boat was too heavy to take overland, as the Indians are accustomed to do with their canoes; nor was it necessary for us, as another could be secured upon the other side of the isthmus. Early in the morning the carriers were at our quarters, accompanied by a crowd of women and children, who, from curiosity, gathered about the door. Every man was paid before he started, each selecting such articles as struck his fancy, from our stock of cloth, arrow-heads, beads, and needles. The display of our wares attracting those who stood about the entrance, the bolder ones pushed themselves within, and the more timid slowly followed, until the room was literally packed, when, with two or three upon each bundle, all diffidence seemed to have been overcome. The lighter packages were arranged so as to be carried upon the head, while the heavier ones were slung upon poles and borne upon the shoulders of two persons.

When the last of the Indian train was in motion, we

frequent both by night and day. The climate of the Upper Rio Negro is somewhat peculiar. The tropical summer, or dry season, is almost unknown, and rains are nearly constant throughout the year. Especially is this true in the districts of the rapids, where the inhabitants enjoy but little of that delightful weather which for several months blesses the valleys of the Orinoco and Amazons. Five or six weeks of freedom from storms during the months of January and February, and a few weeks about June, are the only breaks in the almost constant floods of rain. The waters of the Rio Negro reach their highest level about the end of June. At the cataracts of the river the water rises some twenty feet above its lowest ebb, while at San Gabriel, after having received several tributaries, it is twenty-five or more, and at Bárra the average height is over forty feet. About March, when the Amazons is filled with the floods of its southern tributaries, and while the northern affluents are lowest, the waters of the former block up the mouth of the Rio Negro, causing a stagnation and even retrograde movement of its waters.

On the morning of the 17th, at four o'clock, much later than usual, we aroused our Indians. Several little villages were passed during the day, and at 4 P. M. we were at Guiá, a small Indian settlement, with one Portuguese family, that were bribed by a milreis (fifty cents) to part with a chicken, all the village could offer us. During the afternoon we crossed the equatorial line, and floated upon the waters of the southern hemisphere. Had circumstances permitted, we would have celebrated the event by a sumptuous feast; as it was, we ate from a rock our scanty meal of turtle and mañoca. The river being free from obstructions, we allowed the boat to drift with the current during the night; our Indians sleeping upon their benches. Before morning we passed the Uaupés, a tributary of the Rio Negro, a river which has been made known to the world through that celebrated English traveller, Mr. Wallace, who twice ascended it, penetrating far toward its source amid wild Indian tribes, of which he has given us such graphic and interesting accounts. Five days' journey from the Rio Negro, he encountered the first and most dangerous falls of the Uanpés, above which, he says, " the river became full of rocks to a degree to which even the rockiest part of the Rio Negro was a trifle." After our descent of the Great Cataracts of the Rio Negro, we realized what must have been the adventurous experiences of that bold explorer amid the torrents and cascades of the Uanpés.

We now proceeded with greater rapidity and increasing danger, as we were entering the great rapids, and at length we came to where the river was filled with bowlders and rocky ledges extending from bank to bank. At times we were borne smoothly and swiftly down the dark current; then we went plunging madly through whitened whirlpools, amid rocks and leaping waters. On we rushed down the narrow channels, formed by the islands and rock-masses, often barely escaping destruction from the ledges hidden beneath the sheet of foam. At 1 p. m. we reached San Gabriel, a military post with a fort and garrison. The village occupies quite a commanding position, overlooking the rapids just below, which are the principal ones of the extended series of the river, and more dangerous than those we had encountered. These, after a short rest, we proceeded to pass. Pushing into the middle of the current, we were borne down among the breakers, every man straining at his paddle to keep the boat rightly headed, and to shun the rocks that studded the river. It was with a feeling of relief that we at length saw ourselves riding safely below the obstructions. We continued down the river, plunging now and then into a whirling eddy, without a greater mishap than shipping a quantity of water.

Toward evening we descended a rapid inferior only to the one at the village of San Gabriel, when, drawing up into a little cove upon a sandy beach, we gladly rested from the fatigues and dangers of the day. Early in the morning we passed the last rapid on the river, and our canoe floated upon quietly-flowing waters.

The entire length of these Great Cataracts of the Rio Negro cannot be less than forty miles. Wallace, in his interesting travels on the Rio Negro, thus speaks of them: "The navigation of these falls is of a character quite distinct from any thing in our part of the world. A person, looking at the river, sees only a rapid current, a few eddies, and small breakers, in which there appears nothing very formidable. When, however, you are in the midst of them, you are quite bewildered with the conflicting motions of the waters. Whirling and boiling eddies, which burst up from the bottom at intervals, as if from some subaqueous explosion, with short cross-waves, and smooth intervening patches, almost make one giddy. On one side of the canoe there is often a strong down-current; while on the other it flows in an opposite direction. Now there is a cross stream at the bows, and a diagonal one at the stern, with a foaming Scylla on one side and a whirling Charybdis on the other. All depends upon the pilot, who, well acquainted with every sunken rock and dangerous whirlpool, steers clear of all perils; now directing the crew to pull hard, now to slacken, as circumstances require, and skilfully preparing the canoe to receive the impetus of the cross-currents that he sees ahead."

In the afternoon we stopped at the small village of Victoria, upon the west bank, and endeavored to replenish our exhausted supplies; but, failing, we went without food for the day. Our Indians continued at the paddles until nine in the evening, when they ceased, and the canoe was allowed to drift with the current. This was our usual manner of procedure after leaving San Gabriel; for the river was no longer obstructed by rocks, until far down toward Bárra; and, although the current was not strong, we often made one-half the distance at night that we did during the day.

At daylight on the morning of the 21st we came to Camhosa, a dilapidated village, inhabited by a single Portuguese family, that in this isolated spot of the earth, amid ruin and desertion, eked out a miserable existence. We procured from them some dried beef—a rare luxury in these regions. We had eaten our last upon the Orinoco. A little farther on, and we passed upon the opposite side, to our left, a collection of eight huts, called Wanawacá. Drifting all night, we reached by morning Castanheiro, a nearly-deserted village, like all of the settlements on the Lower Rio Negro. How strange and sad it seems in this land, so greatly blessed by Nature, with a soil so productive that, under the improving hand of cultivation, it would smile with plenty, to see the once populous towns almost deserted and falling to decay, and the few remaining people starving for want of food!

From San Gabriel the river had been growing more picturesque, lovely islands filling the stream in countless numbers, clothed with beautiful verdure in varying forms and colors. The river was rapidly widening, and, when the islands here and there gave way, we looked down the broad expanse of water until the eye rested upon the blank horizon. Great beds of aquatic grass, like floating meadows, went sailing down the current. Birds were more frequently seen than upon the upper waters of the river, still they were not abundant. Parrots, which had made their first appearance upon the Rio Negro near San Gabriel, morning and evening, flew across the river, uttering their hoarse cries. Guacamayas, the largest and most beautiful species of the parrot family, were occasionally seen. One we measured was, from tip to tip, over three feet, with a spread of wings of three feet and eight inches. The plumage of this bird glows in vivid colors of blue, purple, green, red, and yellow, and with its long sweeping tail it presents a gaudy appearance. They generally go in pairs; of the thousands we saw, only once or twice did we observe three in company. Their tenacity of life is marvellous. We once wounded one with a charge of shot, put a rifle-ball into its body, and two more through its immense head, without, apparently, much weakening effect; for it then mounted a log, and showed fight. Our Indians finally dispatched it with their knives; but not until it had nearly succeeded in taking revenge upon its assailants by firing with its claws one of our loaded guns, the ball narrowly escaping one of the party.

One event of the day did not afford many pleasurable emotions. Rowing up for a rest beneath the shade of the forest-bank, a naked Indian was spied gazing out upon us. It was the brother of our guide, from whom he had been long separated, and who chanced upon this spot as we halted. With that cold indifference characteristic of their race, they met as if they had but a few hours before parted. When we were prepared to go, our Indian was motioned to the boat. In words more pathetic than his actions had exhibited, he replied, "Would you separate a brother from a brother?" As the stranger Indian would not accompany us, and argument with the other was of no avail, we reluctantly left with one man less as a result of this unexpected episode, which was not a pleasant one, when we reflected that we were now without a guide or interpreter to navigate an unknown river, encountering Indian tribes and people whose languages were equally strange to us.

On the morning of the 23d we reached San Isabel, another almost deserted village with but three or four

hovels inhabited. We sought, among the few Indians remaining in the miserable huts, swallowed up by weeds and
the encroaching forest, for a pilot to take the place of the
one who had so unceremoniously forsaken us; but none
could be induced to accompany us, nor did we meet with
better success in our many attempts to secure one afterward.

Conucos of India-rubber gatherers were now frequently met with, but all were found wonderfully destitute of
food. We spent some little time at several; observing
with interest the wonders of rubber-making. The tree
from which this product is obtained has a tall, straight
trunk, with a smooth, gray bark, beautiful foliage of ter-
nate leaves, and attains a height of seventy to one hundred feet. The process of manufacturing the *seringa*, or
rubber, is simple. A withe, or slender twig, is bound
tightly around the tree, higher up on one side than upon
the other. Longitudinal gashes are then made in the
trunk, from which a whitish, cream-like gum exudes, and
is caught in a small clay cup placed upon the ground.
Each incision yields daily about half a gill: new gashes
are made every morning. The cups, when full, are emptied by the *seringero*, or rubber-gatherer, into a large
vessel, which is carried at once to his conuco, and the substance immediately formed into the desired shape, as it
quickly coagulates. With a fire built from the small nuts
of the Inagá-palm (*Maximiliana regia*), upon one side,
and his pot of milk upon the other, the seringero seats
himself upon a rough bench and commences operations.
With a cup he pours the fluid over the mold, to which a
thin coating adheres; then holds it for a moment in the
smoke, which dries and colors the rubber, and repeats the
process until his work is completed. The mold is constructed either of wood or clay; if of the first, it is coated
with clay, that the rubber may be more easily removed;

if the latter be employed, it is washed out. Shoes and models of birds and fishes are readily made; but the common form in which the seringa is prepared for commerce is in long sheets or oval pieces, made by using a paddle-shaped mould. For a day or two, while the substance remains soft, it readily receives impressions, and fanciful figures are often neatly traced upon it. The tree yields its gum equally well at all times, but the dry season, or what corresponds to such upon the Rio Negro, the months during which the least rain falls, is generally devoted to the manufacture of the rubber.

Besides the large production of seringa by the inhabitants of the Rio Negro, great quantities of sarsaparilla—the root of a vine found principally along the tributaries of the river—and Brazil-nuts, are annually collected. The last mentioned is the fruit of the *Bertholletia excelsa*, one of the noblest monarchs of the forest. Monkeys, in their perambulations for the wild fruits of the forest, pass these by, as no ingenuity of theirs will gain them access to the nuts, which are enclosed in a hard, ligneous shell, that the natives break open with an axe. The tree requires about eighteen months for the complete maturing of its fruit from the bud. "The fruits, which are nearly as hard and heavy as cannon-balls, fall with tremendous force from the height of a hundred feet, crashing through the branches and undergrowth, and snapping off large boughs which they happen to strike against. Persons are sometimes killed by them, and accidents are not unfrequent among the Indians engaged in gathering them."—(*Wallace.*)

Christmas brought us remembrances of home, and, as we partook of a simple fare, our thoughts naturally recurred to the happy gatherings and joyous festivities which mark the day in our own distant land. It was sunset when we left the island where we had tarried for our meal, and, pushing out into the current, started upon our

nightly float. Noiselessly, and unconscious of any movement, we were borne down the stream, with the outlines of the forest-walls faintly visible in the distance,
and a strange, starlit sky above us. "Nothing," truthfully says Humboldt, "awakens in the traveller a livelier
remembrance of the immense distance by which he is
separated from his country, than the aspect of an unknown firmament." He beholds a new heaven as well as
a new earth. He traces the stars and beautiful constellations that circle the southern pole, and beholds, with
feelings of wonder, the Clouds of Magellan—flushes of
myriads of distant lights that adorn these heavens. But,
of the bright clusters, that of the Cross especially fixes
the attention, and awakens the deepest emotions. "The
Portuguese and the Spaniards are peculiarly susceptible
of this feeling; a religious sentiment attaches them to a
constellation, the form of which recalls the sign of the
faith planted by their ancestors in the deserts of the New
World. The two great stars which mark the summit and
the foot of the Cross having nearly the same right ascension, it follows that the constellation is almost perpendicular at the moment when it passes the meridian. This
circumstance is known to the people of every nation situated beyond the tropics, or in the southern hemisphere.
It has been observed at what hour of the night, in different
seasons, the Cross is erect or inclined. It is a time-piece
which advances very regularly nearly four minutes a day,
and no other group of stars affords to the naked eye an
observation of time so easily made. How often have we
heard our guides exclaim, in the savannas of Venezuela,
'Midnight is past, the Cross begins to bend!' How often
those words reminded us of that affecting scene, where
Paul and Virginia, seated near the source of the river of
Lataniers, conversed together for the last time, and where

the old man, at the sight of the Southern Cross, warns them that it is time to separate."*

Upon the morning of the 27th, we left the northern bank of the river, which we did not see again until the day before reaching Bárra, or Manáos, as called by the inhabitants of the Lower Rio Negro. We were told that the left shore was almost uninhabited, and that we would be unable to secure provisions. We therefore determined upon crossing to Barcellos, and following the southern bank the remainder of the way. The river was now spread out to a great breadth, and filled with islands, so that both banks could no longer be seen at once. We do not recollect navigating through more picturesque scenery; there was a wild beauty in those lovely islands, covered with graceful palm-trees and a growth of vegetation so luxuriant that the eye could not penetrate within their dark recesses. Remove the palms, and we could have fancied ourselves floating through the Thousand Islands of the St. Lawrence. During the forenoon our Indians killed with their palancas a curious, circular, flat fish, called *arraia.* This strange ichthyological creature, fifteen inches in diameter, with a thickness not to exceed three inches, had a cylindrical tail a foot in length, armed with long, thorn-like appendages, which, in its dying rage, it fastened in its body with such force as to be removed with difficulty. It was most unsavory eating, but, for want of something better, we halted at noon upon a playa-island, collected drift-wood for a fire, cooked our game, and enjoyed our only meal for the day. We then continued our wanderings among the forest-islands, in the vain attempt to reach the southern shore, until the darkness overtook us, when we fastened to a point of land and waited in our boat for the morning. Again our Indians were toiling at the paddles, now making way against the current, or wind-

* "Humboldt's Travels," vol. i., p. 135.

ing here and there with it through the labyrinth of channels which constitute the countless arms of this wonderful river. Often, when supposing ourselves alongside of the main shore, we would come to a break in the land, showing that we had only been coasting along an island. Another line of coast would also in turn dispel our illusions by another opening, that indicated the promised land to be still beyond.

Ater a day and a half spent in our attempts at crossing the river, we came in sight of Barcellos; our approach being first made known to us by our Indians commencing to dress themselves, their keen eyes having discovered the town upon a high bluff in the distance, long before it came within the range of our less acute vision. We arrived at a fortunate time, for the inhabitants were gathered from their conucos to pass the Christmas *fiesta*, and the place was well supplied with food for the occasion. Barcellos was formerly the capital of the province of Rio Negro, but is now a sad picture of fallen houses, streets overgrown with weeds and bushes, with a thick jungle that penetrates through the centre of the town. Some thirty houses still remain, with now and then one whitewashed, and covered with a tiled roof. Most of them are occupied during fiestas, but, when these are over, the people are scattered to their conucos through the forest, when the place presents a still more deserted and forlorn aspect. A small church indicated the presence of the padres, who, with indefatigable zeal, have extended their labors to most of the Indian tribes of the country. Blocks of marble lying upon the shore, and bearing the insignia of Portugal, attracted our attention. They had been imported from Europe when Brazil was yet a Portuguese colony, and were intended for government buildings, which, however, were never erected. Seeking the house of the ecclesiastic, we were kindly welcomed; and the padre, upon learning that for two days we had been almost without food, presented us with a large turtle, which our Indians carried to the boat, rejoicing in the prospect of a sumptuous meal. Hospitality is one of the prominent virtues of the people of this country. They often have but little they can give, but that is freely shared with the stranger who chances among them.

Furnishing ourselves with turtles and other supplies sufficient for five or six days, the time supposed necessary in which to reach Manáos, we left Barcellos. When out of sight of the town, our Indians undressed themselves, and, rolling up their garments, tucked them carefully away, for use upon our arrival at the next village. We were now probably upon the widest portion of the Rio Negro. The breadth of the river in its broadest parts has been estimated by some as great as ten leagues. Wallace, in speaking of the river, says he is convinced that in some places it is between twenty and thirty miles wide, and for a considerable part of its course from Manáos to San Isabel, fifteen to twenty. By persons well acquainted with the Rio Negro, we were informed that at Barcellos, where it probably spreads out to its greatest breadth, the opposite shores are about four leagues apart. Our own experiences in crossing the river confirmed us in the correctness of this estimate. In the lower part of its course, the fall is so slight that the current, as you approach the mouth, is scarcely perceptible, and often the voyager is in doubt whether he is ascending or descending the river. In the season of greatest floods many of its islands are beneath its surface, presenting the appearance of forest growing out of the water, while its low banks are, in parts, overflowed, and wide strips of the country upon either side inundated.

On the night of the 28th, our float was interrupted several hours by a strong wind which blew up the river. Breezes on the Rio Negro are but little felt above Barcellos, but below that point they are quite constant up the stream, assisting the upward-bound voyager, but often driving back upon its course, in spite of paddles, the descending canoe.

Upon the morning of the last day of the year, we passed Carvoeiro, and two hours later landed for breakfast upon some granitic rocks, the first of any kind that had appeared below San Isabel. Not far below this point the Rio Branco, the largest tributary of the Rio Negro, pours in its white waters from the north. This river abounds in the great tortuga and other species of tortoises, which, during the season when they resort to the playa to deposit their eggs, draw thither the inhabitants of the Rio Negro, and the settlements that exist upon its own banks, for the purpose of supplying themselves with food against the long dearth of the rainy period. For three hundred miles from its mouth, the Rio Branco is said to be unbroken with rapids, and the country through which it flows, densely wooded.* Above this, obstructions prevent its navigation, excepting with light canoes, and open savannas spread out from its banks, affording pasturage to herds of wild cattle from which the inhabitants of Manáos obtain their supply of beef. A portage of a couple of hours connects the head-waters of the river with those of the Essequibo. †

Late in the afternoon, and several hours below the Rio Branco, we reached Pedrero (sometimes written Pedreiró), a village of twenty houses, the highest point reached by Agassiz in his excursion on the " Ibicuhy " up the Rio

---

* Upon the banks of this river is found the remarkable máraponima, "tortoise-shell wood," a most beautiful wood much employed in the arts.

† Upon the Putaro, a tributary of the Essequibo River, there has recently been discovered (April, 1870), by Mr. C. B. Brown, of the Geological Survey of British Guiana, a fall of over eight hundred feet in height, which is said to have but few rivals in picturesqueness and grandeur.

Negro. On the following forenoon we came to Aidon, a collection of half a dozen huts, and landed upon ledges of sandstone which form the coast. Just before reaching here we had passed rocks of pure hornblende, which jutted out prominently from the bank into the river. Farther down, on the following day, we stopped to examine sandstone cliffs, worn by the action of the water into grotesque caves and excavations. Brown hematite was abundant in the rocks; fragments and smooth globules of which, left by the disintegration of the sandstone, formed the beach. The geology of the Rio Negro is simple. Above the Rio Branco granitic rock forms the surface; at Pedrero this passes into a metamorphic granitoid rock; below that point sandstone covers all indications of granite. Upon this lies a red-clay deposit, often rising into considerable bluffs.

On the morning of the 4th, at a cluster of seven or eight dwellings, we landed in search of food. The time for which we had provisioned our vessel at Barcellos had expired, and our last turtle, with what else we had, was consumed the day before. We learned that we were still three or more days distant from Manáos, with but little prospect of obtaining much in the commissary line before reaching there. In one of the huts we entered the inmates were making a joyous meal upon a young alligator, and in another a couple of monkeys with skins removed, but with hands and heads still attached to their blackened bodies, looking like infants hung up by their heels, were roasting over a fire, preparatory for a cannibalistic feast. Amid this wretched destitution we were glad to secure a small piece of dried *pirarucu*, a monster fish (*Sudis gigas*) common in the waters of the Amazons and Lower Rio Negro. It has a small head, with a body five to eight feet in length, covered with heavy scales. The flesh is exceedingly coarse, excepting portions which are masses

of solid fat.   With mañoca it constitutes the chief article
of subsistence of the inhabitants along the rivers where
found, besides being salted and dried in large quantities
for the Pará market and cities along the coast; the long
strips and broad, slab-like pieces being packed in bundles
for transportation.   The Lower Rio Negro is most thinly
inhabited.   We often went days without meeting a canoe
upon the river; and the country seemed wild and desolate in the extreme.   Our progress was slow, being greatly retarded by the easterly trade-winds sweeping up from
the Amazons, while the rocks which now filled the stream
prevented our drifting with the current at night.   As some
one has truthfully observed, one must be an ardent lover
of Nature to travel through these wild and uninhabited
regions; otherwise but little compensation will be received
for all the toils and privations incident to such a journey.

Apprehensive lest we should be too late for the Amazonian steamer, which we learned, from canoes upward
bound, would sail from Manáos for Pará on or about the
8th of the month, we induced our Indians to work through
the night of the 5th.   The coming day the wind was strong
and against us, and our progress consequently slow and
laborious, notwithstanding we coasted close to the shore,
which rose here in high, abrupt cliffs.   A small piece of
pirarucu-fish, which we divided among ourselves, with a
little dry mañoca, was the only food taken during the
day.   Just before sunset we emerged from the islands
among which we had been confined so long, and entered
upon the open river, that spread out like a lake, ten miles
or more in breadth.   Throughout the night our Indians
continued at their paddles, resting only a couple of hours
toward morning, when they again resumed their places,
toiling all day against a strong head-wind and heavy sea.
Several times we scaled the high bluff in search of food,
whenever a hut appeared at its top; but not a single mor-

sel did we have for the day. At 3 P. M. we came to where
the Rio Negro narrows to a mile in breadth, the waves
breaking in foam upon a wild, rocky coast. The winds
were sweeping so violently through the strait that we were
obliged to delay several hours, and then with considerable
difficulty we made the passage, and entered another great
bay of white-capped water. Night at length came on, but
our faithful Indians did not cease their labors. Extended
playas stretched along the now low and partially-submerged
shores, in passing which our natives would lay in their
paddles and take to the palancas. Hungry from our fast-
ings, we threw ourselves upon the rough poles of our couch.
It was three o'clock in the morning when we were awakened by our canoe grating the beach. No town could be
seen, and we were about to ask the cause of our stopping,
when the ringing of a bell was heard, breaking the stillness of the early morning. It was a welcome sound, for
it told us that our long wanderings of weary months were
at length terminated. We looked around and saw that
our exhausted Indians had thrown themselves upon the
sand. We allowed them to rest until break of day, when
arousing them we rounded the point of land in our front,
and were at Manáos.

The town is pleasantly located upon the left bank of
the river, ten miles from the Amazons. It contains a
mixed population of two thousand, the principal elements
being Portuguese, Indian, and Negro. The town is traversed by two ravines, spanned by quite substantial bridges,
the first we had seen since leaving Valencia. They lend
quite an artistic appearance to the place as viewed from
the river. A large cathedral is also in process of erection,
and has been for the last dozen years. It seems strangely
out of proportion to the present population of Manáos;
but it is probable that some sage padre has had sufficient
prevision to see that the town is destined to become, from

its location, one of the largest and most important in the Amazonian Valley, and that the structure is being adapted to the probable exigencies of the future.

Manáos possesses what is rarely to be found in the heart of the Amazonian valley—a water-fall. So level is this great plain, that the sound of falling water never comes to the ear. The voyager upon the sluggish current of the Lower Rio Negro longs for the sight of clear, leaping water. At Manáos he can have this desire gratified, during certain seasons of the year. A short walk of two miles over a forest-path brings you to a little cascade. We say it may be seen only during a portion of the year, because, as the falls are scarcely ten feet high, when the Amazons rises, they are, as Agassiz expresses it, "drowned out."

In our rambles though Manáos on the day of our arrival, we were not a little surprised to be accosted by a gentleman in English. He was the owner of a large estate upon the southern bank of the Rio Negro, and from him we learned that a party of half a dozen Americans had recently arrived in the place. They were Southerners, and prominent ex-Confederate officers, who had emigrated to Brazil, where, with slavery for their corner-stone, they purposed founding a colony. Dr. Dowsing, the leader of the expatriated party, had obtained for this purpose a grant of land from the Brazilian Government, wherever in the Amazonian Valley he might choose to locate. Others were expected to join them from the States as soon as a site should be selected for a settlement. The Rio Branco had been, at first, decided upon, but some considerations had led to a change of plans, and they were now preparing to ascend one of the southern tributaries of the Amazons.

From this company of Americans we learned that the Quito party of our expedition had, two weeks before, stopped at Manáos upon their way down the Amazons.

This was the first intelligence of them received since our separation at New York. They had succeeded in crossing the Andes, and in reaching the Rio Napo, one of the northern tributaries of the Amazons. But our joy at hearing of their success was saddened by the information that one of their number had been buried upon the Andes. We were unable to determine, from the description of our informants, who were the surviving members of the party. With this uncertainty we left Manáos, January 10th, upon the steamer Belém, hoping to join our friends at Pará before they should sail for home.

Having now crossed the path of the Quitonian party of our expedition, we will close this sketch of the Venezuelian division, to give an account of their experiences among the Andes and upon the Great River.

9

CHAPTER XIV.

FROM PANAMA TO BODEGAS.

WE had been only nine days upon the Atlantic, when we were greeted by the low hills of the Isthmus of Panama, skirting the southern horizon. Clouds hung around the highest points, through which the sun would occasionally break and shoot along the wooded slopes, rendering more vivid the dark emerald coloring of the forest, that contrasted beautifully with the white lines of surf breaking along the shore. A line of low, white buildings upon a marshy coast indicated the site of Aspinwall. Drawing nearer, we could discern the diminutive cabins of the negroes, half embowered by the rank, encroaching vegetation of the surrounding marsh. The luxuriant banana, whose drooping leaves seemed striving to conceal the rich, yellow clusters of ripening fruit, and the palm tossing out from the top of its slender shaft a beautiful tuft of feathery leaves, which dipped gracefully in the slight breeze, stamped the tropical character of the scenery.

Our steamer, in approaching her moorage, unfortunately grounded, and we were obliged to pass the night upon shipboard. The following morning we were placed ashore, and, stepping upon the open, cane-seated cars awaiting us, we were borne swiftly toward the Pacific. What wonders does Nature here present! We felt as though transferred to another world. The vegetation, so different from our northern, so varied, wild, and luxuriant, impressed us at each turn with new revelations of its beauty and prodigality. Springing from the reeking soil stood the palm-like tree-fern, which all our associations had placed far back in those strange, endogenous forests of the carboniferous age; vines festooned them heavily, while brilliant orchidaceous plants enriched the drapery; palms crowned each little rise, lifting their heads above the sea of verdure, formed by trees presenting an aspect similar to that of our northern woodlands, only denser and freer in growth, richer and darker in color. But we must not anticipate; for we shall find all repeated in the vegetation of the equatorial regions, even far surpassed by the tropical forest of the Guayas and Amazons.

After a ride of three hours over a sinuous road, we find ourselves in the picturesque old town of Panama. Besides its old walls, overrun with vines, and its antiquated buildings, it claims the prestige of a romantic history, associating itself with the wild adventures of the bold conquistadores. Panama is pleasantly located. As seen upon an approach from the railroad, it presents quite an attractive appearance, nestled close to the shore, with the bay as a watery perspective; viewed from the harbor, it has a fine background of sloping hills.

Late in the evening of the 11th, the steamer "Panama," of the British South Pacific Mail Steamship Company, moved slowly from her moorings off the little islet of Taboga, embraced by the bay of Panama, and commenced to gently bow to the low, deep swell of the Pacific. It was a beautiful, tropical night; the moonlit bay, one which

vies in picturesqueness with that of Naples and Rio Janeiro, set with islands resting upon their reflection in the sil-
vered water, was invested with a beauty only to be found
beneath a tropical sky. As the land slowly withdrew into
the rich, mellow haze, we fell to watching the bright
sparkle of the moonlight upon the rippling water, and the
dull, phosphorescent gleam playing in our wake, born
from the myriads of animalcula which swarm these
waters.* Each evening we observed with interest the
familiar constellations of the northern heavens, as night
by night they took a lower position, and new clusters appeared above the southern horizon. Just before we crossed
the equator, the polar star, which we had watched as the
last heaven-mark of our northern home, sank from our
view.

In passing from the Atlantic to the Pacific, we left behind us those storms and sudden squalls which render
navigation so unpleasant upon northern waters. The days
were uniformly pleasant, the nights clear and beautiful,
and the heat of a vertical sun was tempered by the strong
trade-winds which met us constantly from the south. The
third day from Panama we passed the point of St. Helena,
the most western cape of Ecuador (or Equator), which
presents the appearance of a vast artificial fortification
frowning threateningly upon the opening bay of Guayaquil. The morning of the 14th we were abreast the Peruvian coast. The long line of crumbling, gray cliffs receded into verdureless plains, relieved only by narrow
bands of vegetation which marked the course of some little
stream, fed by the moister heights of the Cordilleras. In
vain the traveller looks for the towering ranges of the
Andes, for heavy clouds hang enviously about them.

* Phosphorescence has been generally supposed to be the product of
the vital force possessed by microscopic organisms. Darwin, however,
supposes it to be the result of the decomposition of the organic particles.

Entering a small bay, which appeared as though scooped out by the action of the waves, we discovered, crowded between the gray cliffs and the sea, half buried beneath the drifting sands of the desert, the wretched town of Paita. The first question which the traveller suggests to himself, after having surveyed the curious pile of quaint, mud-plastered, tumble-down, bamboo structures, is, "What could possess any people to set up their household gods in such a desolate portion of creation?" It is, indeed, curious to observe where man has sought out a habitation. How often we find him presumptuously planting his little domicile upon the very flank of some restless volcano, which he knows will eventually heap it in rubbish! Deserting the inviting plains of La Plata, he has travelled southward, crossed the Straits of Magellan, and melts with the warmth of his own body the falling snows of the inhospitable Tierra del Fuego; upon the delta of the Orinoco he has swung his house in the trees, when the fertile Llanos and mountain-flanks of Venezuela offer him an enviable home. The only excuse we could find for the existence of Paita was in the fact that it served as a port to more pretentious inland towns.

Going ashore we followed our guide through the narrow streets, which are just wide enough to admit the passing of two pack-animals. Through these contracted passages we wended our way, dodging the careless donkeys which, with cargoes apparently adjusted with no particular reference to the safety of pedestrians, rushed recklessly through the streets. We kept our eyes with ill-concealed apprehension upon the seemingly heavy walls of the houses, the most of which were alarmingly removed from perpendicularity; but the discovery that beneath the plastering of mud, which gave them their wall-like appearance, was only a slight frame-work of split canes, lessened our fears of the evil consequences which might attend the

catastrophe that they seemed disposed any moment to in-
stitute. It being the hour of morning mass, our guide led
us directly to the church. It was a unique structure, and
faithfully characteristic in that it was maintaining its peculiar position in utter defiance of all laws of gravitation.
Without, it was plastered with mud, and thickly thatched;
the interior was pewless, but ornamented with mutilated
tissue paper. About a hundred worshippers, chiefly wom-
en, were assembled, and in the absence of seats were kneeling or squatting upon the floor. As Fletcher has observed
among the Brazilians, so here praying is mostly done by
the women. A negro, armed with a ruinously-impaired
drum, composed the orchestra. The exercises conducted
by the priest were unmeaning genuflections and crossings,
with various manipulations and kisses of the crucifix and
Bible. There was not one word of instruction for the poor
Indian, or a single admonition to the sinful Spaniard.

From the church we strolled on through several narrow streets, and, clambering up the cliffs back of the town,
found ourselves upon the sands of the great Peruvian desert. Treeless and verdureless, it stretched away in vast
undulations, with nothing to arrest the eye save long
trains of donkeys loaded with kegs of water, wending their
way over the glaring waste. All the water used in Paita
is brought from the Piura River, a stream many leagues
inland, born among the snows of the sierras.

The fossil specimens of marine fauna, which enter largely into the formation of the cliff, and which are identical
with species now inhabiting the waters, tell us that this
desert long constituted the ocean-bed; but that internal
forces, so active along the western shore of this continent,
have elevated it to its present position. Portions of this
coast have been lifted nearly one hundred feet during the
last three hundred years. Shells are found high upon the
western slope of the Andes along a line of two thousand

miles. Extensive sea-beaches, at an elevation of over half a mile, indicate long cessations in the action of the elevatory forces, while the waves of the Pacific were beating against and wearing down the rising wall of the Andes. This great desert, extending from the sea to the foot of the Cordilleras, stretches with a varying breadth of ten to twenty leagues, from three degrees south of the equatorial line to the northern portions of Chili, over the whole of the Peruvian coast. The absence of rain upon this coast, and its consequently arid aspect, are due to the proximity of the lofty wall of the Andes, which effectually arrests all storm-clouds from the east, while the prevailing southerly trade-winds drive all the vapors of the Pacific from the coast. As has been often observed, had the physical conformation of South America been changed, the Andes being placed along the Atlantic coast, the greater portion of the continent would have been swept by winds, deprived of all their moisture; and, instead of South America, with its teeming valley of the Amazons, we would have had another Africa with its Libyan desert. But now the Cordilleras, standing close to the Pacific shore, with their cool heights acting as a "great condenser," wring every drop of moisture from the clouds borne upon the equatorial trade-winds from the Atlantic, and throw down their waters in torrential rains all along the eastern slope of the Andes. South America owes what it is—a continent of vegetation—to this mountain-wall along its western border. As one looks up to the whitened summit of those Cordilleras, lifted all along to the line of perpetual snow, he is sometimes led to ask why they were raised so high. The long desert coast-line returns an answer. They are the great wall, lifted by a wise Creator to guard a continent and water the rich garden of the Amazons. As in all of Nature's work we find a beautiful proportion and harmony, we can conceive, before climbing that mountain-barrier, what wealth and beauty of vegetation we shall find within the great Amazonian Valley.

The nights upon this coast are uncomfortably cold; mornings we found our overcoats essential to comfort. This low temperature may be referred to the rapid radiation of heat from the desert, and to the cold ocean-current, which, sweeping from the southern sea, carries the chilling influence of its polar waters almost to the equator. Our collections at this point comprised specimens of the present marine fauna and fossils from the cliffs. The floral kingdom was represented by only two species of diminutive shrubs, almost destitute of leaves, belonging to the natural orders Rhamnaceæ and Leguminosæ. The latter we afterward found upon the highlands of Quito, where it assumed almost arboreal dimensions.

Upon the evening of the 16th, the Favorita steamed into the bay, and stepping aboard we gladly bade farewell to Paita and the Peruvian coast. Just before entering the Gulf of Guayaquil, and eighteen miles below Tumbez, we pass several petroleum-wells, located upon a sterile coast, which are yielding a remunerative supply of oil. One day from Paita brings us opposite the Ecuadorian coast. Ecuador presents a verdant front to the Pacific. Evergreen tropical forests fringe heavily its western shores; for the winds which sweep the Peruvian coast lose their regularity as they approach the equator, and the vapors are distilled in heavy showers. The dark emerald of the vegetation presents a pleasing contrast to the gray cliffs and arid plains of Peru. This tropical forest, replacing the great desert three degrees south of the equator, extends northward, throwing its dense shades along the Guayas, and over the wilds of the Esmeraldas,* and

* The Esmeraldas is the largest river upon the Pacific slope of South America. It is supposed by some to take its name from the emeralds that were obtained in large quantities from that locality at the time of the

stretches to Panama, its western edge bordering the Pacific, while its eastern flank lies high upon the steep slope of the Andes. Under the equator tree vegetation reaches an elevation of about eleven thousand feet,* when it gives place to the *paramos*, or grass-lands, which extend up to the line of perpetual snow, found upon the equatorial Andes at 15,740 feet.

Toward evening of the second day from Paita, we entered the Gulf of Guyaquil, passing the island of Puná, which afforded to Pizarro a temporary station, when seeking an entrance to the kingdom of the Incas. It presents a low coast-line, and is densely wooded. Upon the morning of the 19th, as we mounted to the deck, a novel scene greeted us. During the night we had reached Guayaquil, and were now quietly moored abreast the city. Crowded along the shore were canoes, balsas, and floating craft of every description, laden with an endless variety of tropical fruits, bananas, plantains, pine-apples, oranges, cocoanuts, and mangoes, products of the fertile banks of the Guayas. Heaped upon the shore were also piles of fruit, surrounded by crowds of half-naked, vociferating Indians, with gayly-clad Spaniards and negroes. Meek-looking donkeys pushed their way through the crowd, and occasionally an ungraceful mule-cart rolled along the street. Though our eyes were naturally first arrested by this motley market-scene, they were next caught by the architectural front of the buildings lining the *Malecon*—the river street and principal one of the city. These were two stories in height, the upper furnished with inviting

conquest. There is, however, ground for belief that it was so called by the Spaniards on account of the vivid green of its forests, contrasted with the sterile coast of Peru.

* The polylepis, however, forms an exception to this; groves of this tree are found upon the slopes of Chimborazo at an elevation of 13,000 feet.

balconies, which, jutting over the sidewalk, rested upon columns, forming a low arcade—a shady retreat from the rays of a vertical sun. Constructed of split canes, and plastered with mud, they surpass those of Paita by having added a coating of whitewash, and in exchanging the thatch for neat roofs of tile.

Guayaquil is located upon the Guayas River, about seventy miles from the sea. Almost all imports intended for the table-lands of Ecuador pass through this port; and into it the elevated plains of Quito pour almost all their products intended for exportation. The city comprises a mixed Spanish, Indian, and negro population of about twenty thousand. There is here, as, indeed, throughout Spanish America, no prejudice of race or color; all barriers are thrown down, and the results of unrestrained amalgamation are observable everywhere throughout society.

The climate of Guayaquil during the wet season is exceedingly warm, and pestilential diseases prevail with alarming fatality. The unhealthiness of the city is not wholly the result of an unavoidable conjunction of natural circumstances, as proximity to sluggish streams, long-continued rains, and excessive heat, but of causes superadded to these by the uncleanly habits of the people. An American resident, speaking of the sanitary state of the city, remarked, "The location of Guayaquil is the most healthful in the world." We were led to believe that its unenviable reputation for fevers is largely referable to causes which the observance of the most obvious sanitary requirements would remove. Our advent to the city was during the dry season, which lasts from June to December, during which portion of the year the climate is healthful and cool. The sky is generally obscured the early part of the day; the heavy clouds which hang about the towering summits of the Cordilleras rolling down during the

night over the city to the coast, only receding before
the heat of mid-day, to again suspend their dark veil between the city and the lofty ranges of the Andes. It is
seldom that an opening rent allows a glimpse of the dizzy
heights of the Cordilleras.

Desiring to secure as large collections as possible from
this section, so seldom visited by naturalists, we made
Guayaquil our headquarters, and planned several expeditions upon the different branches of the Guayas. Captain
Lee, an American, who has established steam navigation
upon these streams, kindly offered us the privileges of
his steamers. We had but just commenced our work,
when we were interrupted by fever, which prostrated all
but one of our party. We cannot forbear, in this connection, mentioning our indebtedness to Dr. A. Destruge,
whose kindness and talent proved of great service to us.
Two weeks found us convalescent and preparing for the
passage of the Cordilleras. We were determined to escape as soon as possible the heat of the tropical coast, and
climb the Andes to Quito, the "city above the clouds,"
and, to the joy of travellers, also above fevers, scorpions,
and mosquitoes. As heavy rains are liable to be encountered among the sierras, our baggage was carefully secured
by wrappings of tarpaulin ; while we provided ourselves
with ponchos and overcoats, for severe storms of sleet and
snow often sweep the bleak passes of the Andes. Should
the traveller be fortunate enough to escape these, the
sudden change from the sultry coast to the extreme cold
of the Cordilleras renders this precaution necessary.

These preparations completed, we took passage on one
of the little American steamers which navigate the Guayas
as high as Bodegas, seventy miles above Guayaquil, from
which town the traveller takes to the back of mules. The
scenery of the Guayas is most varied and beautiful; the
banks being heavily fringed with every form of tropical

vegetation. Large plantations of the rustling-leaved banana alternate with extensive forests of cacao, the tree which yields the chocolate of commerce. Twenty-five million pounds are annually exported from Guayaquil, the greater portion of which is produced upon the Guayas and its tributaries. Orange-trees bend under their load of golden fruit, while the magnificent mango and the bread-tree, with its immense leaves, lend diversity to the vegetation. Here and there, seeking the water's edge, waves a grove of graceful grasses. It seems strange to speak of grasses as forming forest; but here that arboreal gramina, the *Bambusa guadua*, which has a deeper social instinct than most species of tropical plants, forms dense, beautiful thickets. The tall, slender stalk, rising forty feet and upward, sways in the slightest breeze, and when swept by heavy winds the groves bend and rock like fields of grain. This gramina is only surpassed in beauty by the stately palm, which we must crown as the "prince of tropical vegetation." So expressive of elegance and grace, it is not strange that it has been the favorite of all poets whose home has been the home of the palm. But Flora's kingdom, varied and wonderful as it is, affords not all of the attractions of these regions. Animated Nature is not lacking in representatives here. Nowhere in South America, not even in the teeming valley of the Amazons, did we observe a greater variety of ornithic forms, or find any characterized by more varied or brilliant plumage. The marshes were whitened with aquatic birds, which also flecked the air. Only a few monkeys, however, were seen; for, of the eighty-six species found in the New World, not more than three or four inhabit the forest west of the Andes. But the sluggish waters of the Guayas afford a congenial home for alligators, of which hundreds lined the banks with their cuirassed bodies, which, upon our approach, would slowly glide into the water, their move-

CHIMBORAZO, SEEN FROM THE GUAYAS.

ments frequently accelerated to an ungraceful plunge by a shot from one of our rifles. Slowly we steamed up the Guayas, stopping to take aboard every native who signalled us from the shores. The bed of the stream often compelled us to run close to the banks, so that occasionally our decks were swept by the overhanging trees. We always enjoyed these brushings, until we ran into a nest of bees, which speedily cleared the deck. After that we enjoyed it quite as much when we were steaming clear of the forest.

But amid the varied scenes of the day was one not altogether tropical. The desire of years was gratified by a view of the mighty chain of the Andes and one of its grandest volcanoes. The sun had already touched the edge of the high forest, and we were seated upon deck, watching the changing hues of the clouds as they were touched by those soft, rich colors so characteristic of the tropics, when a native friend approached, and asked if we saw Chimborazo. "Why, no!" we exclaimed, "is it clear from clouds?" "Look," said he, turning toward the east. We looked, raising our eyes to an angle generally assumed when taking in the summit of mountains. But nothing appeared, save the usual heavy clouds banked high along the horizon. "Where are you looking?" exclaimed our friend, casting a glance at our eyes; "here!" and he pointed away up among the clouds. We looked, and never will we forget that view. Resting upon the high bank of clouds, which seemed to have assumed a marble firmness, stood Chimborazo, its snow-fields four miles above us, flushing gold and crimson from the rich colors of the west. The clouds, parting, rolled either way along the slope of the Cordillera, until the long, dark wall of the Andes stood before us, lifted to the height of fourteen thousand feet, buttressed by a hundred darkened spurs all along its flank. As the clouds were drawn away, the snowy dome of Chimborazo appeared supported upon the dark waves of the sierras—a fitting "crown of the Andes." Vast snow-fields, broken by yawning crevasses, indicated by heavy shading, mantled the summit of the mountain: from the teeming tropics we looked up into the snows of an arctic winter. Between the snow-line and the zone of forest which covered the base of the mountain were dark cliffs, broken and scarred by black lines—deep chasms in the mountain's sides. As the sun sank lower, the golden hue of Chimborazo faded to an ashen white, while its rough outlines were toned to softer shadings; and then the mists of evening again veiled the Cordilleras.

This sunset view of Chimborazo was followed by another scene, if less grand, quite as beautiful. It was the tropical scenery of the Guayas, beneath a moonlit night. The soft reflections from the waters, and the weird gleam of myriads of brilliant glow-flies, sparkling in the dark forest-walls which crowded close to the river, seemed to convert the stream into a fairy entrance to some fabled land, that our reveries, into which we had fallen, pictured as lying beyond, and of which we had caught a glimpse in the fading glories of Chimborazo.

CHAPTER XV.

CROSSING THE ANDES.*

Bodegas.—Beneath the Forest.—Climbing the Cordillera.—Our Mules.—
Above the Clouds.—Descending Trains.—Carmino Real.—Valley of
Chimbo.—Guaranda.—Upon the Crest of the Andes.—Arenal.—The
Snow-line.—Dreary Ride.—Zones of Vegetation.—Coloration of
Flowers of High Altitudes.—Valley of Quito.—At the Foot of Chim-
borazo.—Mocha.—A Posada-scene.—Spanish Curiosity.—Ambato.—
Vespers among the Andes.—Indian Hospitality.—Latacunga.—Plain
of Turubamba.—Glimpse of Quito.

At the head of low-water steamboat navigation upon
the Guayas is located the Indo-Spanish town of Bodegas,
containing about two thousand inhabitants. Here the
traveller obtains mules and guides for the ascent of the
Andes. We reached this place late in the evening of the
first day from Guayaquil, and spent the following in securing animals for the transit of ourselves and baggage
over the Cordilleras: at least one day is required to con-
summate the most trifling business transaction in Equa-
dor. Just at evening all was arranged, and we were in
our saddles, in high expectation of a romantic mule-ride.
Altogether we made up an interesting cavalcade. Five
pack-animals, laden with trunks, boxes, and photographic

* * The equatorial Andes are divided into two longitudinal ranges,
called respectively the Eastern and Western Cordilleras: between these
lie the table-lands of Quito. The term Andes is sometimes applied to the
western ridge alone

apparatus, led the van, while our party brought up the rear—our little mules being almost buried beneath huge rolls of blankets, saddle-bags, guns, and nondescripts indispensable to the traveller among the Cordilleras.

It was a bright moonlit evening, and, riding until quite late, we drew up at a way-side hut, kept by an old negro, and upon inquiry whether we might pass the night, received the usual affirmative of welcome, "*Como no?*" Why not? We knew of no good reason why we should not, and so dismounted. Our *arrieros* (muleteers) unburdened the mules, hobbled and turned them loose to crop the short herbage immediately about our quarters. Climbing up a rickety ladder, we found ourselves in a small apartment, laid with split canes which threatened to break through at every step. Rolling ourselves in our blankets, upon the floor, we were not long in making the discovery that we were in a rich entomological field; which state of affairs above, in connection with an unfortunate conjunction of circumstances below, rendered even the thought of sleeping preposterous. Directly underneath was a wakeful cock, which insisted upon lusty demonstrations at the most unreasonable hours; while a calf, tied to one of the supports of the hut, filled the interludes of the heavily-grunting pigs, which, with other domestic animals, occupied the ground-floor of the cabin.

The shouting of our arrieros, driving in our mules, assured us that it was time to prepare for our day's ride. By sunrise we were mounted and passing beneath the dense, heavy forest which, as we have remarked, shades the Pacific shore, and covers the basal portion of the Andes. So thickly sprang the trees, that our loaded animals forced their way along the narrow trail only with the greatest difficulty. Parasites feeding upon parasites marked the eagerness of vegetation; vines twined upward round tall, branchless trunks, and drooped from their tops in beautiful coronals of leaves and flowers, concealing death and decay beneath life and beauty; heavy clumps of mosses (*Tillandsia*) with pendant tresses, fostered by the humidity of the atmosphere, draped the whole with their gray festoons, giving a sombre and funereal aspect to the scenery; as those forest depths are scarcely lighted by the scattering rays of the sun, which tremblingly shoot through the thick canopy of leaves above. During early morning the forests are resonant with the hum of multitudinous life; but, as the day advances, all grows silent, and one wandering beneath their dark shade feels painfully oppressed by their solitude. We recall now our first ramble in the forest upon the outskirts of Vinces, a little village located upon one of the affluents of the Guayas. The many sounds of morning had given way to the torpor of mid-day, and, as we strolled in the silent wood, our own footfall almost startled us. Rarely is the sense of loneliness so keen as when companionless in the depths of a South-American forest.

For the first half day we forced our way through this wilderness, and by noon reached the foot of the Andes, where we halted for a traveller's lunch, and then commenced to ascend. Our mules scarcely ever showed any indication of weariness. What a blessing have these addicted to wandering over the by-ways of the world found in this patient, circumspect, sure-footed animal! Notwithstanding a long-founded prejudice, we conceived a deep admiration for the species in general, from the good behavior of our own beasts, as they bore us safely over the steep and slippery passes of the Cordilleras. We, however, had a little misunderstanding at first. We addressed them in English, not thinking of their classical deficiencies. The result was, when we intimated to them our desire to stop, they were sure to alarmingly accelerate their movements; and, when, with a halt being finally secured, we told them to move on, they would stand as though they had as much leisure as the generality of Spaniards. The true state of affairs not recurring to our minds, we naturally referred all to their unregenerated nature; and, consequently, our orders were often repeated, perhaps rather peremptorily. We have not the least doubt but that our Andean mules will retain to their dying day vivid conceptions of cogent English. Soon discovering the difficulty, we fell to addressing them in their vernacular; then we got along more pleasantly.

Our course was along a wild mountain-torrent, which came leaping wildly down a rocky gorge, suddenly bursting into view above, only to escape behind some dark cliff below. We were constantly crossing and recrossing its rocky bed, the strong current opposing much difficulty to the passage, sometimes almost sweeping our mules from their feet. We made a rapid ascent, and, as we rose into the cooler heights of the sierras, found ourselves enveloped in heavy mists. We halted for the night at a small *tambo*, having made an ascent of about three thousand feet. The following morning we awoke, chilled by the cool mountain-air. How different the bracing atmosphere and the fresh breezes, from the heated, malaria-laden air of the coast! We now breathed more freely, without fear of inhaling with each inspiration miasma and fever. Every thing conspired to make that morning's ride the most enjoyable of our journey. The temperate air of the mountains infused new life and vigor into our party, and thus rendered us more susceptible to the influence of the bold, wild scenery that surrounded us; which, in its piles of mountains and dizzy heights, compelled us to stand still, just to admire and wonder. Beneath us lay a heavy stratum of clouds, resting along the flank of the sierras, and stretching westward until blended with the sky, concealing the scenery of the lowlands, as it had hid from our view, when we were beneath it, the form of the Cordilleras. We had passed through these clouds the day previous, or rather entered them, for the tambo in which we passed the night was, upon the evening of our arrival, wrapped in thick vapors which before morning had settled about the base of the mountains. As we looked down upon the bright surface of this vapor-sea, beautifully tinted by the rising sun just shooting through the ragged summit of the Cordilleras, with all in our upper world sunshine and brightness, we really pitied those condemned to live beneath its gloomy shade, and to look upon its dark and cheerless surface. It was suggestive to us of human life. Sometimes our sky seems to be darkened, and heaven appears to frown. Our position is at fault; a higher stand-point would show a serene sky and a smiling heaven. The sun had commenced to lift those vapor-clouds, and already we could discern detached masses rolling up the deep gorges, convincing us that, unless we stopped moralizing, and proceeded to climb upward, we would very soon be wrapped in cold, unpoetic mist.

Slowly we mounted the Cordilleras. Such was the confidence with which our sure-footed mules had inspired us, that we threw the bridle over their neck, and surrendered to them the privilege of choosing their own way. We had less apprehension when astride them, passing along knife-edged ridges and by dizzy precipices, than we should have had if trusting to our own feet. Long trains of donkeys and bulls, laden with products of the table-lands, rushed recklessly down the precipitous path, causing us to hug closely the cliffs, to avoid being overturned or crowded over into the abyss. One drove safely passed, we turned our eyes upward only to see another train, winding down the seemingly perpendicular sides of the mountains. The llama is seldom employed in transporting burdens over the Cordilleras of Ecuador—we met but one in our passage—but farther south, among the Andes of Peru, the traveller encounters long trains of these "mountain-sheep," which are admirably adapted to traversing the bleak, broken passes of those snowy sierras.

By ten we reached Camino Real, a collection of half a dozen Indian huts. Unrivalled was the view which our position afforded. The heavy clouds, that in the morning lay at the foot of the Andes, now hung but a few hundred feet below us, and we seemed to stand upon a precipitous coast, the vapor-sea dashing its light waves about the mountain-peaks which rose like islands from the surface of this cloud-ocean. Such was the view to the westward. In our front towered still higher ranges of the Cordilleras, pushing their crests boldly upward till the low, shrubby growth, struggling up the gentler slopes of the valleys, gave way before the summit was nearly reached, leaving their tops scarcely clothed with Alpine grasses. High above all towered the peerless Chimborazo. Such are the elements of grandeur entering into a view among the Andes. The mind is actually oppressed by the exhibition of power, feels a sense of uneasiness, and in vain looks for repose amid the liftings of the hills.

Delaying at Camino Real only for a hasty refection, we again remounted and rode slowly along the brow and down the slope of the sierra. The chilling winds, sweeping from off the ice-fields of Chimborazo, rendered grateful the warmth of our ponchos. Scattered along our path were the whitening bones of animals, and frequently the eye would fall upon a grim human skull, crowded into a small excavation in the bank, or bound to the arm of a rude cross, half-buried beneath the pile of votive stones thrown about it by the superstitious arrieros. In a single decaying trunk we counted seven of these relics of the sufferings of the poor muleteers upon these bleak passes.

A little more than half-way up the slope of the Cordilleras lies nestled among the hills the picturesque valley of Chimbo. We had scarcely left Camino Real, and turned the summit of Pizcureu, before we were brought in full view of that truly mountain-picture. The sight of cultivation was refreshing, after our having passed over the forest-trail which leads from the coast. We anticipated scenes wild and grand among the Andes, but our imagination had never placed there the repose and beauty of such a vale. The sierras, shaded about their base with dark forests, encircled it, as if to guard against all approach, little villages clustered amid the fields, checkered by cultivation, and hedged by lines of aloes, or century-plants. Descending from the ridge of Pizcureu, we stopped for the night at the little village of San Miguel. The houses are more firmly and warmly built than those of the coast, the walls being two or three feet in thickness, and constructed of *adobes*, large mud-bricks dried in the sun; the roofs are thatched with *paja*, the long grass afforded by the paramos. It was here that we first slept upon beds, which, we think, and sincerely hope, are confined to the Andes. They consisted of narrow, mud projections, about eighteen inches in height, running around the sides of the room. We were musing what earthly purpose they could subserve, when our host came in and intimated that they were to be our bed. We have seen better sleeping arrangements. In the court-yard of the building was a black bear, an animal found on the high slopes of the Andes, but which seldom descends to the *tierra caliente*.

A short ride through the valley of Chimbo brought us to Guaranda, a town of two thousand inhabitants, and the half-way station between Guayaquil and Quito, where the traveller must exchange his mules for others; as those coming from the coast are not allowed to enter the colder heights of the sierras. This village lies at an altitude of

little less than nine thousand feet ; just the zone, under the
equator, of eternal spring. Five thousand four hundred
feet higher is the bleak pass leading over the highest
range to the plains of Quito. From the outskirts of the
town Chimborazo towers upward with one unbroken,
dizzy sweep of over twelve thousand feet. The trail
which we must follow leads us up to within seven thousand feet of the summit of the mountain. Our Guayaquil-
ian friends had admonished us to cross the crest before
10 P. M., as later the winds sweep violently down the sides
of Chimborazo, and driving storms imperil the traveller
upon the pass. Although we charged our arrieros to be
ready to start by five in the morning, it was nine before
they were prepared to move. Once mounted, we made
a rapid rise, occasionally catching a glimpse, through the
drifting masses of clouds, of the icy sides of Chimborazo.
Rising higher and higher, we became enveloped in cold
mists, and, approaching the snow-line, chilling winds
rushed down the mountain, driving the falling sleet directly in our faces. Accustomed to the enervating heat
of the *tierra caliente*, we were doubly susceptible to the
piercing cold, which completely benumbed our bodies.
The summit of the pass was gained by scrambling up a
steep slope of sand and gravel. The extreme rarefaction
of the atmosphere at this great elevation of almost three
miles (14,250 feet) rendered every exertion most fatiguing.
A large train of heavily-laden donkeys were being urged
up the precipitous bank ; many, completely exhausted,
had sunk upon the ground, and refused to rise, in spite of
the shouts and blows of the arrieros. When lifted to
their feet they would climb up a few steps, and then again
drop, as if lifeless, upon the sand.

The highest point reached, and we were upon the dreary waste of the Arenal—a belt of coarse sand and gravel
lying upon the sides of Chimborazo—a few hundred feet

below the line of perpetual snow. Its formation seems to indicate a glacial origin; it appears like the vast terminal accumulation of some glacier that may have flowed down the slopes of Chimborazo during a period when the snow-line was lower than at present. We now find it upon the equatorial Andes at 15,748 feet, while in latitude 18° south it is 17,000 feet, and in Tierra del Fuego it descends to within 3,500 to 4,000 feet of the sea. The elevation of the line over a thousand feet, as we proceed southward from the equator, is caused by the arid nature of the Peruvian coast. South of Concepcion, latitude 37°, the climate changes, as is marked by the forests which there cover the base of the Andes, and the snow-line rapidly descends, until in latitude 40° it lies at an elevation of only 6,000 feet. At great heights snow is probably not thawed, but evaporated. Darwin was informed that, during an unusually long and warm summer, the snow, doubtless removed by evaporation, entirely disappeared from Aconcagua, the highest peak of the Andes.

It is a dreary trail that leads over the icy foot of Chimborazo. We shall not soon forget the feeling of utter desolateness experienced while crossing that mountain-waste. Having lingered behind to collect specimens of the few Alpine plants that outlive the cold of those bleak heights, we became separated from the party and its Indian guides, and for eight hours rode companionless over the dreary Arenal and a lonely paramo. Upon the former all traces of vegetation finally disappeared; a more stern desolation the imagination could not picture. Occasionally the clouds would gather and drive fiercely over the barren slopes. It is Nature, in such solitudes as these—

"Such majesty of lofty loneliness "—

that stirs the deepest feelings of the soul.

While upon the summit of the Andes, we could not

but recall the different zones of vegetation through which we had passed. Nowhere in the world does Nature crowd together such a diversity of climate, as there directly under the line of the equator. Just above where we stood reigned the snows of an eternal winter, below, the constant heat of the fervid tropics, while the vales between enjoyed the freshness of perennial spring. In three days we had passed from the rank, stimulated growth of the *tierra caliente*, to the stunted vegetation of a few hardy Alpine plants, struggling for an existence amid the melting snows of Chimborazo. The decrease of vegetation as we ascend mountain-slopes, as well as its inferior organization, is the result not only of a diminution of heat, but also of the existence of less carbonic acid in high regions of the atmosphere. Lichens, " children of the rocks," are starved as well as frozen. It is curious to observe the wide range of conditions to which vegetable organizations are adapted. With our plants gathered amid the snows of the Andes, are some found growing under the peculiar conditions afforded by the crater of Pichincha, and still others taken from the Stygian waters of the hot springs of Valencia. Specific characteristics adapt each variety to these widely-diverging conditions of life. Finding species so admirably fitted to circumambient conditions, the question is naturally suggested, how far these adaptations are referable to individual adjustment, rendered possible by the plastic nature of primal forms. This is one of the most interesting questions awaiting the solution of naturalists.

The bright color of the flowers of these high altitudes is refreshingly attractive to the eye of the traveller; rendered doubly so by the gray, sear, sombre appearance of the scene which they deck like sparkling jewels. A beautiful deep blue and bright yellow are the favorite colors of these Alpine plants. The cause of the peculiar coloring of flowers of lofty elevations is the more intense actinic properties of the unstrained light; for, at the altitude of a little over three miles, the rays have passed through only one-half the quantity of air that those must traverse which are unobstructed by mountain elevations before reaching the ocean level. This peculiar coloration of flowers—the predominance of blue and yellow—has been observed by Bowles among the Rocky Mountains, at an elevation exceeding only by a little one-half that at which the phenomenon is most distinctly marked upon the Andes. This would seem to indicate a less absorptive power of the lower strata of the atmosphere of the temperate zones, as compared with that of the tropics. The pale shade, and often delicate white, of our early spring flowers, and the richer and more gaudy hues of summer and autumn, are doubtless the result of the varied chemical properties of the light during different portions of the year. We observe that the humming-birds which flit so constantly in the unstrained light of the lofty regions of the Andes are more brilliantly colored than those found upon the lowlands. May this also not be referred to the same causes that effect the coloration of plants? That other birds of high flight are sometimes of a dull color, may be explained, perhaps, by the counteracting influences of peculiar habits of life.

From the paramo of Chimborazo the traveller looks down upon the plateau of Quito, which, at this point, is about twenty miles in width. To the right lies the renowned city of Riobamba, in the midst of an apparently well-cultivated plain. A dreary ride over a dreary moorland, gradually descending, and we turned into the courtyard of the tambo of Chuquipoys. The prospects afforded by the miserable mud hovel were cheerless; but it was at least a comforting reflection that the bleak pass was crossed. and we were over the Western Cordillera, although Quito was yet distant one hundred miles up the valley to the north. That was a memorable night passed at the foot of icy Chimborazo. With the exception of a single cane-arrangement, our room was destitute of sleeping-accommodations; even the mud-projections were absent, consequently we spread our beds upon the ground, and, rolling in our blankets, endeavored to obtain a little of "Nature's sweet restorer," but the cold was too intense. With the first indication of light we were up, wrapped in our ponchos, and out reconnoitring our position. Dreary was our upper world. Snow had fallen during the night upon Chimborazo and the surrounding ranges, mantling them far below the usual snow-line; but the clouds were now broken and driving with a wintry aspect through the heavens. The winds were bitterly cold, and our poor animals, confined in the court-yard with only a low mud-wall for a protection, were trembling from their night's exposure, and seemed anxious to be mounted. Chimborazo, free from clouds, towered majestically above us; although we stood at an elevation of over two miles, this colossus of the Andes lifted itself more than nine thousand feet above our tambo.

From Chuquipoys, a ride of nine miles over a paramo, clothed with heavy tufts of wiry grass called *pajo*, brought us to Mocha, a sorry-looking town, the most miserable of any passed upon our route. The low mud-huts, with thatched roofs, were common habitation for pigs, poultry, donkeys, and guinea-pigs, which, with half-naked Indian children, strayed in and out of the opening that served as a door. Breakfasting at a wretched hovel, which made some pretensions as a *casa posada*, we prepared to remount, and then was enacted the soul-trying scene of settling accounts with our host. The Ecuadorians have a most peculiar way of transacting such business. A bill is generally made out for each article, and presented separately. Upon this occasion, however, a bill of six reals was handed us, accompanied with the assurance that it was "*por todas cosas*" (for every thing). Congratulating ourselves that we had at last found one of sufficient tact and enterprise to make one job of breakfast-charges, we quickly cancelled the indebtedness. But scarcely did we feel ourselves in our saddles before *cuatro reales mas* (four reals more) was demanded for the breakfast of our arrieros. Expostulation was useless, and the bill was paid only to be followed by another of two reals for *yerba* fed the animals. Protest of course we did, till our by no means superfluous stock of Spanish expletives was completely exhausted; and then we made another drain upon our pockets; after which we were informed that the two reals only paid for the *yerba* given the *bestias de silla* (saddle-animals), and that a like amount was due for the *bestias de carga* (pack-animals). Having paid for the damages done by the cargo-beasts, we put spurs to our mules, thinking to be conscientiously absolved from further payments, for the very good reason that we should hear of no more bills being presented. But we were arrested by the shouts of our arriero, our host having laid violent hands upon the gun, which had been committed to his charge, announcing his intention to retain it as payment for the services of the Indian who had brought the *yerba*. The last instalment which we made toward the discharge of the debt contracted that morning for breakfast was to redeem our favorite rifle from the hands of the insatiable posadero.

Besides the peculiarities of posaderos, there is another annoyance to which the traveller is here subjected. This is the curiosity of Spaniards, all laudable enough in itself, only objectionable in the means adopted for its gratification. We are indebted to our friend and fellow-traveller, Bushnell, for the following: "It is an old saying that the more people know the more they want to know, and that the more intelligent they become the more curious they are. The first statement is undoubtedly true, but one's faith in the latter is certainly shaken, after having travelled for a time among the ignorant class of Spaniards. No people can be more curious for curiosity's sake than are these. If a traveller stop at one of their houses, they commence at once by asking, 'Whence do you come, where are you going, what is your business, how long will you remain in the country, when will you come to see me again?' After this introduction, they pass to more personal matters, and desire to know your name, whether you are married, and, if so, your wife's name, whether you have any children, if boys or girls, and their names, whether you have any brothers and sisters, and what their names are, whether they are married, and, if so, their partners' names, whether their parents be living, and, if so, what their names are. If not married, they want to know if you are in love, if the young lady is pretty, the color of her eyes and hair, what her name is, and the name of her parents. Nor does their curiosity become satisfied when all these questions are satisfactorily answered, for they immediately begin upon another strain, viz.: 'Do they use horses in your country?' 'Are there any hens there, and do they lay eggs as ours do?' 'Are the people of your country white or black?' 'Do they drink coffee?' 'Do they have any schools there?' 'What is the religion?' 'What is your religion?' 'Are there any cities in your country?' 'Do the people speak Spanish?' Thus they pass through the whole category of questions that the mind, memory, and imagination, can devise. Even the servants and muleteers have the audacity to question a traveller upon such matters, and think themselves greatly insulted if every query is not fully and respectfully answered."

From Mocha our trail descended gently, and, as we

escaped the chilling influences of Chimborazo, cultivation gradually appeared. Unexpectedly the beautiful city of Ambato burst into view, lying in a deep, cañon-like valley; an abrupt descent, and we were within the town. It was inspiring to hear the clatter of our animals' hoofs upon a well-paved street. The houses are substantially built, with mud-walls four to five feet in thickness, and but one story in height, in order to better withstand the *terremotos*, or earthquakes. Its climate is a little milder than that of Quito, and it is a place of frequent resort during the season of fruits, for which the Ambato valley is justly celebrated. Its population is eight thousand. The evening of our arrival being unusually clear, just as the sun was disappearing, we clambered up out of the ravine, anticipating a view of Cotapaxi, which we were now approaching. Our anticipations were more than realized. Around us stood three of the grandest peaks of the Andes, divested of the heavy clouds which for several days had hung darkly about the summit of the Cordilleras. To the south Chimborazo towered heavenward; the light clouds, which lay in white bars across its breast, sullying its whiter robe of snow, which fell far down its sides; eastwardly the beautiful volcanic peak of Tunguragua broke the uniformity of the eastern wall of the plateau; while, farther to the north, Cotopaxi raised the most perfect cone in the world, its summit mantled with snow. The light smoke-wreaths curling innocently about its crater was all that told of the deeply-hidden forces which so often shake the Andes from base to summit. We sat long, watching the changing hues of the mountains, as the sun, that had just hidden itself behind the Western Cordillera, colored them with a rich crimson, which slowly faded to a ghostly white. The whole scene was one of that majestic repose so characteristic of the landscape of these mountain-hemmed plains. Grandly those mountains lifted their snowy altars about us—we felt it to be the hour and place for reverent worship. Just then we observed several groups, slowly making their way up the steep path which wound from the town, to render their evening devotions before the crucifix planted upon the brow of the hill, and around which a small number were already gathered in the attitude of prayer. There was something pleasing in that vesper service. We thought it a fitting scene of the closing day, enacted there before Nature's own altars, with the glories of that mountain-temple stilling the soul in adoring wonder and reverence.

We spent the Sabbath in Ambato. This is the great market-day of the week. Our observations confirmed the remark of a friend at Guayaquil, that the Sabbath never found its way across the isthmus. There is a deplorable lack of veneration for the day throughout Spanish America. Early in the morning, the Indians of the country surrounding Ambato come pouring into the city with fruits and produce of every variety; the women carrying the burdens upon their backs with their infants perched on top, while their lords trot along empty-handed. By ten o'clock the *plaza*, or public square, is packed with a motley throng, and presents a busy scene during the remainder of the day. Next to the plaza, the little stream that runs through the town presents the most unique and animated scene. Its banks for a long distance are flecked with drying garments, while at the bowlders in the stream stand the Indian washerwomen, using the rough stones as scrubbing-boards. Having no linen in "the wash," we looked on unmoved as the stout, swarthy señoras rubbed the clothes upon the rocks, whipped them about the bowlders, or pounded them with the smaller stones.

A few days' rest at Ambato, and we again resumed our journey. We were necessitated to make easy stages, as the sudden change from the *tierra caliente* to the high table-lands, combined with the severe ride over the Cordillera, while still weak from the effects of fever experienced at Guayaquil, had completely exhausted Colonel Staunton, who, unable longer to endure the fatigue of riding, was carried in a litter borne upon the shoulders of four Indians. Our *cholo*[*] guide made use of the authority of his position, to impress into the service of bearing the litter any Indians whom we happened to meet. He had mounted the colonel's horse, and possessed himself of his gun, and, thus equipped, rode about with an air of the gravest dignity. Observing an Indian in the distance, he would put spurs to his horse, and, displaying his weapon, would soon come up to and order the man to the relief of one of the bearers. Some of the Indians, doubtless mistaking him for a recruiting-officer—for thus they recruit in Ecuador—often led him in a hot pursuit across the plain. After one had accompanied us a few miles, we would reward him with a calabash of chicha, the Indian's national beverage, when, doffing the remnants of a wool hat, he would say, with a low bow, "*Muchas gracias, señores*," and go on his way rejoicing.

Our road led across a barren plain, the dreary region over which reigns the restless Cotopaxi. All day long we rode slowly over this arid waste, drooping listlessly in our saddles, our faces veiled to protect them from the glare of the scoriæ-strewn plain. The only sound that arrested the ear was the foot-fall of the Indians, who bore the litter with slow, measured tread before us. The desert aspect of the plain was occasionally relieved by straggling aloes and cactuses, that seemed to find a congenial home in the burning sands. Condensed in their solid rosettes of thickened leaves or columnar shafts, they flourish during seasons of protracted drought, when other plants be-

---

[*] Cholos are the offspring of whites and Indians. In most of them the Indian element largely predominates.

come withered and scorched through rapid evaporation. The aloe, as we have remarked, furnishes an admirable substitute to the native for needle and thread. One day our blanket unfortunately became unrolled, and fell beneath our mule, which very carelessly put his foot through it, making a serious rent. We deplored the accident the more because the hole would just correspond with the slit in our poncho when both were wrapped about us at night. But one of our Indians, stepping to an aloe, broke off a spine, drawing out the attached thread, and then sat down and quickly repaired the damage.

While passing up the valley, we were, at times, the recipients of Indian hospitality. We never had a greater effort made to contribute to our comfort than at one of their huts, where we chanced while suffering from an attack of the fever, which still clung to us. A bed was immediately provided, which, although only a blanket spread upon the ground, with a piece of pumice-stone for a pillow, was still their best. A fire was kindled, but, the fuel being ill-cured grass, it imparted little heat, but puffed out clouds of smoke, until we were almost suffocated. Then an attempt was made to administer, for our fever, a calabash of fiery aguardiente. Afterward soup, the constituents of which we could never divine, was furnished; and sympathetically the dishevelled Indian and her little naked ones stood by while we were partaking. It was kind in them, but we confess that their proximity to our soup was any thing but appetizing. We survived their kindness, and have often since recalled, with gratitude, alike their good intentions and our escape.

The second day from Ambato we reached Latacunga, a town of fifteen thousand inhabitants, situated fifteen miles south of Cotopaxi. Half the city lies piled in ruins by the terrible earthquakes which have frequently visited it. Pumice-stone, tossed out by Cotopaxi, forms the principal building-material. This rock is also obtained from a quarry two leagues distant from the town. The quarried stone is of a more fibrous, silky nature than the fragments ejected by the volcano, and its color is of a bluish gray. Leaving this city, our road gradually ascends, until we find ourselves upon the bleak ridge of Chisinchi, a transverse range which lies across the plateau, separating the waters of the Pastassa and Esmeraldas. The latter flows northward about fifty miles, and then, breaking through the Western Cordillera, leaps down to the Pacific; the former runs an equal distance south down the valley, then bursts the Eastern Cordillera and hurries down the slope of the Andes to the Amazons. Descending from Chisinchi, the aspect of the country suddenly changes, and the beautiful vale which we enter the fourth day from Ambato, gradually spreads out into magnificent plains, where the yellow glow of ripening fields, contrasted with the deep green of growing grain, gives evidence of a perpetual spring. These are the plains of Turubamba; and our arrieros, pointing up the plateau, tell us that a few leagues more will bring us in sight of the city of Quito.

Late in the afternoon of the 29th of August we gained a gentle rise, which allowed the eye an extensive sweep up the valley. Upon the left of the plain before us rose Panecillo, a dome-shaped hill, symmetrical as though formed by art, and joined to the Western Cordillera. From behind this hill stretched out toward the east a long, broken line of white walls—the outskirts of Quito. Already Pichincha was throwing its deep shadows over the plain, and hastening forward we were soon passing rapidly through the streets of the capital, and shortly entered the court-yard of the *Casa Frances*, where, in the warm welcome from the members of our party who had preceded us, we forgot all the weariness of our journey over the Andes.

CHAPTER XVI.

QUITO.

CROSSED by the equator, and fenced round by lofty,
snow-clad mountains, lies the beautiful valley of Quito.
It is over two hundred miles in length, and twenty to
thirty in breadth. The scenery of that mountain-walled
valley is of unrivalled grandeur. Three degrees south of
the equatorial line the Andes divide into two cordilleras,
which, running parallel to each other until again united
north of the equator by the mountain-knot of Los Pastos,
encircle those lofty table-lands. Set round upon those
trachytic walls are the noblest peaks of the Andes, which,
wrapped in their shrouds of eternal white, standing against
the horizon, seem in their majestic repose to be the faithful guardians of the once favorite home of the Incas.

Here, fifteen miles south of the equator, close under the
shadow of the Western Cordillera, and resting partly upon
the flank of the volcano Pichincha, lies the far-famed city
of Quito. Its altitude is nine thousand five hundred and
forty feet; just three thousand two hundred and fifty feet
higher than the summit of Mount Washington. Upon
the north and south are unfolded the plains of Añaquito

and Turubamba, the most fertile of any embraced by the plateaux of the Andes. Above is spread a deep, soft sky, shedding the influences of an everlasting spring. In the climate of Quito we observe a fine illustration of the fact that meteorological phenomena are determined not less by elevation and relation to mountain-ranges than by position in latitude. Considerable portions of so-called tropical America do not enjoy, or rather suffer, a tropical climate. The lofty cordilleras of the Andes, culminating in height near the southern line of the tropics, with their broad, elevated table-lands, carry a temperate, and, in isolated instances, a frigid climate to those intertropical regions. Thus western equatorial America is as truly temperate as tropical. The mean annual temperature of Quito is fifty-nine degrees; you here never feel the inconvenience of heat or cold. The entire variation during the year is only twenty-five degrees, while in our Northern States it is over one hundred and thirty. Under this equable and salubrious climate epidemic diseases are almost unknown; cholera, yellow fever, and consumption, never find their way into these elevated valleys. In respect to scenery and climate, Nature has done much for the city of Quito. But man has done his part less well. He has defaced this spot with a city so devoid of beauty, so filled with filth and guilt, that, should Pichincha bury the whole beneath its lavic floods, we would have no trouble in interpreting the providence. Let us review hurriedly the history of Quito, and then speak briefly of the present city and the character of Quitonians.

Quito has been the proud capital of four successive civilizations. Centuries ago, almost beyond the reach of tradition, it was founded by the Quitus race. Five hundred years before the Spanish invasion, the Carans, who ascended the western slope of the Andes, by way of the Esmeraldas, conquered the Quitus nation, and established

in the valley the dynasty of the Scyris.* Temples and
palaces of barbaric splendor, and ambitious *tolas*,† or
tombs, rose throughout the valley. Second only to the
civilization of the Incas was this early one of the Carans.
They were familiar with implements of bronze, and possessed some knowledge of astronomy. The sun, as with
the Incas, was the central object of their worship. But,
while the mountain-peaks which stand about the plains of
Quito were witnessing the high civilization of the Scyris,
there was springing up in the highlands of Lake Titicaca
an indigenous civilization which nowhere found a parallel among the primitive nations of America, except upon
the table-lands of Mexico, and which was speedily to ab-
sorb the Quitonian kingdom.

The great Inca empire had its origin about the year
1100, four hundred years before the Spanish conquest.
An island in the mountain-girdled lake of Titicaca, where
tradition says Manco Capac and Mama Oella, his sister
and wife, "Children of the Sun," first appeared, is to-day
held sacred as the birthplace of the Inca kingdom. But
of the Empire of the Incas we need speak but briefly, for
the pen of Prescott has made all familiar with their romantic history. By conquest and the assimilating forces
of a wise and paternal polity, they soon extended their
kingdom to the domains of the Scyris. The Inca Tupac
Yupanqui, jealous of this rival kingdom, led his warriors
against the king of the Carans, and wrested from him the
southern portion of his dominions. Both kingdoms now
changed rulers. Cacha the Fifteenth came to the throne
of the Scyris in Quito. Huayna-Capac succeeded his
father, Tupac Yupanqui, in Cuzco. Capac made an heroic
defence of his empire. Overpowered by numbers and

* The king of the Carans was called Scyri. The language of this
race was the Quichua, the national tongue of the Incas.

† See "Four Years among Spanish-Americans," Hassaurek.

treachery, he was swept up the plains of Quito. Mocha, Latacunga, and the capital, fell successively into the hands of the victorious Inca. Upon the plains of Hatuntaqui, in the province of Imbabura, the most northern part of the Quito valley, was fought the terrible battle which decided the fate of the Caran nation. "To the *borla*, the emblem of Peruvian royalty, was added the emerald of the Scyris." Quito now became one of the capitals of the Inca empire. During the reign of Huayna-Capac, the Peruvian kingdom attained its culminating point of grandeur. It embraced the principal Indian tribes of the plateaux of the Andes, and stretched for more than two thousand miles along the Pacific coast, while claiming as its subjects many of the tribes of the tropic interior. It was by this Inca that many of those great works of internal improvement, whose remains are still so magnificent, were constructed. Quito was joined to Cuzco by that royal road which swept the entire length of the kingdom. "As prudent and highly politic," says Hassaurek, "as the conduct of Huayna-Capac is generally reputed to have been, so imprudent and impolitic was the division of the empire on his death-bed, bequeathing his paternal dominions, Cuzco, to his first-born, Huascar, and to Atahuallpa, the kingdom of Quito." From that unwise division may be dated the fall of the Peruvian empire. Jealousies speedily kindled into war, and for the first time Inca joined battle with Inca. Huascar was taken prisoner in the battle of Quipaypan, and Atahuallpa seized the entire kingdom.

Just at this moment, while the kingdom was convulsed by these internal strifes, the western shore of the empire was startled by the Spanish invaders. We need not tell of the cruel crushing of the Inca nation, the confinement of Atahuallpa, the golden ransom, the perfidy of the conquerors, the sad fate of the last of the royal line of the

Incas, and the establishment of Spanish supremacy in
South America. Quito was one of the last cities to fall
into the hands of the invaders. After the death of Atahuallpa, his chief Rumiñagui collected the army, shattered in the battle of Quipaypan, and prepared for the
defence of the capital. Sebastian de Benalcazar, with
only a handful of Spanish soldiers, but having a strong
force of Indian allies, crossed the Cordilleras, and, after a
series of fiercely-contested battles, arrived at Quito; but
only to find it a heap of ruins. Rumiñagui, removing the
treasures from the temples, had destroyed the city, and
retreated to the northern provinces of the valley. Through
this desperate act of the Indians, and the vandalism of the
Spanish iconoclasts, themselves baser devotees, as some
one has well said, of a baser idol than ever found a place
in the temples of the religion they warred against, not a
trace was left of the former magnificence of the city of
the Incas.* Thus fell Quito while enjoying a civilization
superior to that of Rome during the reign of the Tarquins;
equal to that of the Britons at the time of the Saxon invasion. Upon its ruins was founded, in 1534, the present
city.

Its long, instructive colonial history we will pass in
silence. But a change at last came. Spain, by impolitic
diplomacy, by arrogant assumption of colonial jurisdiction, at length forced her American colonies to revolu-
tionary measures. During the war for independence,
Ecuador joined her fortunes with those of New Granada
and Venezuela, but shortly after the close of the struggle,
in 1829, this union was dissolved, and since that time Quito
has been the capital of the *República del Ecuador*. Revolutions, and rumors of revolutions, make up the history of

---

* "Of the ancient buildings of Quito no stone was left upon the other,
and deep excavations were made under them to search for hidden treasures."—(Hassaurek's "Four Years among Spanish Americans.")

the city under the *régime* of a republican government.
Varied has been its past; unsatisfactory is its present;
may the future bring it days equal to those when it was
called the " City of the Incas ! "

Quito, as we find it to-day, presents a melancholy contrast to its former magnificence. The city lies upon the
projecting spurs of the volcano Pichincha, which rises out
of the Western Cordillera. The buildings, generally two
stories in height, are constructed of adobe, the walls being
two to three feet in thickness, as a precaution against earthquakes. The upper windows are furnished with balconies,
and the roofs covered with tiles. In consequence of the
incombustible nature of the building-material, there are no
conflagrations. You could as easily fire a beavers' village
as the mud squares of Quito. Some of the houses enclose pleasant court-yards, around which run verandas
about ten feet in depth, and above these second galleries
of equal width, furnished with low balustrades. The
government buildings and churches are the only edifices
that make any architectural pretensions. The façade of
the Jesuit church is the most elaborate work of art the
city affords, being constructed of the porphyritic rock of
Pichincha. One of the marked features of Quito, as of
all Spanish towns, is its plazas, or public squares. Of
these there are three, each being furnished with a stone
fountain which graces the centre. The *Plaza Mayor* was
formerly, as the remaining two, the *Plaza de San Domingo* and the *Plaza de San Francisco*, are at present,
destitute of trees; but President Moreno converted it
into a park in order to unfit it as a place for bull-fights, or
rather bull-baitings. Quitonians now view this amusement from the balconies of the San Francisco plaza. The
last-named square, with that of Santo Domingo, is used
as a market-place. Throughout the city are shattered
walls and unseemly piles of rubbish—traces of frequent

earthquakes.   This was true at the time of our visit, and,
should we pass through the city now, we would find many
a ruin added by the late terrible earthquake of August
16, 1868, which entirely destroyed its sister cities, Ibarra,
Otovalo, and Atantaqui, situated in the northern provinces of the valley.

Quito contains a mixed Indian and Spanish population
of forty thousand; the Negro element being scarcely represented.   This city, in the preservation of the aboriginal
inhabitants, presents, in common with most other Hispano-
American towns, an anomaly in the history of colonization.   In North America we witness the indigenous
population swept away before the tide of Anglo-Saxon
civilization; in Australia and New Zealand the primitive
inhabitants are rapidly becoming extinct upon the advance
of Europeans; Southern Africa presents a repetition of
this same fact; in the East-Indian Archipelago the natives
of many of the islands have been extirpated by the more
energetic Malay race; in Van Diemen's Land the entire
population was swept from the island in less than thirty
years after its settlement by Europeans, a portion being
removed to save them from entire extinction.*   In viewing such facts as these, we are almost led to the adoption
of what has been termed the "Spencerian theory," and to
look for the future of mankind only in the "survival of
the fittest."   But Hispano-America, as we have remarked,
presents an exception.   There the native population was
spared, all barriers between the races were thrown down,
and the way left open to unrestrained and unparalleled
amalgamation.   The deterioration attending this commingling of Spanish and Indian races is painfully apparent.   We observe a loss of intellectual force, a union of
the worst qualities of both, of which there is no lack in
either, and an elimination of all the essential elements of

* "Naturalist's Voyage round the World," Darwin.

a broad and vigorous manhood.   And such seem ever to
be the results of a blending of races.   The objector may
point to the Anglo-Saxon, as an instance of a people of
acknowledged intellectual energy springing from an unex-
ampled commingling.   But we must draw a distinction
between what are popularly termed races and the varieties, or branches, of these.   The blending of varieties of
the same race is always attended with elevatory results;
and it was only in accordance with this law that the union
of the obstinate firmness of the native Briton with the
impulsive energy of the Teutonic tribes gave birth to
that mental strength characteristic of the Anglo-Saxon.
But the amalgamation of the races, as the Latin with the
Indian, or the Indian with the African, presents less satisfactory results.   The labor and triumph of the race constituting the leading civilization of the world will be in
preserving and lifting to its own level less favored ones,
while maintaining uncontaminated all its own intellectual
expression and energy.   How is this to be secured?   History tells us that, in the presence of a strong people, a
weaker one will be crushed out in the strife for existence,
unless beneath the selfish shield of slavery, or preserved
by amalgamation.   Recourse again to the first alternative,
in order to secure from extinction an inferior race in the
fierce struggle for life, can never be had; when we speak
of the second, the experience of South-American civilization leads us to hesitate.   Amalgamation, such as we observe in almost every Hispano-American city, produces
equality; but chiefly at the expense of the elevatory
power, by pulling down the higher, not by lifting the
lower.*   This problem of the races presents a question as
interesting to the ethnologist as important to the philan-

* "The hybrid between white and Indian, called Mammeluco in Brazil, is pallid, effeminate, feeble, lazy, and rather obstinate ; though it
seems as if the Indian influence had only gone so far as to obliterate the

thropist. In seeking its solution, while claiming positively equality of rights, let us be careful, in entering another sphere, that we do not pass those lines that Nature has drawn, and which she will not allow to be disregarded with impunity.

Of the mixed population of Quito, about one-fifth constitutes what is termed the white population, an evident misnomer, as probably not a score of them could count back two generations without encountering an Indian; and this fact their physiological characteristics do not fail to reveal. This class form the upper circle of society, and assume the affairs of state. The purely Indian element, comprising about one-fourth of the inhabitants, is condemned to manual labor. *Cholos*, or *mestizos*, descendants of Spaniards and Indians, make up by far the larger portion of the population. They constitute the soldiers and the business class of Quito, and, while superior to the Indians, are as much inferior to those who comprise the first and leading class.

In every thing, especially in ideas of progress and enterprise, degenerate Quito is several centuries behind the age. And how could we expect that it should be otherwise? Offspring of imbecile and retrogressive Spain, posted above the rest of the world almost two miles, fenced in by mountains which only a mule or a llama can scale, with the hereditary antipathy of its people to modern innovations, affording a still more effectual barrier than those mountain-walls to the introduction of modern thought and improvement, what else could it do but fossilize? As their fathers did, so do they. Fletcher, in his brilliant "Brazil and the Brazilians," tells the following story, which is so applicable to Quitonians, and illustrative of Spaniards, that we cannot forbear repeating it: "Once

higher characteristics of the white, without imparting its own energies to the offspring.—("A Journey in Brazil.")

upon a time, Adam requested leave to revisit this world; permission was granted, and an angel commissioned to conduct him. On wings of love the patriarch hastened to his native earth; but, so changed, so strange, all seemed to him, that he nowhere felt at home, till he came to Portugal. 'Ah, now,' exclaimed he, 'set me down; every thing here is just as I left it.'" The sequel would have been the same had the good angel taken him to Quito: Adam would have had a longing to be set down there at once.

The religion of Quito is an intolerant Catholicism. The city is crowded with churches and conventual edifices, where, under the garb of religious sanctity, is hidden a mass of corruption, whose influence is felt throughout every grade of society. Daily mass, carnivals, and public processions, constitute religion here. The fête-days are legion, and often must the images of the Virgin and saints be borne through the streets. We witnessed one especially brilliant procession in honor of *la Virgen Maria del Rosario*, the special patroness of the San Domingo Church. The evening preceding the day for the ceremonies, the façade and dome of the church were brilliantly illuminated, and within, hundreds of wax-candles glistened amid tinsel and drapery. About ten, upon the following day, the plaza presented a gay appearance. From the balconies hung flags, shawls, ponchos, and bed-quilts, of every hue and size. Amid the jingling of bells, and crackling of fireworks, the procession issued from the church, preceded by the images of the saints, borne upon the shoulders of Indians, impressed for the occasion. Following the monks were the high officials of state, including the President, the military bringing up the rear. This subservience of the State to the Church is the curse of Ecuador; the present illiberal position of the government toward Protestants being maintained through the influence of religious intolerance and bigotry. Having occupied about two hours in passing around the plaza, the saints, who doubtless enjoyed the airing, were borne into the church in good time to escape a rising shower. Such religious ceremonies as these are illustrative of Catholicism as we find it in Quito, and, indeed, through a large portion of South America. So supremely ignorant are the people, so thoroughly indoctrinated in the superstitious teachings of native and foreign priests, that any reformatory movements, leading to a religion less material and of higher spiritual conceptions, must necessarily be slow.

Of social life in Quito, of the customs and character of its inhabitants, their vices and virtues, we will not speak, as we have already dwelt upon these in our description of Caracas, and life in one of these Spanish capitals is but a photographic picture of that in the other. We must allude, however, to one cause, beyond its inefficient population, which must ever tend to retard the prosperity of the city. We can hardly predict for it the glorious future which some foresee. Nature, although she has done much for the city, has failed to give it the one thing needful—a stable soil. There must necessarily be a stagnation of all enterprise, an ever-present discouragement to the entering upon any great public or architectural work, where, in every few decades at least, the movements of the earth pile the most labored of man's works into ruins; and, without these, to give expression to a people's progress, no advancement has ever been rendered permanent. Quito's isolation and earthquakes are balanced against its delightful climate and magnificent views.

Distant from Quito about three hours' ride is the celebrated Hacienda of Chillo, which must be noticed in connection with our hasty sketch of the capital. To reach it we cross the Puengasi Hills, which border the city upon the east, and then pass through the beautiful valley of

Chillo, one of those lovely little vales into which the plateau is broken by the low transverse and longitudinal ranges, between the two main cordilleras. It is closed upon the south by the rugged walls of Rumiñagui, while opening to the north into the valley of the Esmeraldas. In the quiet and picturesque character of its scenery, it is the rival of the valley of Chimbo, that lies upon the western slope of the Andes. The Hacienda of Chillo was established as a Jesuit mission station soon after the conquest. The building has been often remodelled, but is still undermined by old vaults and passages. Its architecture is that of the sixteenth century; corridors extend nearly the entire length of the building, the walls being decorated with fresceed paintings of the Muses and various designs. A vaulted entrance leads to the chapel, which occupies the centre of the building. It is small, but sufficiently large to accommodate the Indians, about two hundred in number, belonging to the hacienda. This church contains Titian's beautiful painting, "The Crucifixion," which was brought here by the Jesuits, and has been retained, notwithstanding several efforts that have been made to remove it to Spain. During one of the late revolutions in Ecuador, it was secreted in the vaults of the hacienda, and suffered considerable injury from dampness. The surrounding grounds are tastefully laid out, ornamented by a lively fountain, and rendered fragrant by lemon-trees, white with blossoms, while loaded with mature fruit. During a recent earthquake, a tower and clock occupying the centre of the building were thrown down, and have not since been rebuilt. While upon our excursions about the capital, we were often here entertained; and thus many of our most pleasant recollections of the Quito valley are connected with this interesting Hacienda of Chillo.

CHAPTER XVII.

MOUNTAINS ABOUT THE VALLEY OF QUITO.

Groups of Volcanoes.—Quitonian Peaks.—What gives them their Interest.—Chimborazo.—Its Summit gained by M. Remy.—Sangai.—Cotopaxi.—Antisana.—Pichincha.—Our Ascent.—Wild Scene from its Summit.—Down its Crater.—A Thunder-storm within.—Climbing out.—Lost upon the Volcano.—Return to Quito.

THE volcanoes of the New World—unlike those of the Old, which are generally placed upon the islands—are situated upon the continental land, in connection with its great mountain-axes; and, moreover, curiously disposed in five great linear groups. Humboldt, in a geognostic and geographic description of the volcanoes of the Americas, designates these as the group of Mexico, of Central America, of New Granada and Quito, of Peru and Bolivia, and of Chili.* More than ninety volcanoes are embraced by these series, of which number forty-eight still give evidence of activity. The distance between the most northern in Mexico and the most southern in Chili is almost five thousand miles; the greatest distance between any two of the groups is found separating the clusters of Quito from that of Bolivia, a stretch of nine hundred and sixty miles. The volcanoes in each assemblage have a linear meridional disposition; those in Chili being set along

* See "Cosmos," vol. v., pp. 265, 283.

ANTISANA AND COTOPAXI, AS VIEWED FROM SALTO.

a stretch of one thousand miles, while those about Quito are crowded upon a line of four hundred and seventy-two miles. The group of Central America comprises the greatest number, having twenty-nine volcanic peaks, of which eighteen are still active. But Chili claims the honor of having the highest mountain of the series, Aconcagua, which rises 23,200 feet above the Pacific—1,700 feet higher than Chimborazo, yet 6,000 feet below the summit of the highest peak of the Himalayas. The Peruvian and Bolivian group names the snowy peaks, Gulatciri, Sahama, Sorata, and Illimani, that look down upon the loftiest table-lands of the New World—the Plateau of Bolivia. Here is Lake Titicaca,* lifted up in the air to a height twice as great as the elevation of Mount Washington.

But the grandest of these groups is the one which circles, with its snow-mantled peaks, the valley of Quito. The volcanoes of this cluster are found between Sangai, two degrees south of the equator, and the *Volcan de Tolima*, five degrees north, a distance, before stated, of four hundred and seventy-two miles. They are set in two lines, along or near the axes of the two main cordilleras, into which the equatorial Andes are divided. Along the Western Cordillera rise Caraguairazo, Iliniza, Pichincha, and Cotocachi; while fronting them in long line stand, upon the Eastern Cordillera, eight noble peaks, stretching from the fiery Sangai upon the south, to the beautiful peak of Imbabura upon the north. About the centre of this row, advanced a little out upon the plain, stands Cotopaxi, the most symmetrical of Andean volcanoes.

Grand did those mountains appear to us, as, having

---

* The elevation of this lake is 12,795 feet above the ocean-level. It empties its waters by El Desaguadero into Lake Aullagas, which has no outlet, its waters being removed by evaporation. Both these lakes, like Lake Valencia, in Venezuela, are undergoing rapid desiccation.

crossed the western range from the Pacific, we journeyed between them up the plateau. On either side, stretched along the unbroken walls of the Eastern and Western Cordilleras, and upon their crest, stood those ice-crowned peaks, which, kindled by the sunset, seemed like beacon-fires set along the darkened battlements of the sierras. Often have we watched the effect of the evening sun upon the snow-fields of those lofty volcanoes. As the light wanes, the prismatic tints of the snowy peaks almost imperceptibly blend with the roseate colorings of the clouds, which form the background to the mountains. 'Tis an arctic scene, painted with all the rich hues of the tropics. Rarely does Nature so blend the elements of beauty and sublimity.

The mountains about the valley of Quito are exceeded in height by several of the Chilian and Peruvian groups. Chimborazo, of the Quitonian series, is surpassed by at least four of those lofty peaks, if we may rely upon the estimated elevation of those mountains, which is as yet somewhat unsatisfactory. But the volcanoes of Quito have a deeper interest attached to them than belongs to their loftier rivals, on account of their associations with the labors and triumphs of the most devoted heroes of science. "Wherever intellectual tendencies prevail," reflects Humboldt, "wherever a rich harvest of ideas has been excited, leading to the advancement of several sciences at the same time, fame remains, as it were, locally attached for a long time." Nature seems almost without expression, unless animated by human thought and achievement. As eternal as are the mountains of Quito, so enduring will be the names Humboldt, Condamine, Bouguer, and Boussingault, whose indefatigable labors among the equatorial Andes have made such valuable contributions to physical science.

Of the twenty-two peaks of the Quitonian group,

which push above the line of perpetual snow, but nineteen are properly volcanoes, and the grandeur, even of the larger number of these, consists not in the play of volcanic forces, for sixteen of these have either become extinct or dormant. For ages these have stood inactive; some with broken walls, others with their sides scarred by dark streams of lava.* Of all the peaks, volcanic and otherwise, that stand about the valley of Quito, Chimborazo is the grandest; Cotopaxi (some, however, think Tunguragua) is the most nearly perfect type of a volcanic cone; Antisana is peerless in beauty; Sangai is the most active; and Pichincha, from its association with science, possesses, perhaps, a greater interest than any of the others. Let us look at each of these.

Chimborazo, the most southern of the peaks of the Western Cordillera, first claims our attention. It rises 21,422 feet above the Pacific. We have already spoken of the impression produced upon the mind by this mountain, when viewed from the western coast. Seen from that stand-point, it appears like a truncated cone; from the table-lands it presents an irregular outline. The mountain seems to have suffered terrible convulsions, and now stands as a shattered dome, supported by gigantic buttresses of trachytic rock. Chimborazo has been classed by some as a volcano. But there are no traditions of its activity, and, as Humboldt has observed, it presents none of the distinctive characteristics of a volcano, and is destitute of any crater-like opening. That careful observer says: "I reckon as volcanoes, besides those which are

* In the Eastern Cordillera, almost opposite Chimborazo, stands the beautiful volcano called Altar, the walls of whose crater have fallen in, leaving portions still standing, so that the whole presents the appearance of a ruined fortification. Although most of the volcanoes of the Andes throw out during their eruptions only streams of water and mud, yet we find four immense lava-streams upon the slopes of Antisana, and one marks the sides of Tunguragua.

11

still burning and active, those volcanic formations whose old eruptions belong to historic times, or of which the structure and eruptive masses (craters of elevation and eruption, lavas, scoriæ, pumice-stone, and obsidians) characterize them, without reference to any tradition, as volcanoes which have long been extinct. Unopened trachytic cones and domes, or unopened long trachytic ridges, such as Chimborazo and Iztaccihuatl, are excluded." * No "banner of smoke," or thunder of volcanic fires, inspires our reverence for Chimborazo. Its massiveness, its dizzy sweep of precipice, its heaven-piercing height, the storms that break about its summit, do this. Words are powerless to convey any conception of the feelings of awe and wonder inspired by the massive form and towering height of that peerless mountain. Upon the top of our own Mount Washington place Etna, a mountain over ten thousand feet in height, and upon that pile Vesuvius, and you will still fall several hundred feet below the summit of the giant of the Andes. Although standing beneath the ardent sun of the equator, where tropical forests girdle its base, over five thousand feet of its height are wrapped in the snows of an eternal winter. Wrote Colonel Staunton, the lamented artist of our expedition, after watching, with all the enthusiasm of his nature, the first unveiling to us of the Andes: "The clouds lifted just at sunset, and permitted us one view of the hoary head of Chimbo-

* Prof. Orton, we observe, in his enumeration of the principal peaks of the Ecuadorian Andes, classifies Chimborazo as a volcano. This difference in classification may result from different views respecting the distinctive characteristics of volcanic mountains. We cannot but regard, however, as most nearly correct, that based upon the geologic structure of the mountain, rather than that dependent upon accidental phenomena. The rocks mentioned as found upon the flanks of Chimborazo are not exclusively volcanic products; also the hot springs upon its north side afford no evidence in favor of its being a volcano, for these are often found far removed from volcanic mountains.

razo; but that is enough for a lifetime." It is a feeling of reverence that one experiences, as he has unveiled to him this Colossus of the Andes. By no other exhibition of herself does Nature so overpower us with her greatness and grandeur. Shortly after our return from our wanderings among the Andes, we were privileged to visit the Falls of Niagara. It was our first visit. We were disappointed. We viewed them from every stand-point: we looked down from above; we looked up from below; we watched them from the front; we went behind the sheet of water; but the rush, and plunge, and roar of Niagara, failed to inspire in us those feelings of sublimity that we felt as we stood in the silent presence of the mighty Chimborazo. Nature is never so grand, so awe-inspiring, as in the awful repose of her giant mountains.

During early morning Chimborazo is generally free from vapors; but later, as the heated columns of air rise from the plains, and come in contact with its icy sides, the dome is quickly capped with clouds, swept and whirled by the frigid currents which push down the slopes of the mountains. What an Æolus indeed it would be, had it been placed in the Boreal regions, instead of under the tropics! Its crest has been reached but once by man; yet the condor, the "kingly bird of the Andes," often soars, on balanced wings, far above its summit. Humboldt and Bonpland attempted its ascent in 1802, but failed. In 1831, Boussingault and Hall reached a point only eighteen hundred feet below the summit, three hundred feet higher than the elevation attained by Humboldt and his companion; but difficulty of respiration, and the density of the clouds, forced them back. But upon the third of November, 1856, its summit was first reached by M. Jules Remy and Mr. Brenckly. The view, however, was entirely cut off by heavy clouds that enveloped the mountain. These travellers determined, by the boiling of water (at 171.5° F.), the height of the mountain to be 21,467 feet, forty more than obtained by the trigonometrical measurement of Humboldt, made upon the high plain of Tapia, near Riobamba, in 1803.

Situated in the Eastern Cordillera, a little out of the axis of the range, in a southeast direction from Chimborazo, is Sangai, the most terrible volcano in the world. It is 17,120 feet in height, and, although in a state of constant activity, it is perpetually wrapped in snow. It frequently sprinkles with ashes the forests of the Pacific coast, and, during its eruptions, it makes its thunders to be heard one hundred miles around.

Cotopaxi, whose position relative to the Eastern Cordillera has been given, is a peak with which Chimborazo must share its honors. Its height is 18,880 feet; yet it seems scarcely half that estimate. But we must not forget that it stands upon elevated table-lands, the height of which Vesuvius, piled upon Mount Washington, would fail to measure. About three thousand feet of its summit are covered with snow. Since 1742, there have been seven eruptions of the volcano, all of which have been accompanied with ejected floods of water and mud, or by storms of sand and ashes, which have devastated the surrounding plains of Callao, Mulalu, and Latacunga. It has never thrown out lava-streams. When in a state of rest, as at present, only light smoke-clouds, at times almost imperceptible, float about its crater. These, with its occasional deep mutterings, are the only indications of the slumbering forces beneath. When in actual eruption its explosions can be heard at a distance of over five hundred miles, and ashes, pumice-stone, and plutonic rocks, are hurled from its crater and scattered over the plains for leagues around. Rocks fifteen feet square have been tossed a distance of nine miles. Until 1870, its crater was unseen by man. During the summer of that year, a party of Spaniards scaled the mountain, and affirmed that they found seven craters!

Going north from Cotopaxi, we come to the dome-shaped Antisana, towering to a height of 19,137 feet, its summit heavily capped with eternal snows. Down its deeply-furrowed sides run immense streams of lava, poured from its crater long ages before the conquest; we traced one of these far down into the wild forest upon the eastern slope of the Andes. The portion which is covered with snow is beautifully rounded, so that in the sunset it appears like a vast golden dome. Upon the flanks of this volcano, 5,600 feet higher than the Hospitium of St. Bernard, is situated the famous hacienda which bears the name of the mountain.

In the Western Cordillera, rising abruptly from the outskirts of the city of Quito, stands the interesting volcano Pichincha. Situated almost directly under the equator, its elevation of nearly three miles (15,827 feet), which, in a temperate climate, would render it a snow-crowned mountain, here scarcely raises its summit above the line of perpetual snow. Its eruptions, the last of which occurred in the year 1660, have always been attended with much damage to the city of Quito, located as it is upon its very base. It is a mountain not without an historical interest; for on its elevated slopes was fought, in 1819, the celebrated battle of Pichincha, by the republicans, under Simon Bolivar, against the Spaniards, at an altitude of 10,800 feet; probably the greatest height at which any battle was ever fought.

An intense longing to have a peep into the crater of this volcano led us, while at Quito, to mature plans for a trip to its summit. Ascending by a gentle grade the side of the mountain, we soon left far below us the fine and well-cultivated plateau of Quito; its undulating plains, spreading out more than forty miles in breadth, broken by

mountain-spurs and isolated ranges. Situated in a pleasant valley through which we passed, is the Indian town
of Lloa, comprised of mud-huts, thatched with long grass.
From here a short ride brought us to the Hacienda of
Lloa, formerly a Jesuit mission-station, where we stopped
for the night, intending to take an early start the following morning for the crater. The building has an antiquated appearance, with its old archways, tiled roof, and
environs of crumbling walls, overrun with vines. We were
in the very heart of the Andes; yet, despite the wildness,
the evening scenery possessed an unusual aspect of repose
and beauty. The clouds which had hung about the summit of the volcano during the day broke away just at
sunset, and the golden hue imparted to the mountain-
ridges contrasted beautifully with the deep green of intervening valleys and forests.

Some time before the light indicated the approach of
morning, we were astir; for, in order to obtain a good
view of the crater, it should be reached by sunrise, before
obscured by rising mist. Subjected to considerable delay
in procuring a guide willing to accompany us into the
crater, it was late before we were mounted. Once started,
we ascended rapidly by a forest trail. A short ascent
through this zone of tree-vegetation brought us upon a
paramo, or moorland, which sweeps up to within a few
hundred feet of the scoriæ-covered summit of the volcano.
From this point the view was grand. We were above
the clouds, through which rents torn here and there
would allow us a glimpse of the valley of Quito, far below. The volcanoes of the Andes stood out like islands
from the clouds that concealed their bases. Cotopaxi
never appeared more grand than standing, as it did, with
its cone raised more than a mile above the clouds, with
light columns of smoke issuing from its crater. Antisana
and Sincholagua, with several other snow-crowned moun-

tains, appeared half immersed in the clouds, which were now rolling up the sides of Pichincha, threatening to destroy our view of the crater. Apprehending this, we spurred on our horses as rapidly as possible, being obliged to ascend the sides of the mountain in a zigzag course. The effect of the rarefied atmosphere was very apparent upon our animals, which breathed with great difficulty. Arriving within a short distance of the summit, we were obliged to dismount, the sides growing very precipitous, and covered with ashes and scoriæ, which afforded only a treacherous footing. Securing our horses to some rock-masses, that had been arrested in their fall by a transversal depression in the slope of the mountain, we commenced to ascend on foot. Light snow a few inches in depth covered the *débris*, rendering our progress exceedingly toilsome; so that we could mount but a few yards, when, breathless, we would sink upon the snow. Half an hour was thus consumed in reaching the summit; when, exhausted with the ascent, we threw ourselves upon the edge of the crater, and gazed over into the frightful opening, which appears about a mile in diameter, and, according to barometrical observation, is over twenty-five hundred feet in depth, its precipitous walls rising, in some places, almost perpendicularly from the bottom. From the deep, sulphur-incrusted crevices rolled slowly up heavy columns of steam and smoke. It was a scene of the wildest and most awful grandeur. The clouds below cut us off from the world beneath, and we were standing upon a fiery island, an illimitable sea rolling away on every side, its expanse relieved only by the ice-crowned summits of the volcanoes, which pierced its surface like vast icebergs, rendering the whole a most dismal arctic scene. Cotopaxi, with its smoke-clouds, was the Erebus amid the drear desolation of ice, and cloud, and smoke. The easterly trade-winds swept over the mountain, but with little momentum;

for at the top of Pichincha the air is only about one-half (0.568) as heavy as at the sea, consequently the force of the winds is proportionally less. Occasionally we would be startled by the dull, heavy rumbling of the rocks, which, loosened from the sides of the crater, plunged with fearful leaps into the gulf below.

We had determined to reach, if possible, the bottom of the crater, and, after resting a few moments upon the edge, we commenced the descent. Twice before we had attempted it, but failed. The first attempt was made by Prof. Orton and an assistant, but, after reaching a point several hundred feet below the summit, they were stopped by a sudden precipice, which rendered farther progress impossible. The second was made by Bushnell and the writer; we had scarcely commenced the descent, when heavy clouds closed round the mountain, filling the crater, and rendering objects invisible at a distance of a few feet, thus making the attempt utterly impracticable. Our third united attempt proved more successful. We entered the crater upon the southeastern side, and, following our Indian guide, scrambled down the steep cliffs, shrinking close to the rocky walls, as we saw the stones loosened, plunging over precipices, setting others free, until a perfect avalanche rushed and thundered down a thousand feet below us. At times, a chasm or precipice would confront us, and we were obliged to drop and receive one another from ledge to ledge. Our hands became so benumbed, from clinging to the icy rocks, that they were of little service, and our footing was so slippery that often it would give way, causing a momentary thrill, as we shrank closer to the cliff. Thinking only of reaching the bottom, the thought how we were to scale these precipices again scarcely occurred to us. In several instances, those in advance narrowly escaped the rocks loosened by those behind. At last we reached the *talus*, or steep slope of *débris* at the foot of the cliff. Down this we hurried, half sliding, till, breathless with excitement and our exertions, we stood upon the bottom. This consisted of a plain about seven hundred yards in diameter, piled round the edges with the rocks broken from the cliffs, which towered up half a mile on every side, except upon the west, where there was a deep depression, or gorge. Varying a trifle from the centre of the plain, was a little hill, about two hundred feet in height, broken by deep fissures, incrusted with sulphur, deposited from the vapory exhalations which rise from the openings. We found a few plants scattered over the bottom of the crater, which served in a measure to relieve the chaotic, life-forsaken aspect of that rock-walled caldron.*

Within those amphitheatral walls Nature enacts, without a spectator, her grandest and most thrilling scenes. It was indeed a strangely wild and chaotic scene, when the rain, that had been threatening, broke over our heads in a fearful storm of thunder and hail. Heavy clouds drifted over the edge of the crater, and, settling within, shut out the sun and hid from view the upper portion of the surrounding walls. We were seated upon some rocks, partaking of our breakfast, which consisted of bread, steamed over the fissures exhaling vapors heated almost to the boiling-point, when a low growl of thunder, and the deep rumbling of loosened rocks, told us that a fearful storm was gathering round the volcano. The rain and hail forced us to the shelter of some shelving ledges. The storm increased; the thunders growing louder and rolling heavily along the cliffs, while the rocks were constantly

* The following is a list of plants found within the crater; several of these species were also observed growing without, just at the base of the scoria-cone : *Lusula Peruviana, Valeriana plantagina, V. Bonplandiana, Calectium longifolium, Diplostephium rupestre, Senecio ericafolius, Pernettya parifolia*, also a species of Festuca, and Lupinus.

crashing from the walls, which swept up in dark, unbroken precipices more than twenty-five hundred feet above us. The winds hurled the clouds within in eddying masses, or drove them fiercely over our heads across the crater. The ground, filled with vents, emitting hot, suffocating vapors, appeared ready to give way beneath us. It seemed as if Pluto and all the infernal gods had conspired to punish our intrusion on their domains. We may forget the circumstances attendant on many a hurried lunch, while forcing our way through tangled forests, or while upon lonely rivers, but always vivid will be our recollections of the little party, and each incident connected with the meal spread upon the plutonic rocks within the crater of Pichincha.

We remained within the crater about an hour, securing some interesting mineralogical specimens, and also obtaining representatives of the peculiar species of plants that we found growing at the bottom, and then commenced climbing out. The ascent was extremely toilsome; for, while it had been raining at the bottom, snow had been falling above to a considerable depth, and this rendered our footing doubly insecure. The rarefaction of the atmosphere also caused almost complete exhaustion to follow our exertions. Up we climbed, slowly mounting, at times, by the assistance of our guide. Gaining a ledge where we might rest, we would throw ourselves down almost in despair of reaching the summit. At length, after three hours of hard climbing, we once more stood safely upon the rim of the crater, and, as we looked back into the abyss whence we had escaped, we gave joyful expression to our gratitude by singing the good old doxology :

> " Praise God from whom all blessings flow,
> Praise Him all creatures here below,
> Praise Him above, ye heavenly host,
> Praise Father, Son, and Holy Ghost."

As the cliffs sent back the words, we felt a thrill never caused by the same echo, so often listened to before, when thrown from the walls of a temple of man's own rearing. If any one can stand upon that awful altar and watch the incense-clouds of smoke as they ever pour toward the heavens; feel the rush of the winds, as, unbroken by any obstacle, they hurry almost noiselessly past; look round upon the scarred ramparts of the amphitheatral walls; listen to the falling rocks, as they tell of the ruin of the mountain by the lapse of time; permit the eye to drop three miles down the terraced slope of the Andes toward the Pacific, or to range eastward across the valley of Quito to the great cordillera that piles itself all along the horizon; and watch the play of the light upon the ice-mantled peaks of Chimborazo, Cotopaxi, Antisana, Cayambi, and Cotocachi—if any one can stand surrounded by such an exhibition of Andean grandeur, and not feel a deeper reverence for Nature and her great Architect, then she has, for him, no scene to fire the soul with inspirations of awe and homage.

From the summit of the mountain we descended the cone to where we had left our horses, brushed from our saddles the snow that had fallen during our absence in the crater, and set out upon our return. Night overtook us while bewildered in the forest that covers the basal portion of the volcano. Having lost our trail, we wandered several hours in hopes of extricating ourselves; but were obliged to pass a wearisome night upon the slope of the mountain. The following morning discovered to us the lost trail, which soon brought us upon the plateau, and shortly after we passed under the old arched gateway, and were once more in Quito.

CHAPTER XVIII.

Resting high upon the eastern slope of the Andes,
lies the flank of the great forest which throws its dense
shade over the larger portion of the Amazonian Valley.
From the Andes it stretches two thousand miles eastward
to the Atlantic, and from the Llanos of Venezuela upon
the north sweeps southward, without a break, to the Pampas of Buenos Ayres. The depths of that primeval forest
have, for ages, been known only as the home of warring
tribes of wild Indians; the hum of civilization has scarcely
approached its borders, and to-day its deepest solitudes
are unbroken save by the never-ceasing rush of its hurrying rivers. So impenetrable is that tropical forest, that
the interior of South America would have been forever
closed against man, were it not for the paths ploughed by
powerful rivers through its tangled mazes. A hundred
streams, leaping down from the Andes, tear open passages
all along the western front of the forest, and then join

their waters to swell the Great River, which ploughs a broad pathway for over three thousand miles through the very heart of the wilderness.

After spending two months in the valley of Quito, we commenced preparations for our journey down the eastern slope of the Andes, through this forest to the Atlantic. Our intended route was the same as that pursued in 1541, by Francisco de Orellana, the treacherous deserter of Gonçalo Pizarro, the brother of the conqueror of Peru, in his journey of unparalleled suffering, through the wilderness, in search of " El Dorado." He found not the " Gilded King," but discovered what was of infinitely more value to the world—the Amazons.* Knowing that all supplies of provisions might be withheld by the Indians, we were obliged to take from Quito sufficient to last us until our arrival at one of the frontier Brazilian towns upon the Amazons—a distance of one thousand miles through an unbroken forest. The traveller in those wilds must place but little dependence upon his rifle for food. The fact that where the vegetable kingdom is over-luxuriant the animal is subordinated, is there fully illustrated ; even the natives, with all their skill, secure only a precarious subsistence. Monkeys and jaguars are there ; but you will probably only hear the howl of the latter, and catch unsatisfactory glimpses of the former, trooping gallantly and safely through the tops of the forests one hundred feet overhead. Moreover, all Ecuadorians were in blissful ignorance of that portion of their country. There was, indeed, in Quito, one delineation of the Oriental portions of Ecuador, by Dr. Villavicencio ; but, like Mark Twain's maps, it had been gotten up with more reference to picturesqueness than geographical accuracy.

* The mouth of the Amazons was discovered as early as 1500, by Vincente Yañez Pinzon ; but Orellana was the first to navigate its waters, and to make known to the world the grand proportions of the river.

No reliable information could be obtained concerning the obstacles we might encounter, or estimate made of the time which would be consumed in penetrating the forest. This uncertainty also constrained us to see that our supply was sufficiently large to meet any emergency.

Our provisions being obtained, and carefully secured in sealed cans, to preserve them from the excessive humidity of the forest, the next difficulty was respecting means of transportation. Indian arrieros and peons without number are always ready for a trip down the occidental slope of the Andes; but an excursion down the opposite side is what few of them care to undertake. To secure carriers we were obliged to send among the tribes inhabiting those regions. The curate, who possessed ecclesiastical jurisdiction over the Indians of the interior, was the only person through whom we could negotiate with them. After several weeks' delay, every thing was arranged, and just one day before the close of October we were assured positively, for the last time, that mañana, horses and guides, from Papallacta, a little Indian village upon the eastern slope of the Andes, just at the commencement of tree-vegetation, would arrive at Quito to take us to the former place, where, discarding our horses, we were to reorganize our train for the march through the forest to the Rio Napo, one of the northern affinities of the Amazons.

Upon the appointed morning the cavalcade—over a dozen animals—accompanied by twice the number of uncouth Indians, came clattering into the court-yard of the Casa Frances. From the mingled herd five of the best beasts were selected for our party, and the best again from this chosen number for the heaviest member of our company, who even then had little occasion to feel proud of his Tartar. The others were by no means imposing in appearance, or superbly decked, but were plainly capari-

OUR ARTIST'S GRAVE.

soned with cow-hide bridles and curious saddles with huge wooden stirrups. Having started our baggage in advance, each stepped astride his Bucephalus, bowed low as he passed under the archway leading from the court-yard, and we were galloping through the streets of the capital. Quitonians gazed in mute astonishment upon what they had seen but once before, an expedition bound for the *Oriente*. Many were the prophecies that we would never be heard of again.

Leaving the outskirts of Quito, our path led us across the beautiful plain of Iñaquito, which spreads out to the north of the city. There is always a saddened feeling that steals over one, when he knows that he is taking a last farewell of scenes which, by long and pleasant associations, have become familiar. Such were the emotions we experienced then; still they were awakened not alone by the fading view of the capital, but our thoughts were turned to feelings of subdued sadness, because one must be left behind. During our short sojourn at Quito we had laid one of our little party, Colonel Staunton, in a foreign grave, and it was just to our right, upon the plains of Iñaquito, that we passed the little cemetery where lay that friend who had shared in the early labors of the expedition, and participated with us the delight of viewing, for the first time, the beauty and grandeur of tropic scenes. Turning from a gentle rise for a last view of the "City of the Incas," our eyes wandered from its towers and domes, and lingered upon that sacred spot; and, as there came pleasant, sad memories of the past, our hearts alone could whisper the word—"Farewell!"

Colonel Phineas Staunton was Vice-Chancellor of Ingham University, Le Roy, New York. He had cherished, with an artist's longing, a desire to visit the tropics; especially did he wish to sketch the wondrous scenery of the Andes. Said he, "Church has painted the '*Heart* of the Andes;'

I shall paint its *spirit*." But he had another object in visiting our southern continent, which, had he been permitted to realize it, would have been of incalculable value to science. As you enter the large Memorial Hall, sacred to his memory, in Le Roy, New York, you observe, just over the entrance, portraits of three noted North-American Indian chiefs. They are paintings by Colonel Staunton. Impressed with the conviction that the aboriginal inhabitants of the New World were doomed to speedy extinction, or that, at least, all their physical characteristics would soon be obliterated, he proposed to go into the wildest portions of North, and also of South America, in order to obtain the best representatives of the race. When the importance of these to the future ethnological student recurs to our minds, stranger still seems the Providence that took him from us in the midst of his unfinished plans. When our expedition was organized, he joined it as its artist, and had but just entered into the work, with all the enthusiasm of his nature, when the fever contracted upon the coast took him from us. We laid him just beneath the shadows of Pichincha, and to-day there is a lonely grave, to which our hearts oft revert, amid the guarding mountains of the Andes. It is a fitting resting-place for the artist, with the snow-crowned mountains, symbols of his own purity, standing as silent sentinels about his grave.

> " O, beauteous Earth ! his worship didst thou know,
>   That thou shouldst take him to thy very heart,
> And set thy mountains, with their sun-kissed snow,
>   To guard his precious dust, of thine a part ?
> Once to behold that vision of delight,
>   To breathe the air of thine eternal spring ;
> And then his soul, exultant, took its flight,
>   To dwell forever with its Lord and King.
> Grieve not, O Earth ! immortal was thy child,
>   And, springing from his consecrated grave,

> Behold a flower, whose splendor undefiled
>   May yet thy darkened people cheer and save.
> Its starry rays are lighted from above,
> And, in its heart, the crimson Cross of Love." *

We feel impelled, in this connection, to speak of the intolerant spirit of Roman Catholicism, which pervades and animates the republics of South America—republics, yet often suppressing liberty of conscience. Prof. Orton, before the open grave of Colonel Staunton, around which were gathered the remaining members of the expedition, and a few friends, residents of Quito, spoke the following words: "Yonder city of Quito has stood for three hundred years, but has never seen such a day as this—a Protestant burial in a Protestant burial-ground." The import of this remark will be understood when we observe that the Ecuadorian Government has, under ecclesiastical influence, occupied so illiberal a position as virtually to exclude all but the Catholic faith, refusing even to enclose a burial-place for Protestant foreigners who might die within the country. But our late minister to Quito, Hon. W. T. Coggeshall, supported by protestations from our government, succeeded in inducing the Quitonian authorities to set apart the little cemetery to which we have alluded, and that was to be devoted to the use of the Protestant residents of Quito. Just a few days before the death of our friend, the cemetery was completed, and his was the first "Protestant burial in a Protestant burial-ground" in the Catholic city of Quito.

That day inaugurated a new era for Ecuador. It marked the first step taken in abandonment of that blind and suicidal policy which has so long hermetically sealed her against the entrance of that foreign element which

---

* These beautiful lines were written by a friend of Colonel Staunton, upon the receipt of the intelligence of his death and burial at Quito. They accompany a little volume *in memoriam* of the artist.

alone will ever develop her vast natural resources. As a
result of the fanatical prejudice against Protestants, there
are, at present, only three or four American residents in
Quito. Nominal religious freedom is now enjoyed in most
of the republics of South America, though trammelled by
meddling and arbitrary legislation, and often rendered in-
operative by the fury of an impressible populace, led by
the fanaticism of an ignorant, bigoted, and intolerant
clergy. Let us not be misunderstood. Not one word
would we say against Catholicism. All that we speak
against is unkind intolerance. All that we ask is a kindly
recognition of the right of every man to form an individual
opinion upon every question involving individual responsibility, and countenance and protection in the enjoyment
of that opinion. This, we believe, will soon be secured
throughout South America. There are many there who
feel that the time for religious intolerance and exclusive-
ness has passed. There are many causes at work, among
which are none stronger than the demanded commercial
relations that must soon be assumed, which will speedily
break down and remove those factitious barriers that have
so long hedged about the prosperity and advancement
of the republics of our sister continent.

From this digression let us return to our journey. As
Quito lies close under the Western Cordillera, we had to
traverse the entire width of the plateau, which, at this
point, is about thirty miles. These table-lands are not, as
might be inferred, level plains, but, besides being broken
by projecting spurs of the main Cordilleras, they are
traversed by deep cañons, with banks so high and precipitous that we were often obliged to follow their course a
considerable distance before finding a practicable crossing.
Our road was, at times, a single foot-path; at others, an
innumerable number of deep ruts or paths, anastomosing
so as to form a broad net-work, leading across uncultivated

plains, almost destitute of vegetation. But a portion of the valley formed a pleasant contrast to these desolate stretches, being clothed with cactuses and several species of mimosa, that interesting family of sensitive-plants so largely represented in the tropics. In our own States we have only a few species, but here they are often the most numerous and conspicuous forms, towering high above the other vegetation. We have already described the Saman del Guere, near Valencia, in Venezuela, a member of this family, forming, from its gigantic size and graceful proportions, the central object in the beautiful scenery of the valley of Aragua. In Southern Brazil, Fletcher tells us of whole groves of these sensitive-plants, which, upon the approach of evening, fold their leaves, and open them again only with the light of the morning, some even anticipating the coming day. This family of plants are, by a wise provision, furnished with sharp prickles, which constitute an effectual protection from rude approach. Why they should fold their leaves at the approach of evening is inexplicable.* It tells of a strange sympathy existing throughout Nature, animate and inanimate—of the laws of which we are yet ignorant.

Late in the evening we arrived at the Hacienda of Itulcachi, a cattle-farm and bread-factory, situated at the base of the Eastern Cordillera. Learning that our baggage had not arrived, we resolved to pass the night here, in hopes that it might come up during the evening. There is something interesting in these old haciendas; perhaps the same interest that attaches itself to any ruins, for they are generally fallen into decay, with their broken

---

* "One fact, among others, showing that the changes are not *caused* by the light, but by some power in the plant itself, is this: The leaves of the sensitive-plant close long before sunset, but they expand again before sunrise, under much less light than they had when they closed. Besides, in this, as in many other plants, the leaves take the nocturnal position when brushed or jarred."—*Gray.*

walls mantled with vines. A portion of this one, however, was in a good state of preservation; the principal court-yard, used as an enclosure for trains of donkeys and mules, being surrounded by a pleasant arcade, which had suffered but little from the effects of time. The room furnished us afforded no conveniences for sleeping, except several huge bread-trays, and, each selecting one adapted to his length, we spread our blankets within, and found them quite comfortable. The night passed pleasantly, but it was unfortunate for our morning nap that the next was baking-day; and early the Indians came in for their kneading-troughs. Not wishing to retard culinary business, we turned out, the trays were lifted through the low window, into the back court-yard, and the process of bread-making commenced. Then we paid a visit to the mill. It was a primitive affair, attended by an ugly squaw, who was wading barefooted in the flour, which was allowed to fall directly upon the floor, from all sides of the uncovered stones.

Part of our baggage having come up during the night, and being assured that by evening all would reach Tablon, a small Indian village upon the sierra, several thousand feet above Itulcachi, we set out in advance, and reached the place early in the afternoon. Beneath us lay the valley of Quito, and beyond stretched along the wall of the Western Cordillera, broken by the towers and pinnacles of Pichincha, Atacatzo, Corazon, and Iliniza. Its deeply-serrated ranges seemed to have been torn and tossed, by the Titanic power of a tremendous upheaving force, into a thousand rude piles of rock and earth. From Tablon we had a most glorious sunset. We never wearied viewing sunset among the Andes. The great elevation of the Quito Valley has an influence upon the rays of the sun, so that the landscape, under a waning light, is un-rivalled even by that beneath the classic skies of Italy.

The heavens also present a peculiar character of "mild effulgence and repose."* That we knew was our last sunset view in the valley of Quito, for the following day we were to climb to the crest of the cordillera, and commence our descent to the Amazons. Perhaps it was this thought that led us to sit longer than usual in the chill evening air, while the shadows of the Western Cordillera grew longer and deeper upon the plain below. Slowly the light faded away from the great hills, till the snowy peaks stood in ghostly paleness about us. As we watched the shades of night stealing over that valley, once the favorite home of the Incas, was it strange that our reveries carried us back to the past, and we were viewing another scene—watching the light of the empire of the "Children of the Sun" dying away from those same hills, and the chill and darkness of a spiritual night falling upon them? With what feelings of undefined sadness is the history of the Incas always recalled, since the pen of Prescott has invested their strange story with so romantic an interest! The ruins of their works now lie scattered upon the sierras or throughout the val-

* Humboldt, in speaking of the aspect of the heavens viewed from the table-lands of Peru, says: "On an average the fixed stars appear only to scintillate when less than 10° or 12° above the horizon. At great elevations they shed a mild, planetary light." This observer refers the phenomenon of scintillation to "luminous interferences," caused by the rays of light passing through strata of air of unequal density. In the tropics the atmosphere is more uniform as respects distribution of heat and humidity, consequently the twinkling of the stars is less observable. If, now, in that uniform atmosphere, we take our position upon the lofty plateaux of the Andes, thus placing more than a third (by weight) of the atmosphere beneath us, we can readily perceive why the stars should present that planetary appearance. The same authority, whose views we are presenting, in speaking of planets, observes: "The absence of scintillation in planets with larger disks is to be ascribed to compensation and to the neutralizing mixture of colors proceeding from different points of the disk." See "Cosmos," vol. iii., pp. 99, 101.

leys of the Andes. Along the flank of the Eastern Cordillera may be seen to-day remnants of the great road which once connected Lima, Cuzco, and Quito, the three great centres of the Peruvian kingdom. Upon the table-lands, massive ruins of the temples of the sun mark the devotion of the people to their religion. As we might expect, traditions of their former state of happiness exist among the Peruvian Indians, who still look for the restoration of the Inca dynasty, longing for its mild, paternal sway, while crushed by Spanish oppression. The corrupting influence of this foreign civilization has wrought a great change upon these Indians. A certain chief being asked why he shunned civilization, replied: "What you call civilization is simply a collection of vices; before you came among my people they were pure and good; see what your civilization has made them."

It is interesting to observe that every instance of high, indigenous civilization among the primitive nations of the New World was looked down upon by the loftiest peaks of the highest mountain-ranges. Witness the civilization of the Quitus and Carans, guarded by the noble mountains which stand about the Quito Valley; and, again, that of the Incas, nourished into national strength and vigor amid the peerless peaks of the highlands of Titicaca, and later spreading itself over the Quitonian valley; observe, also, the civilization of the Montezumas, walled in by the cordilleras of Mexico. Shall we consider the influence of their mountain-home as the originating and moulding power which determined those characteristics that so widely distinguished the Indians of the plateaux of the Andes, and the table-lands of Mexico, from all other American tribes? So Ruskin would. He would tell us that, as we find the dweller of the plain sharing in his nature the tameness of the scenery about him, so we must expect the mountaineer to partake of the stern energy of the hills. With him, "mountain gloom and glory," aside from climatic considerations, are formative forces in determining national character. There is certainly enough gloom and glory there; and while we would not ignore their influence, still to those elevated table-lands, carrying a temperate climate under the tropics, must be largely referred all these remarkable instances of aboriginal development.

From Tablon we climbed up a steep paramo, until, at the height of over two miles, we entered a dense group of polylepis, which, thinks Dr. Jameson, flourishes at the greatest elevation of any tree upon the globe : it is found upon Chimborazo, thirteen thousand feet above the sea. Upon these lofty slopes also grow representatives of the genera valerian and potentilla, and some shrubby compositæ. We made a short halt for refection, in an open spot of the forest, at an altitude twice as great as the summit of Mount Washington. Resuming our journey, we soon issued from this polylepis forest upon an open paramo, which afforded pasturage to large herds of wild-cattle.* As we mounted higher, vegetation, with the exception of a few tufts of wiry grass, almost entirely dis-

* As we have already remarked, the wild cattle and horses found in South America are not the offspring of those that roamed its plains during the geologic period immediately preceding the present. As is well known, fossil remains of a species of horse, elephant, and mastodon, have been found upon both continents. The last two are found in the valley of Quito upon the Andes. Fossils belonging to these same genera have also been taken from the deposits of northern Siberia. This wide geographical distribution of these genera, ranging over three continents, has led to the supposition that Asia and North and South America were connected at no remote geologic period. Darwin conjectures that, over land now submerged near Behring's Strait and in the West Indies, these animals found their way from the northern plains of Asia into North America, and then into the southern continent. All these species have become extinct. The existing cattle and horses of the Americas are introduced European species.

appeared. The only sign of life upon these elevated, barren tracts is the condor, that may often be seen sweeping in majestic circles far above the highest peaks. The home of this bird is between the elevations of two and three miles; but in its flights it frequently rises to a height of over four miles, and yet at that immense altitude it soars as easily as when it sweeps, as occasionally it does, through the dense air of the low coast. Humboldt estimates that he saw it at an elevation of over twenty-three thousand feet; the greatest elevation attained by any living thing, with the exception of some microscopic insects, which are often carried much higher by upward currents of air. The spread of wings of the condor is from nine to thirteen feet. Notwithstanding this great expanse, such is the elevation to which the condor rises, that we have observed it, when we were standing at a height of sixteen thousand feet, to appear as a mere speck, projected against the sky above us. When in the air its wings are motionless. It is difficult to conceive how a bird of so great a size can support itself, seemingly without any effort. "In the case of any bird soaring," says Darwin, "its motion must be sufficiently rapid, so that the action of the incline surface of the body upon the atmosphere may counterbalance its gravity." This motion he supposes to be given by the movement of the neck and body of the bird. The same authority says that it is frequently captured at night by the Chilenos while it is perching in the trees upon the low coast. We were told of a different method more generally employed by the Indians. A low palisade is formed, enclosing a circle within which is placed the body of some animal, that soon attracts these keen-sighted vultures. After they have gorged themselves they are unable to rise, on account of the contracted circle, as they cannot leave the ground without taking a run of some distance.

After climbing upward the greater portion of the day, we at length stood upon the very crest of the Cordillera, at an elevation of almost three miles, and looked down into the tropical valley of the Amazons. Not more perfect could have been the contrast between that view and our last of the valley of Quito. The Quitonian plains presented a scene of perfect repose; with the clouds lying in heavy banks in the transversal valleys, or resting in long drifts upon the flanks of the Western Cordillera. Over the summit of the ridge, in the Amazonian Valley, the trade-winds were dashing heavy clouds against that gigantic mountain-wall, or sweeping them wildly up the steep slopes of the paramos. It was only through the rents, torn in the clouds, that we could catch a glimpse of the great forest, which seemed to roll like a dark sea into the deep valleys between the outlying spurs of the Andes.

Starting down the eastern slope, our horses leaped across a rivulet, the first waters of the Amazons, now a little stream half lost in the tall grass of the moorland, before reaching the sea a majestic river, presenting to the voyager a blank horizon of water and sky. We passed the night at a tambo two thousand feet below the summit of the cordillera. Snow whitened the surrounding mountains, as, the following morning, we set out for Papallacta, the terminus of our ride. A short distance from our tambo we found ourselves upon the borders of a little lake, formed by a stream of lava from Antisana flowing across the bed of a mountain-stream. After leaving this lake, our trail became fearful, even for the Andes, often dropping down by means of steps formed of the trunks of trees, laid transversely, down which our trained horses carefully descended sidewise. At times we rode along the wall of the ancient lava-stream which poured down the slope. Reaching Papallacta, we were greeted by the Indian governor, who received us in his own hut, spread

12

our dripping blankets—for we had been riding in a drench-
ing rain—and, as we squatted about the fire, built in the
centre of the room, provided each with a calabash of welcome cordial.

The day of our arrival was a sad one for the little vil
lage of Papallacta; for death had entered the tribe. According to custom, the funeral was at night. The entire
village having assembled within the rude church, they
marched slowly to the grave, where the women chanted a
plaintive song. The mingled group, their dusky faces,
seemingly sad, revealed by the weird light of the torches,
presented an interesting scene; while the stillness, and the
gloomy shadows of the dark, amphitheatral hills, seemed
in fit keeping with the ceremonies.

The village of Papallacta consists of about thirty huts,
with a population of scarcely one hundred. The day following our arrival the governor collected the inhabitants,
and with them squatted before our hut to negotiate for
the trip to the Napo. It was arranged that, in consideration of one hundred pesos, we were to have a train of
twenty Indians, each of whom was to carry seventy-five
pounds; we were to start *pasada mañana*, day after to-
morrow (nothing is done in this country until to-morrow
or next day), and, upon the ninth day from Papallacta, we
and our baggage were to be safely delivered into the hands
of the Indians of Archidona, a village only one day's journey from the Rio Napo.

CHAPTER XIX.

BENEATH THE FOREST.

Leave Papallacta.—Wretched Trail.—Torrents and Land-slides.—Our
Camp.—Baeza.—Fording the Hondachi.—Separated from our Train.—
Archidona and Archidonians. —Photographing Indians. — A New
Train.—Tropical Forest.—Scarcity of Animals.—Sight of the Rio
Napo.

Upon the morning appointed, the 5th of November,
we turned our backs to Papallacta, and, with our Indian
train, which, by the addition of several of the wives of
our natives, had increased to thirty, we entered the dense
forest that for two weeks was to shut out every satisfactory view of the sky above. The trail which we followed
was all but impassable: at times it led us up almost perpendicular acclivities, then dropped to the bottom of some
fearful ravine; sometimes we floundered through matted
marshes, or forded, with the greatest difficulty, the torrents which rushed across our trail; frequently the rocky
cliffs, or tangled forest, so closely hemmed the streams
that the trail would be forced into the current, and waist-
deep in water we would follow down their courses, or
tread our way upon the detached rocks along their banks.
In order to form any conception of the torrents which rush
down the eastern slope of the Andes, it must be remembered that we have here, not the water-system constituting
the drainage of a short hill-side, but that of the sloping

roof of a vast mountain-range, that lifts its ridge to an
average elevation of almost three miles, and which per-
mits scarcely a single drop of water to pass its summit.
All the vapors gathered by the equatorial trade-winds, as
they sweep from the Atlantic over the teeming valley of
the Amazons, are thrown down upon the eastern side of
this great refrigerator. Of the severity of tropical storms
we have already spoken. After a short continuance every
rivulet is converted into a mountain-torrent, and the greatest danger attending the descent of the Andes is the lia-
bility to be suddenly cut off from retreat or advance by
swollen rivers. Although the general descent of the oriental slope of the Andes is more gradual than the occidental,
yet the flanks of the ranges, which stand as gigantic buttresses along the main longitudinal cordillera, seem quite
as precipitous; and frequently, upon their almost vertical
declivities, could be seen the long scar of the land-slide,
which had torn its way down from a great height, throwing a vast pile of *débris*—rocks and crushed trees—across
our trail.

At an early hour of the afternoon of our first day's
march, we halted for the night. We had made a considerable descent, indicated by the vegetation, which was
more tropical than that of Papallacta, many palms being
interspersed through the forest. Our Indians quickly constructed for us a rancho, simply a roof formed of palms,
or the broad leaves of a parasitic plant that grows here in
abundance. Our natives always encamped near us, and,
building a large fire before their rude shelter, would stretch
themselves side by side in a semicircle, with their little
ponchos drawn up over their heads, and their naked limbs
extended toward the fire. Our day's march had been a
fatiguing one, although we had made scarcely a dozen
miles, which was our average day's journey. We were
drenched by rain, and soaked from fording rivers and

marshes, but, after bathing, and donning dry clothes, we felt in humor for a good supper, drawn from our commissary stores, after which we rolled ourselves up in our blankets and dreamed of home.

The morning of the 6th of November was clear and bright, and by seven we were making an easy ascent, which was soon alternated by a precipitous descent and a torrent, and then followed two hours of almost perpendicular climbing, that placed us upon a dizzy ridge, flanked by immensely deep valleys, threaded by the white lines of torrents, which, in their hurrying course, were dashing themselves into foam. Westward we had a splendid view of Antisana. We had never appreciated its height before, for we had always viewed it from the elevated table-lands. We almost shuddered as, having lifted our eyes to its lofty summit, we dropped them to the bottom of the deep ravines. We passed the night at a camping-place called Pachamama, and the following day reached Baeza, a hamlet consisting of two Indian huts, and, as our natives desired a rest, we tarried here one day. From the family occupying one of the dwellings our Indians purchased a pig, and we gratified them by dispatching it with our rifle, when they singed it, then all day long held high carnival. We opened our cans and concocted some flapjacks, and baked and ate, and ate and baked, till we fairly astonished our natives.

Upon the 9th, continuing our march, we pushed on to the Rio Cosanga, a broad, rapid stream, upon the banks of which we encamped for the night, and were lulled to sleep by the roar of the torrent. The next day's march of twelve miles up the left bank of the stream was made with the utmost difficulty, the trail being poorly cut, and the mud often to our knees. Toward night we reached a rudely-constructed Indian bridge, which spanned the most formidable portion of the torrent. By this shaky structure we crossed, and encamped upon the right bank. The next morning one of our Indians was suffering from a sprain, and we were compelled to remain in camp for the day. A heavy rain, that had set in the night before, continued throughout the day, until the Cosanga became so swollen as to sweep away the bridge by which we had crossed the evening previous. Fortunate was it for us that we had not encamped upon the opposite bank. The following day found our Indian no better, and, not daring to delay longer, we left him in a little ranch, with a supply of provisions, to await the return of the others from Archidona. For the greater part of the day we made a gentle descent, the trail running along the crest of Guacamayo ridge, which radiates from the main cordillera. Descending from this range, we crossed the Cochachimbamba, and passed the night at a camping-place which rejoiced in the name of Guayusapugaru.

Early the following morning we reached the Hondachi, a broad stream, rushing down an inclined bed, broken by huge bowlders. In attempting to cross, it was with the utmost difficulty that our Indians, accustomed as they were to fording torrents, retained their footing. We scarcely realized the danger of the attempt until one poor fellow was swept from his feet and borne down the rapids; fortunately, he caught a projecting bowlder, and was assisted ashore. In fording streams, instead of leaning against the current, as we very naturally did, before initiated, our Indians would lean with it. With the body in this position, the water tends to press the feet upon the bottom. Lacking the dexterity of our Indians, we deemed it prudent, before attempting the passage of the maddened Hondachi, to have stretched across the torrent a rope, with which we were fortunately provided. This, being too short to span the river, was held at either end by an Indian, who, standing a short distance in the stream, braced himself with a

CROSSING THE HONDACHI.

couple of poles. Thus was bridged the strongest part of the current. Our precaution was not unnecessary, for, upon reaching the middle of the stream, with the water nearly to our neck, our feet were swept from the bottom, and, but for the aid of the rope, we would doubtless have gone down to the Amazons.

With fording rivers, and floundering through swamps, that day's tramp was a hard one. In our order of march a small party of three or four generally proceeded several miles in advance of the main train, in order to select a camping-place for the night, and to construct a ranch. We generally attended the main company, but this day we took a middle position. It was growing dark when we found ourselves separated, no knowing by what distance from our baggage, a part in advance, and the remainder behind. Whether to attempt to overtake the leading party, or turn back to meet the other, was a perplexing question; but the thought of passing twice more over the trail we had come decided our wavering, and on we pushed. As we dragged ourselves wearily along, we thought of Bayard Taylor, who, while traversing some distorted portion of the world, tells us of one of his *agoyats* exclaiming: "I was never in this country of Maina before. If I should happen to be fettered and brought here by force, I might see it again; but of my own will, never!" If ever we see the orient of Ecuador again, it will be from reasons as cogent as those required to secure a revisit to Maina by that dragoman. We could not also help commending the decision of two associate travellers of Dr. Jameson, who, having accompanied him from Quito to the Rio Napo, determined, rather than go back across this trail, to descend the Napo and Amazons, a distance of three thousand miles, and sail for the States from Para, instead of Guayaquil, as they had intended.

At length we were gladdened by the sight of a rancho,

with a fire in front, surrounded by four of our Indians. One was a mere boy, who had carried a pack of eighty pounds! How the little fellow had brought it along the trail, which led across rivers, up precipices, through jungles and dense forests, which hemmed the path so closely that we, unembarrassed by any load, found it almost impossible to force our way, was ever a mystery to us. The same pack was, during one long day's march, carried by a woman. Our provisions, blankets, and dry garments, were with the other party. This was pleasant! But there was no alternative, and we threw ourselves in our wet clothes upon the ground, crowded together, and—waited for the morning. It did come at last, and cold, stiff, sleepy, and hungry, not knowing whom to blame for our discomfort, we sat crouching over a little fire which we had succeeded in building, waiting for our Indians to come up. They arrived a little after sunrise, and we had soon prepared the best breakfast our stock of provisions would afford. Leaving this camping-place, often to be recalled during the remainder of our tour, we recommenced our march for Archidona, where we arrived early in the day. Here we received a cordial welcome from the bishop and padre, Jesuit missionaries laboring among the Indians.

Archidona lies just at the foot of the Andes, upon the banks of the Misagualli, and contains an Indian population of about five hundred. Buried in the midst of the great forest, it is almost completely isolated from the rest of the world, and can be reached only by Indian trails. The huts are low, the thickly-thatched roofs reaching nearly to the ground. The Archidonian Indians in physical development are superior to any with whom we came in contact in South America. The men are taller than those of the table-lands of the Andes, are slightly and even delicately built; their long, dark, sometimes curling hair, falling over their shoulders, giving them a peculiarly feminine appearance. The women in both form and feature are, as Dr. Jameson observes, inferior to the men. Darwin remarks the same in speaking of the personal appearance of the Tahitian women. The only clothing of the men consists of a narrow cloth about their waist, and a light poncho, both of a coarse cotton manufacture, obtained from Quito. This dress is especially becoming to the little boys, who, with delicately-formed limbs, painted a deep red with annotto (*Bixa orellana*), and with every movement natural and unrestrained, are really interesting; and, often, the charming simplicity of these children of the forest is graceful and winning. A life freer from care than that led by these Indians can hardly be conceived. To supply their wants they have only to gather the fruit of the palm and the plantain, or secure with their poisoned arrows game from the surrounding forest. Far removed from moroseness, their disposition is cheerful and active. Their minds, however, are unable to grasp abstract ideas, and seem scarcely susceptible of cultivation—a fact well attested by the padres, who have labored among them for two hundred years, yet with no perceptible results beyond keeping them docile. We could not but think that should these assiduous and self-denying teachers adopt the method pursued by our own missionaries in fields quite as unpromising, and teach these Indians the virtue of industry, to cultivate the rich soil, manufacture fabrics from the productions of their virgin forest, and encourage them to secure for themselves the comforts of civilized life, their success in developing and training their spiritual nature might be commensurate with their untiring and praiseworthy zeal.

While at Archidona we were quite successful in increasing our collections. We were assisted in our work by the Indian boys, who, as soon as they got an idea of what we wanted, brought us large numbers of insects, with occasional specimens of fishes from the Misagualli. Being desirous of obtaining all the representatives possible of the latter, we would reward them with a *medio* (a Spanish coin worth five cents) for each specimen. On one occasion two little fellows came to us, one with the head and the other with the tail of a fish which they had neatly halved. The head being presented first, the manager of the department of ichthyology was rejoicing over a new species, for never before had he seen an ichthyological specimen end so abruptly; but, with the tail being handed in, by the other youngster, the relations of the two became apparent.

While here, we determined upon taking a photographic view of Archidonians. This was attended with some difficulty. These natives were not all as willing to be "taken" as the groups about the Congress of Saratoga. The whole population, men, women, and children—the women each with two babies, one slung before and the other behind—were assembled and drawn up in a semicircle upon the plaza in front of the little church. The men enjoyed it; but to the women the camera was clothed with terrors, they thinking it an *escopeta* (gun); and, as soon as the operator took position behind the instrument, they broke in a run for their huts. The good padres succeeded, after much persuasion, in again forming them in line—but again they broke. At length they were induced to stand within range sufficiently long for a hazy view.

November 17th, with a train of Archidonian Indians, our others having returned to Papallacta, we again resumed our journey to the Napo. A few miles from Archidona we forded the Misagualli, and about noon the broad and rapid Tena, upon whose banks was a little Indian village, bearing the name of the river. We were now at the foot of the Andes, and the vegetation assumed a more tropical character than that of the higher slopes. Stately palms lifted their heavy crowns throughout the struggling mass; arborescent ferns,* which spring, with a palm-like growth, to a height of forty feet, although native to the temperate heights of the cordilleras, were still occasionally seen; the equisetum, a cryptogamous plant, congener of our northern scouring rush, attained a height of twenty feet; while arborescent grasses, shooting up forty feet above us, impressed us with the capabilities of a tropical nature. These familiar illustrations will enable one to form some conception of the luxuriance of the vegetation here, and the gigantic size attained by specific forms. But these do not constitute the frame-work of the forest. This is formed by the trunks of exogenous trees similar in appearance to northern arboreal forms. The diameter of these is not so striking as their great height. This framing is filled in with every form of vegetation; parasites and epiphytes, the aërial roots of the latter often reaching down from the highest trees to the ground, load the branches; while gray, sombre, arboreous mosses lend a peculiarly melancholy aspect to the old forest-monarchs; vines encircle the trunks, and, looping, twisting, and intertwining, form a perfect maze of cordage. Humble plants of strange types form the lower stratum of the forest, constituting an almost solid mass of vegetation, through which it is often impossible to penetrate. As the sun scarcely enters the depths of these primeval forests, every thing is saturated with moisture, which humidity affords one of the chief requisites for that giant vegetation which we find upon the flanks of the Andes and throughout the valley of the Amazons. We found the forest at least

* We obtained sections of this gigantic plant eight inches in diameter. Darwin measured some in Van Diemen's Land six feet in circumference. The species are numerous, and, as Humboldt observes, are confined almost exclusively to the tropics, but there preferring temperate altitudes.

grander in proportions upon the slopes of the equatorial Andes than in the heart of the valley. The same is observed in crossing the continent from the mountains upon the north. The forests of the Rio Negro seem dwarfed in comparison with those of the Venezuelian cordilleras.

One of the most striking peculiarities of these forests, and one which every botanist quickly observes, is the absence of flowers. We journeyed sometimes for days without meeting with any conspicuous inflorescence. The few flowers we found were small and of a dull color. The sunlight is too much excluded to allow Flora to paint her forms with those rich, brilliant hues with which she decks the flowers of the unshaded table-lands, and even the shrinking rosettes of the mountain paramos. The inflorescence is above and along the walls of the rivers. Animated life, also, as we have intimated, is extremely scarce. During our entire journey from Quito to the Napo, a distance of nearly two hundred miles, upon which trip we had anticipated adding largely to our zoölogical collections, we saw but few birds; only one company of monkeys, and these were going through the tops of the forest as if to fulfil an appointment; one serpent, that was so unfortunate as to get into our alcohol-can; and a jaguar, which one evening ran through our camp—startling our natives.

Our Archidonian Indians led us rapidly over the trail, that our journey might be completed before night. Just at evening the forest suddenly opened before us, and we stood upon the banks of the Rio Napo. The turbid stream appeared almost stagnant, compared with the furious torrents of the cordilleras, and, in its slower march seemed as if wearied with its leaping, hurrying course down the Andes. We greeted it with delight, for it told us of the end of weary marches over wretched trails, and we now imagined ourselves floating dreamingly down to the Amazons. Strange were our feelings as we stood upon the banks of that lonely river. We realized then a full sense of our isolation, and felt, as we never had before, the loneliness of the great wilderness. We scarcely know why, but we always felt more lonely when upon the rivers than when far removed from them in the forest; perhaps, because we had learned, in our northern land, to associate with rivers the picture of cities and the life of commerce; and then, when we saw the desolateness of these forest-walled rivers, we felt the strangeness of the contrast.

CHAPTER XX.

CANOE-VOYAGE DOWN THE RIO NAPO.

NEAR the point where we emerged from the forest is located the Indian village of Napo, comprising about thirty straggling huts. It stands at the head of canoe-navigation upon the Rio Napo, six hundred miles from its confluence with the Marañon, as the upper portion of the Amazons is called. In front of the town the current of the river, as we have remarked, is smooth, but a short distance above and below it breaks, in formidable rapids, over sandstone ledges.

A short hour's walk from the village, upon a little island formed by the Yusupino, a small affluent of the Napo, we found an American, Mr. George Edwards, who had lived here, almost isolated from the world, for fourteen years. We shall long remember our visit to his little island-home, and the hearty welcome received. It was, indeed, a miniature paradise, such as we scarcely expected to find in the depths of these wild forests. It could be reached only by fording an arm of the river.

His dwelling was similar to the huts of the Indians, but more commodious, while the grounds surrounding were filled with tropical fruits—bananas, pineapples, plantains, and lemons. We were especially interested in the vanilla-plant, which he was successfully cultivating. Since our return to the States, he, acting upon our suggestion, has been attempting to domesticate some wild bees, obtained from the forest. In a letter recently received, detailing his experience, he says: "Shortly after you left, I obtained two swarms, which I have preserved in the manner you directed. They have been busy since secured; but they show no indications of swarming. One of the swarms is of a black color, and are called by the Indians *cushillo mishke*, or monkey-honey, because, I suppose, of their resemblance in color to that animal. The others, which are yellow, they call *rara mishke*, or corn-honey. It is curious that the Indians have no word for bees, only for their color and for honey. The black species is said to make the most honey, and the yellow the best." We believe this is the first attempt to domesticate native bees in the valley of the Amazons. We are confident that their culture in those forests will be attended with satisfactory results.

Bees are indigenous to South America; hence the reason of our finding them so far removed from civilization. In the northern continent they were introduced by the colonists, and have preceded civilization by only a few miles as it has advanced westward. European species were introduced into the temperate portions of Southern Brazil in 1845, and have there been quite successfully cultivated. There are about one hundred and fifty species of native bees in South America. The largest number are destitute of stings, or have them but imperfectly developed —one thing in their favor, certainly. Some of these species inhabit hollow trunks, others construct their homes under-ground, while upon the Llanos of Venezuela is a kind that construct a nest similar to a wasps'. A few species collect sour honey. Large quantities of wax are gathered in the different provinces of Brazil, by the natives, who are experts in finding a "bee-tree." In Agassiz's "A Journey in Brazil" we observe the following, relative to the mathematics of the bee, displayed in the construction of its cells: "The bees stand as close as they can together in their hive, for economy of space, and each one deposits his wax around him, his own form and size being the mould for the cells, the regularity of which, when completed, excites so much wonder and admiration. The mathematical secret of the bee is to be found in his structure, not in his instinct." This statement is incorrect, and the inference wrong. In South America are species of bees that, while possessing forms quite as perfect as European varieties, still display less accuracy and economy in the construction of their cells. We are at a loss to conceive how, if the shape of the cell of our own hive-bee be dependent upon the structure of the insect, that should give it its peculiar hexagonal form. A few moments' observation before an open hive shows us the true *modus operandi*. The bee, instead of depositing the wax about its body, takes a position upon the comb, while the scale of wax, secreted from its body, is placed upon the edge of the cell, and carefully moulded into shape. The mysteries and mathematics of the hive must be sought in the instinct of the bee, and not in its structure.

The Napo Indians, at the time of our arrival, were celebrating one of their festivals—a curious amalgamation of their own customs with innovations introduced by the padres, during their semi-occasional visits among them. While delayed here several days, in making preparations for our trip to the Amazons, we were entertained by a constant drumming, the essential accompaniment of an Indian pow-wow. To drum and drink chicha are the central ideas of these fiestas, which are maintained by the Indians for weeks together, until the failure of provisions compels them to set out upon long hunting-excursions. Their villages are then deserted, and we find them scattered in little tambos along the banks of the lagoons and minor water-courses, obtaining a precarious subsistence from the streams and forests.

There are two principal tribes dwelling upon the Rio Napo: the Záparos, upon the southern bank of the river, and the Napos, upon the northern. The latter have been partially civilized by the padres, and, in almost all their little villages, the rude church, occupying the most prominent site, indicates their presence. The nomadic Záparos, from the fact that they do not congregate in towns, have not been brought under the influence of civilization. They are the most abject and miserable Indians that we encountered in the interior. The Quichua is the language of the Napos. Singularly enough, in Quichua the word for mother is the same as in English. It seems strangely odd to hear these children of the forest calling " mammá!" The tongue of the Záparos is, doubtless, judging from certain affinities, a dialect of the same. In common with many other American tribes, their system of numeration contains traces of decimal arrangement. However the tribes beyond the Quichuas may have come in possession of their somewhat imperfect system—whether by contact with higher civilization, or by originating it among themselves—the rigid notation of these Indians bears the impress of Peruvian culture, and illustrates how language is moulded and retains the impressions of the genius of a people long after all other traces of it are lost. The monuments of the civilization of the Incas, which rose upon the table-lands of the Andes, now lie scattered over those plains, in unintelligible ruins; while here, in their language, we find a monument that will endure ages beyond

the time when the last representative of the Peruvian
people shall have ceased to speak the tongue of his ancestors.*

* The Hindoo origin of the Incas has been inferred from the similar-
ity in grammatical construction of the languages of both; between two
and three hundred of these coincidences have been pointed out.   The
Quichua abounds in compound words ; the conjugations and declensions
are formed by particles, and by the use of different words.   From the
admirable work, "Cuzco and Lima," by C. R. Markham, we take the following specimen of Incarial verse, to illustrate the advance made in the
department of poetry by the early Incas.   It was taken down from the
lips of the Indians, soon after the Spanish conquest.

A chieftain had fallen in love with the daughter of an Inca, but had
been refused her hand by her father, and the daughter herself (Cusi Coy-
llur) had been severely reproved, when she is represented as indulging in
this lament :

> " Ay Ñustallay! Ay Mamallay!
> How can I fail to mourn ?
> How can I fail to weep ?
> My father so dear to me,
> My guardian so beloved,
> In all these days and nights,
> In this my tender age,
> Has quite forgotten me,
> Without asking for me.
> Ay Mamallay ! Ay Ñustallay !
> Ah, my adored lover !
> In the morning that I came here,
> The day became dark,
> The sun seemed obscure in the heavens,
> As if it were shrouded in ashes.
> The clouds of burning fire
> Announced my grief.
> The resplendent star Chasca [1]
> Sped out its rays,
> All the elements were weary,
> And the universe was tired.
> Ay Mamallay ! Ay Ñustallay !
> Ah, my adored lover !

-----

[1] Venus.

We experienced considerable difficulty in persuading the Indians to break off their feast for a trip to the Marañon; but at length succeeded in obtaining a sufficient number to man three canoes, which were to take us as far as Santa Rosa, a little village eighty miles below Napo, where we might obtain canoes and Indians to convey us to the mouth of the river.

Upon the morning of the 20th of December we embarked, and were borne swiftly down by the strong current, which sometimes became dangerous rapids, over which our little canoes would shoot with fearful velocity, our Indian paddlers dexterously avoiding projecting rocks and breakers. The recollection of the fact that a party in descending these same rapids, a few years previous, had been wrecked, and lost every thing, was far from a comforting thought, as our canoes went plunging down between the rocks, or, as caught in a little eddy, they would tremble for a moment as poising for another leap, and rush through the foaming sluices. The appearance of our naked Indians, their long hair streaming in the wind, and their wild shouts mingling with the roar of the waters, with the rolling of our little bark, rendered the shooting of these rapids unique as well as exciting navigation. Passing safely all these rapids, toward evening we reached the old site of Santa Rosa, which had been abandoned on account of its unhealthfulness, the Indians believing that it had been cursed by the padres. Drawing our boats ashore, we landed. It was sad to see the little huts of the deserted village, almost lost in the rank vegetation that had sprung up around them, with no traces of their former occupants; none to gather the falling fruit of the scattered orange-trees, but all silent and desolate. As the gloom of the approaching night settled over the deserted spot, our Indians motioned us to the canoes, unlashed and quickly pushed them from the bank into the strong current, and in the deepening twilight we swept on down between the dark forest walls.

About fifteen miles below the old town, we found the new Santa Rosa, containing one hundred and fifty Indians. The rapidity with which we had descended the river may be inferred from the fact that in seven hours we had come a distance of eighty miles, making a fall of three hundred and fifty feet. The Indians here were also engaged with their feast, and we again experienced much difficulty in obtaining any to accompany us to the Marañon, but at length secured two canoes and four Indians, paying them in *lienzo*—cloth of a coarse cotton manufacture, which we had brought from Quito. We delayed at Santa Rosa several days, in order to allow our Indians time to prepare a sufficient quantity of the yuca-root to last them during the long voyage. The yuca-shrub yields a large cluster of tuberous roots. These, when used for the manufacture of chicha, are bruised or ground into a pulpy mass, and then allowed to ferment. A large handful mixed in a calabash of water makes a thick, nutritious, and not unpleasant drink. It was upon this that our Indians chiefly subsisted while passing down the river, secreting large quantities from time to time upon the islands, to be used upon their return trip.

The night preceding our departure from Santa Rosa our Indians spent in drinking chicha, so that the following morning, when ready to start, they were, as the Spanish alcalde expressed it, decidedly "irrational." Bidding adios to their friends, they shoved our canoe into the stream, and, with the coolest indifference, stretched themselves in the bottom, with the exception of the governor, who, as pilot, settled himself in the stern, and commenced blasting away upon an old cow's-horn. But such an arrangement, although doubtless highly conducive to comfort, was decidedly incompatible with our idea of safety, as the canoe was drifting among snags and down rapids, with but little consideration for the right of the bow to go foremost. Finding all expostulation useless, they being supremely ignorant of the English and Spanish languages, and we as indifferently posted in regard to their *kita-wa-wa*, as a last resort we tried a vigorous application of one of the shovel-shaped paddles, which had a most exhilarating effect upon the happy sleepers, and suddenly attracted the attention of the musical governor to piloting duties. After this drunk, our Indians were always obedient and faithful, generally working at the paddles with a ready good-will.

Early in the first afternoon from Santa Rosa we reached Suno, a collection of four or five tambos. The night was excessively sultry, for the river, hemmed in by the high forest, does not receive the influence of the easterly tradewinds which prevail upon the Amazons and Lower Napo; and the burning rays of the vertical sun, pouring in during the entire day, render the air so oppressively hot that one feels as though in an oven. We disposed of ourselves for the night, by two of our number sleeping in the canoes to guard our trappings, while the others swung their hammocks between the trees upon the bank. The following day we passed Coca River, one of the largest tributaries to the Rio Napo, and stopped at the small Indian village of Coca, a short distance below their confluence. In coming from Napo village we had been obliged to sit cramped up in the bottom of our canoe, under a low cover of palm-leaves; but, all the rapids being now passed, we determined upon a more pretentious and comfortable mode of navigation. Firmly lashing our canoes about eight feet apart, we covered the intervening space with a bamboo floor, and, constructing a roof over the whole, we had a craft such as had never floated upon those waters before, and which we christened "Zápara," in honor of the wild Indians upon the right bank of the river. Having completed all much to our satisfaction, we placed our baggage on board, and early in the morning of the 28th of November—Thanksgiving—we cut loose our craft, and once more started for the Marañon.

After the confluence of the Coca and Napo, the latter spreads out beautifully; and, as there are no mountains to wall it in and confine it to a single channel, it has cut numberless paths through the forest, embracing with its broad arms many beautiful islands, rendering a view up or down the stream extremely picturesque. The banks are uniformly low, and torn by the action of the water, which gradually undermines them until a long strip of the forest falls with a tremendous crash into the river, strewing the shore with long lines of its ruins. As we drifted down we never wearied noting the varied grouping of the pendant masses of vegetation which fringed the islands and river-banks. Yet there was one thing we missed. The hills were gone. How lonesome one feels without the mountains! We know not what part of the education of our feelings we owe to the hills. Should they be levelled, we would soon find that they were raised for purposes other than irrigation, or those which the so-called utilitarian discovers.

We only realized this after having travelled for weeks beneath dense forests, where only now and then we could catch a glimpse of the sky above, and upon a river where the tall, prison-like walls of the forest shut us in day after day, until we longed for just one look upon the world outside—longed for some elevated position, that our eyes might range over the tops of the forest, and rest satisfied with seeing the blue lines of distant hills. But no mountains break the uniformity of that forest-level, which bears away thousands of miles to the Atlantic, relieved only by some slight elevations toward the mouth of the Ama-

zons; so that we knew, when we, some time before, bade
farewell to the Andes, that the first mountains which would
cheer us would be our own native hills. Imagine, then,
the surprise and delight with which, as the sun arose upon
the 28th of November, we saw it faintly tracing to the
westward the outlines of the Cordillera, and the beautiful
shaft of Cotopaxi, seeming lofty as ever, though now two
hundred miles distant. We had bidden adieu long since
to the volcanoes of the Andes, thinking we had seen them
for the last time, so that it was with double pleasure we
once more recognized the familiar form of our favorite,
Cotopaxi; which did not now, as when we looked up its
snowy sides from its foot, appear cold and stern, but
through the long distance of the heated tropics it threw
a warm and softened look. The rising mist soon drew a
light veil over it, and shut out our last view of the Andes.
The scene naturally recalled our first view of Chimborazo
from the Pacific coast, as one evening, just at sunset, the
clouds lifted from the Cordilleras. Those views of the
Andes, our first and last, as they welcomed us through the
opening clouds, in the bold, rugged outline of Chimborazo,
and bade us farewell through the beautiful form of Cotopaxi,
awakened emotions which the lapse of time will not lead
us to forget. We feel such scenes, we take them with us
through life; we recall them often, or, rather, they come up
uncalled; but words will not permit us to tell them to others.

Our passage down the river was a pleasant one. During the day, when our Indians were not working at the
paddles, we would allow our craft to float just as suited
its own fancy, stern-foremost or sideways, and, as we
drifted thus leisurely with the current, two of our number
would put off with the little canoe, which, when not in
use, we kept lashed to the side of our "Záparo," in pursuit
of birds, monkeys, and peccaries. The last-named (*Dico-
tyles labiatus*), a species of wild-hog, in common with the

puma, is one of the few South-American animals that have found their way into the tropical portion of the northern continent.

Among the many beautiful birds upon the Napo, the guacamaya, belonging to the parrot family, is the most conspicuous. We kept one of these birds for some time upon our craft, as a pet, having clipped its wings. It was more beautiful than amiable; and, having acquired a habit of climbing to the roof, and of tearing holes through the thatch, and, upon our going for it, of falling overboard, we disposed of it, preserving its skin to grace some future museum. The toucan is often seen upon the Napo. It is a prettily-colored bird, but all ideas of proportion are forgotten in its rostral development. What a beak for such a bird, or for any bird! We think it is Goldsmith, in his "Animated Nature," who says that, after we have seen a thing, we begin to reflect upon its "uses, purposes, and inconvenience." We fell into a train of reflection, as every one else when he sees a toucan always does, but no use, no purpose, could we divine. Had we never been able to discover but one of these comical creatures, we should have solved the problem instanter, by shouting, "*Lusus naturæ!*" At last we wished for Darwin, that he might tell us to what process of "natural selection" we were indebted for this ornithological absurdity.[*]

We found but few species of humming-birds upon the

[*] "It has been assumed by some writers on natural history, that every wild fruit is the food of some bird or animal, and that the varied forms and structure of their mouths may be necessitated by the peculiar character of fruits they are designed to feed on; but there is more imagination than fact in this statement: the number of wild fruits furnishing food for birds is very limited, and birds of the most varied structure, and of every size, will be found visiting the same tree."—*Wallace.* This applies to the toucan; we cannot account for its immense beak by supposing it the result of adaptation to certain habits of life; it feeds with birds that have bills as widely different as possible.

river.   The elevated valleys of the Andes are their favorite home.   There are about four hundred known species of hummers, all of which belong to the Americas, and, with the exception of about half a dozen, are confined to the southern continent.   They are frequently found as far south as Tierra del Fuego.   Their chosen *habitat* is the zone of vegetation which lies just below the paramos of the Cordilleras.   Those living in the shade of the forest of the Amazonian Valley are destitute of that brilliancy of coloration which characterizes the hummers of the high slopes of the Andes.   They probably feed but little upon the nectar of flowers, but frequent them for the insects there found.   Like other fissirostral birds, they frequently catch insects in the air.   The full beauty of the hummer is only displayed when it is upon the wing, flitting in the bright sunlight, when every change of position gives brilliant metallic flashes from its irisated breast.

From the playas, or sand-bars of the river, we obtained large quantities of turtles' eggs, which served a good purpose, as our stock of provisions brought from Quito was becoming much reduced.   On approaching a playa which promised to afford eggs, our Indians would cry, "*Lulun, lulun!*" "eggs, eggs!" and, pulling vigorously for the island, we would soon be running over the hot sand, each with a stick, which he would thrust into every suspicious-looking depression, the nest being discovered in this way.   It was with a satisfaction nearly akin to our boyish pleasure of hunting hens' nests in the hay-loft, that, after digging through a foot or eighteen inches of loose sand, we would discover the pile of round, white eggs, stowed away to the number of eighty or one hundred and twenty; and then roll them out in handfuls upon the sand.   The turtle which deposits these eggs does not exceed two feet in length, attaining a weight of about eighty pounds.

These playas frequently afforded us stopping-places for

13

the night; our Indians always preferring encamping upon them, to landing on the wooded bank, as they were more free from insectile pests. But do not think these islands were "Elysian Fields." Far from it. The sancudos (mosquitoes) were even there in strong force. Our Caracas party have complained of meeting a few in Venezuela. There may be a few up there on the Orinoco, but there is not the least doubt in the world but that they have their headquarters upon the Napo. It was impossible to withstand their attacks, and, upon the approach of evening, we were driven beneath our nettings, where we would lie nervously watching the swarming insects, which we could see against the light of the sky, gathered in large groups, or walking about upon the outside of our *mosquiteros*. Nor were we always favored by having them without. Somehow they would gain admittance; either by entering with us, or by searching out some hole ever undiscoverable to us.

While we always spent the night upon our craft, our Indians would sleep upon the playa. Let us stroll over to their camp, discovered by that little fire built of driftwood, which they have collected from the island. Their spears are stuck in the sand a few yards from the fire, before which is squatted the pensive old governor, holding upon his knees a little Indian baby, while a young squaw is stirring, with a rough stick, the contents of an earthen pot placed over the fire. This is their supper; being a conglomeration of meat, turtles' eggs, bananas, yucas, and annotto. The other members of the party are seated about the fire, or a little distant, listening, with some degree of excitement, to the least splash in the water, or noise in the forest, which might indicate the presence of game. After disposing of supper, they will stretch themselves upon the sand, beneath a rude shelter of palmleaves. Such is the life of these wandering Indians. We pity them. Still they are content, for they know of nothing higher, nothing better.

We were often amused by the oddities of our Indians. Like all natives of the tropics, they manifested a decided aversion to clothing. Having resolved one day to modernize our crew, we gave to them some cast-off garments. Their attempts to put themselves inside, comically betrayed their lack of acquaintance with such articles. It was decidedly entertaining to see them climbing into the pants wrong end up, and getting the other things on upside down; but, with the fit about the neck not being good, trying again, bringing them on inside out, or wrong side before. To the governor, who was freely perspiring with his exertions in the sweltering heat, we gave an overcoat, and so lugubriously did he survey himself, that for once our other Indians shouted with merriment. They kept themselves inside but a short time, and then tore the things to pieces to subserve other more important purposes.

December 1st.—To-day we saw the first representatives of the *genus homo* since being upon the "Záparo." They comprised a party of eight or ten Indians—namesakes of our craft. More unhuman they seemed than the monkeys of the forest. Almost their only clothing were strips of bark; their bodies were blackened and blotched with the attacks of insects, and their whole aspect indicated a life of the lowest degradation. We afterward saw two other canoe-loads; but, as soon as they caught sight of our craft, they pulled into a side-channel of the river and disappeared. Upon the 4th we overtook a Spanish trader on his way to the Marañon, with a quantity of sarsaparilla and hammocks. Wishing to secure some of the latter, we drew alongside of his canoe, and opened negotiations. To our first question, put in Spanish, respecting the value of his hammocks, he replied in English, which was such a murderous attempt upon the language, that we impulsively informed him that we did not understand English. With Spanish grandiosity he then set forth the virtues of his hammocks. We purchased several, and floated on.

Upon the night of the 8th we were aroused by a severe storm, that threatened, for a time, to unroof our craft. We encountered these squalls frequently upon the Lower Napo, and they were a source of constant apprehension. Moreover, we were now among wilder Indian tribes, for we had passed beyond the limits of the Napos and Záparos. Consequently, upon the night of the 9th, we instituted a watch. There is more pleasant employment than watching for wild Iquitos, Orejones, and Putumayos in the Napo forest.

The Napo, during its lower course, becomes a majestic stream, and, forgetting its former haste, moves slowly down; and so we were borne leisurely alongside its forest-borders. We have spoken of the impressiveness of tropical vegetation. Yet we think we are in accord with all travellers in intertropical America when we say that, in the forests of those regions, we find but little of the quiet beauty of our northern woodland scenery. We admire them because of their many individual stately forms, their boldness of growth, their wildness, and their luxuriance. But the one element, color, which must enter largely into any landscape view calculated to produce æsthetical effect, is here almost entirely wanting. We have remarked the scarcity of flowers in these dense, primeval forests. Then the rich, autumnal tints of our own northern woods are here unknown; throughout the months there is the same eternal, unvarying green. Not willingly would we exchange our own forest scenery for that of the tropics.

Upon the morning of the 10th of December we discovered a few huts upon a low bluff of the river, and, landing, found we were at Camindo, a little Indian village, only a short distance from the Marañon. That the mighty river was almost reached, and a life-long desire to be gratified by a view of its majestic stretches, awakened every feeling of anticipation. One more bend of the Napo, and the great river was before us, rolling its broad volume of turbid water down between the wall-like forest, which stretched away in the distance until only broken lines rested upon the water, which soon gave way to an unbounded horizon. It was the strange solitude which most strongly impressed us—the silently-flowing waters, the deep forest buried in the torpor of mid-day, their only possessor the apathetic Indian squatted at our feet.

Drawing ashore upon the point of land just where the two rivers commence to mingle their floods, we hastily photographed the scene, with the broad expanse of the Amazons as a watery perspective to several beautiful islands, lending picturesqueness to the view. Reëmbarking, we bade farewell to the Rio Napo, and our little craft drifted into the strong current of the Amazons.

CHAPTER XXI.

THE UPPER AMAZONS.

WE can form only vague conceptions of the magnitude of the majestic Amazons. Observe its great length, stretching across the continent almost from ocean to ocean. Taking its rise less than one hundred miles from the Pacific upon the west, it runs a distance of almost four thousand miles, to pour its floods into the Atlantic upon the east. But its breadth impresses us most deeply with its oceanic proportions; one thousand miles from the sea it has a width of three miles; at a distance of five hundred it spreads out ten miles in breadth; and mingles with the Atlantic along a line of one hundred and fifty. It has poured into it all the waters rolled down the eastern slope of the Andes along a stretch of two thousand miles, and all the floods from the highlands of Guiana upon the north, and the table-lands of Brazil upon the south. So gentle is the slope of the valley, from the foot of the Andes to the ocean, that the Amazons has an average fall of only six and one-half inches to the mile, and for the last two thousand miles of its course its fall is less than two inches to the mile. But notwithstanding this almost absolute level of the river-valley, so vast is the volume of water that presses toward the sea, that the Amazons sweeps down with a current that tears away its banks with their load of forest, and mottles its floods with islets of grasses and with trees torn from its shores.

Although we apply the general term Amazons to the whole river, the natives designate different portions by different names. From its mouth to the Rio Negro it is termed Amazons; the part between that river and Tabatinga, or the Peruvian frontier, is called Solimoens; while from Tabatinga to the Andes it bears the name Marañon. All are familiar with the origin of the name Amazons—how Orellana, having deserted Pizarro upon the Napo, floated down that stream, and reported to have seen, upon the banks of the great river, a tribe of female warriors, that naturally suggested the fabled Amazons of the Afric Hesperia, or of the Thermodon of Pontus; hence the application of the name to the river upon which they were encountered. The foundation for this story of a nation of women-warriors is clearly shown by Wallace, in the following observations upon the Indian tribes of the Uaupés, one of the tributaries of the Rio Negro: "The men, on the other hand, have the hair carefully parted and combed on each side, and tied in a cue behind. In the young men, it hangs in long locks down their necks, and, with the comb, which is invariably carried stuck in the top of the head, gives to them a most feminine appearance; this is increased by the large necklaces and bracelets of beads, and the careful extirpation of every symptom of beard. Taking these circumstances into consideration, I am strongly of opinion that the story of the Amazons has arisen from these feminine-looking warriors encountered by the early voyagers."

We found navigating with our little craft more dan-

gerous upon the Amazons than upon the Napo; we were
in constant danger from the sudden squalls which swept up
the river from the east. For greater safety, we kept close to
the banks, that we might more quickly run the "Záparo"
into some sheltered spot, upon the approach of a storm. In
many places the banks were lined with fallen trees, marking the encroachment of the river upon the forest. Swiftly
we were borne down the Amazons, and upon the second
day from the mouth of the Rio Napo we reached Pebas,
a little Indian village located upon a high bluff on the
left bank of the Ambiyacu, a small stream flowing into the
Amazons from the north. We here met Mr. Hauxwell,
an English naturalist, who was making this place his temporary home while engaged in securing collections. Here
we delayed several days, awaiting the arrival of the steamer
from the upper Peruvian waters. The town of Pebas is
rendered healthful by its elevated position, which gives
it the influence of the easterly trade-winds. The population is made up of Orejones and Yagua Indians, who, for
the greater portion of the time, are scattered in the forest,
upon the banks of the little streams and lagoons, engaged
in fishing and hunting, as the immediate vicinity of the
village affords insufficient game. These Pebas Indians we
found the most abject and indolent of any that it was our
misfortune to be dependent upon east of the Andes. As
far as we could ascertain, they seem to have no idea of a
Good Spirit; yet they entertain vague conceptions of an
Evil Spirit, that is the source of all ill-success in their war
and hunting excursions. The Yaguas, upon the death of
any member of their tribe, bury the deceased in his own
hut, which is then deserted, and all his other possessions
destroyed.

Here we found, interstratified with the clay of the
bluff upon which Pebas is situated, a stratum of ma-

rine shells;[*] .the supposed bearing of which, upon the interpretation of the geologic facts of the Amazonian Valley, has been made known by Prof. Orton. There is here an interesting question relative to intertropical glacial phenomena. Prof. Agassiz, after careful and extended examination of the deposits, concludes that an ancient glacier once ploughed through the Amazonian Valley. From the report of a paper on the valley of the Amazons, read August 20, 1870, by Prof. Orton, before the American Association for the Advancement of Science, we quote the following: "The conclusion reached was that facts were incompatible with the existence of an equatorial glacier, and even of an intertropical cold epoch." Setting aside all generalizations, let us look at naked facts—see what evidences of glacial action have been found in these tropical regions.

The geologic formations of the Amazonian Valley have been carefully studied by Agassiz, and are given by him as, first, a coarse arenaceous material, resting upon a cretaceous formation, indications of which appear about the edge of the valley; then a deposit of finely-laminated clays, overlaid by sandstone, fully eight hundred feet in thickness. This has been subjected to denuding agencies, which, toward the lower portion of the valley, have removed, in some instances, the entire thickness of the deposit, leaving isolated, flat-topped mountains, such as the hills of Almeyrim, which form the most conspicuous ob-

---

[*] Mr. Conrad, to whom these shells were submitted for identification, gives the number of species as seventeen, all extinct, belonging to nine genera, only three of which are now represented. The following list contains the most important; others may yet be added : Isaea Ortoni, I. Lintea, Liris laqueta, Ebora crassilabra, E. bella, Hemisinus sulcatus, Dyris gracilis, Neritina Ortoni, Bulimus linteus, Pachydon (Anisothyris) tenuis, P. carinatus, P. obliquus, P. erectus, P. cuneatus, P. ovatus, P. altus, and a bivalve allied to Mulleria.

jects in the scenery of the Lower Amazons, and mark the thickness of the formation. Resting unconformably upon the sandstone thus denuded, lies a deposit of clay, of a brownish-red color, showing slight traces of stratification. Agassiz, finding in these vast deposits no fossils of any kind, with the exception of a few leaves, disposes of the question of their origin, by supposing them to be glacial formations, deposits in a vast fresh-water lake, into which the valley was converted upon the breaking up of the glacier, which, flowing from the Andes, crowded between the highlands of Guiana and Brazil—the mouth of the valley being closed by an immense moraine barrier. By these peculiar circumstances, under which Agassiz supposes these formations to have been deposited, he accounts for the absence of fossils in them; and to the giving way of the barrier, and the escape of the waters of the lake, he refers the origin of those "hills of denudation" to which we have alluded, located in the lower portion of the valley.

The finding of marine or brackish-water shells at Pebas militates against this theory, unless it can be shown, as Agassiz suggests, that they are accidental, or belong to a post-glacial formation, resulting from a submergence of the continent, such as is known to have taken place in North America, after the close of the ice-period. But, although these shells prove the marine or estuary origin of the formation with which they are identified, yet they prove nothing more. We should be cautious, and not proceed in advance of our facts. These, as we now possess them, simply allow us to limit glacial action here. They may permit us, perhaps, to infer that portions of the formations, or even that the main deposits of the Amazonian Valley, are not of fresh-water or glacial origin. But we are committing an error, if, from these data, with a hasty examination of the equatorial flora, with reference to a determination of the question whether or not there has been an intermingling of different floras, such as is thought would be attendant upon a cosmic winter, we make the assertion that there has been no "intertropical cold epoch." The question respecting the origin of the principal deposits of the Amazonian Valley affects only a theory, while the one of an intertropical winter brings us in relation to facts. No theory which militates against facts, pronounced as such by our most accurate observers, can prove subservient to the cause of truth. The fact of the existence of ancient *local* glaciers in the tropics will not admit of a hasty denial. Let us note some observations made by explorers of the valley. We make from "A Journey in Brazil" the following quotation, which gives the results of Prof. Agassiz's researches among the serras of Ceará, near the picturesque little village of Pacatuba: "On this very serra of Aratanha, at the foot of which we happen to have taken up our quarters, the glacial phenomena are as legible as in any of the valleys of Maine, or in those of the mountain of Cumberland in England. It had evidently a local glacier, formed by the meeting of two arms, which descended from two depressions, spreading right and left on the upper part of the serra, and joining below in the main valley. A large part of the medial moraine formed by the meeting of these two arms can still be traced in the central valley. One of the lateral moraines is perfectly preserved, the village road cutting through it; while the village itself is built just within the terminal moraine, which is thrown up in a long ridge in front of it. It is a curious fact that, in the centre of the medial moraine, formed by a little mountain-stream, making its way through the ridge of rocks and bowlders, is a delicious bathing-pool, overgrown by orange-trees and palms." Upon the side of the serra of Ereré, on the northern shores of the Amazons, opposite

the hills of Santarem, are erratic bowlders, masses of
hornblende. Upon the Rio Negro, just below Rio Branco,
we discovered ledges of compact hornblende, to which we
have already alluded.* Will not these throw some light
upon the origin of the bowlders of Ereré? In collating
all the evidence of ancient glaciers, found in the mountains about the valley, we must not fail to mention a fact
obtained by Agassiz from the careful and reliable observer
Dr. Felice. He states that in the southeastern part of the
valley, running from Serra Grande to the Rio Arucaty-
Assá, is a wall-like accumulation, composed of the usual
débris of moraines, which has an extent of one hundred
and eighty miles. Passing from the valley of the Amazons, but still remaining within the lines of the tropics,
we find other unmistakable traces of glaciers. In the vicinity of Rio de Janeiro, Agassiz found the surface of
the rocks upon which the drift rests characterized by
those peculiar undulations recognized as one of the distinctive marks of moving ice-masses, and which are termed
roches moutonnées. Erratic bowlders fill the drift, differing so essentially from the rocks in place as to leave no
doubt as to the fact of their transportation from a distance. Among the equatorial Andes we find evidence of
the snow-line having formerly been lower than at present.
We have already alluded to the vast accumulation of sand
and gravel, termed the *arenal*, resting upon the flanks of
Chimborazo, several hundred feet below the line of perpetual snow upon that mountain. Its whole character
indicates a glacial formation. Dr. Loomis found traces
of glaciers, such as ground and striated rocks, and moraines, upon the Peruvian Andes. We certainly must not
ignore such facts as these, in our search for an interpretation of intertropical geology. These facts appear to indicate an intertropical winter—at least, such a reduction of

* See page 189.

the temperature as to cause a lowering of the snow-line upon the Andes, and the formation of local glaciers among the serras of Brazil. What are required, in order that we may be able to read correctly the geologic history of South America, are more careful research and greater caution in making hasty generalizations from insufficient data. If we may rely upon the facts gathered, the question is one not respecting the existence of an "intertropical cold epoch," but simply of the *limitation* of glacial action, or ice-phenomena, under the tropics.*

* Since the above was written and placed in the hands of our publishers, a new volume has appeared from the pen of Prof. Hart, of Cornell University, who is at present (November, 1870) in Brazil, having charge of an expedition from the university above named. This work, "Geology and Physical Geography of Brazil," is the most accurate and exhaustive account of the geologic and topographical features of that country that has ever been given to the public. Every part shows the presence of the careful and discriminating observer. Upon an examination of the work, we were pleased to find that what we have said above, relative to glacial phenomena, is fully corroborated, and all fairly placed, by the researches of this eminent geologist, beyond conjectural ground. To the evidences of glacial action in equatorial America, gathered by Agassiz, and which we have given above, Prof. Hart adds a long series of phenomena, as the results of his own explorations during two journeys in Brazil. Upon page 29 he says: "I desire to record here the fact that I began my studies of the Brazilian drift with a conviction that Prof. Agassiz was wrong, and I feel much gratified that my independent observations have so fully confirmed the results of his own." After speaking of the phenomenon, so observable in Brazil, of the decomposition of gneiss rock *in situ*, and the marks that distinguish the material thus resulting from true drift, he goes on to give, in different portions of his work, evidences of drift found in the coast-provinces of Brazil, "from the Bay of Rio Janeiro to the Amazons." Prof. Hart regards the sandstone and clays of the Amazonian Valley as tertiary deposits, thus limiting glacial action, as we have supposed, in our remarks above, facts demand in South America; yet, in exact correspondence with the views we have ventured, he says: "My conclusions, after all, do not affect his" (Agassiz's) "theory of the former existence of glaciers under the tropics, down to the present level of the sea, a theory which I hold as firmly as he." But, for

Upon the afternoon of the 16th of December the steamer "Morona" arrived from Iquitos, a thriving little town about one hundred and fifty miles above Pebas, upon the left bank of the Marañon. It was like bidding farewell to an old friend, to part with our little "Záparo," which had so long been our pleasant home, and that had floated us safely through six hundred miles of the great forest. We left it moored in the waters of the Ambiyacu, with our Indians busily engaged in tearing it to pieces, in order to disencumber their canoes.

The first line of steamers upon the Amazons was established between Pará and Manáos, in 1853; the second, from the latter town to Tabatinga, upon the Brazilian frontier, in 1858; the third, in 1862, whose vessels navigate the head-waters of the river as high as Chosoba, in Peru. The presence of steamers upon the Amazons, in connection with the Pacific and Atlantic lines which girdle the continent, have done, and are doing, more for the development of that country than all other influences combined. It has been the absence of means of inter-communication that has rendered the progress of South-American states so slow and unsatisfactory. Brazil has at length awakened to the truth that rapid and cheap transportation, the consequent outgrowth of untrammelled competition, is the most effective agent in securing national wealth and growth. On September 7, 1867, she threw open the Amazons to the competitive commerce of all nations. The steamers upon that river and its tributaries are transforming the country. Their shrill whistle seems to awaken the slumbering natives. Quite a heavy trade has already sprung up in India-rubber, Brazil-nuts, cacao, coffee, cotton, sarsaparilla, tobacco, horses, cattle,

farther information relative to these interesting questions, we must refer our readers to the work itself, which is a valuable and permanent contribution to the geology of our southern continent.

dried meat, hides, pirarucu-fish, turtles, turtle-oil, copaiba, and guarana.

The "Morona," which took us aboard at Pebas, was a swift iron steamer, especially adapted for navigating the rapid Peruvian waters. At nearly twenty miles an hour she dashes down the river, her engine driving the more strongly when the current strengthens, in order to render her control by the helm possible. Captain Raygado was acquainting himself with the intricacies of English, while his associates, who were Englishmen, were returning the compliment by familiarizing themselves with Spanish; the cook was from the Celestial Empire; consequently there was a babel of languages upon the "Morona." Three hours from Pebas brought us to Maucallacta, a small Indian village, where we anchored for the night, and took in wood. Upon the first introduction of steamers on the Amazons, these Indians, as might be imagined, were fearfully alarmed. They had been sufficiently long under the instruction of the padres, to have fire and smoke vaguely associated in their minds with that region which it would be desirable to avoid. So, when the steamer came ploughing up the river, puffing out columns of black smoke, and occasionally giving a terrible scream, they very naturally supposed that the agent of the Evil One had come for them; and, when "the devil's boat"—which their distorted imagination pictured the monster to be—approached their towns, they took to the forest, and not until convinced that the thing couldn't run on land, did they become reconciled to what seemed to them an infernal contrivance.

From Maucallacta we dropped down to Caballochocha, where we passed the night of the 17th, and the next morning steamed down to Loreto, the last Peruvian town met in descending the Marañon. It is located upon a bluff, and, with its church and the whitewashed walls of its huts, presented a pleasing contrast with the villages we had hitherto passed. Thus we spent several days dropping slowly down the river; and finally, upon the 20th, we cast anchor off the frontier Brazilian town of Tabatinga. This village consists of eight or ten buildings, only a portion of which, however, are visible from the river, as they stand a little back from the edge of a high bluff. Tabatinga is a military post, and from some rude earthworks several guns look down upon the river. The commandante of the post, sharing the enthusiasm springing up throughout this new and undeveloped country for collecting natural-history specimens, had gathered quite a menagerie, which he proposed sending to Rio Janeiro.

Late in the afternoon of the 20th, the Brazilian steamer "Icamiaba" arrived from Manáos, and, bidding farewell to the "Morona," we embarked upon this vessel, and the following day steam and current were bearing us swiftly down the river. Travelling upon the Amazons is attended with as few discomforts as are experienced upon our own northern waters. We lived upon deck. This was covered and arranged with a table through the centre, where our meals were taken, so that we might enjoy the grateful breeze created by the movement of the boat. We found the deck also a delightful place to swing our hammocks at night.

Late in the evening of the first day from Tabatinga we reached San Paulo, a collection of huts inhabited by Ticuna Indians, where we received a little freight, and again weighed anchor. Notwithstanding the extreme darkness, we ran all night, and about ten the following morning arrived at Tunantins, a village of a score of houses, located upon a stream of the same name, whose waters are black from being steeped in the forest that rises directly out of the stream. Early in the morning of the 23d we anchored in front of Fonte Boa, located

upon the Cayhiar-hy, several miles from the Amazons.
The naturalist Bates speaks of it as fearfully infested by
mosquitoes, and not without reason; for, no sooner had
our steamer stopped, than these pests boarded our vessel,
and drove us from our hammocks, which arrangements
afford admirable facilities for such attacks upon all sides.
This village is situated midway between the Atlantic and
Pacific civilizations, receiving the influence of neither;
the last not extending beyond Loreto, the most eastern
Peruvian town, and the former being felt but little above
Manáos, at the mouth of the Rio Negro. From Fonte
Boa we steamed down all day, without finding the least
indication of life, until late in the evening, and then only
by leaving the Amazons and steaming up one of its southern tributaries, the Teffé, where we found the town of
Ega, containing a mixed Portuguese, Indian, and Negro
population of about one thousand. Leaving Ega we
again entered the Great River, and steamed on and down
between the eternal walls of eternal green.

We miss upon the Amazons the sloping banks and
beautiful villas so characteristic of our northern rivers.
As we glided down day after day, there was always the
same blank horizon ahead, the same torn and crumbling
banks rising but a few feet from the water's edge, and the
same giant forest walling the river upon either side. To
us, accustomed to northern scenery, there was a strangeness to that tropical nature, which always produced a feeling of loneliness, and constantly reminded us of the distance of our home. We recall now a little incident illustrative of this, that occurred upon the morning of the
25th of December. We were swinging in our hammocks,
which were, as usual, suspended on the deck, when the
familiar wish of “Merry Christmas,” from one of the more
thoughtful members of our party, suggested with unusual

vividness home and distant friends, and suddenly transported us to the midst of a cheerful winter scene. But the strange exotic nature that surrounded us called back our thoughts, and told us that our home was far distant. Dark, tangled forest, overtopped by palms resting their drooping heads against the bronzed sky, the air quivering with the heat of the advancing day, and wide stretches of water, mottled with green masses of floating grass, was the scene that ushered in Christmas morn to us, upon the lonely waters of the Upper Amazons.

Early in the afternoon we reached the mouth of the Rio Negro, with whose black waters the yellow Amazons refuses to mingle, and sweeps proudly by, crowding the waters of the Negro close to the northern bank. The eye can distinctly trace for some distance down the stream the line which separates the waters of the two rivers. This strange aversion of these waters to joining is repeated in other fluvial systems; thus the red floods of the Missouri manifest a decided antipathy toward uniting with the inky waters of the Upper Mississippi. Before the confluence of the Rio Negro and Amazons, the latter, from a width of several miles, contracts to a breadth of less than one, makes a bold sweep to the north, and meets the former almost at a right angle; then, as it passes its mouth, turns again to the east, giving the Negro the appearance of being the main stream, and, were it not for the different coloring of their waters, one would be sure to mistake the relation of the rivers, and the Amazons would be pronounced the tributary. The mouth of the Rio Negro is twenty miles in width; but we enter a channel only two miles wide, formed by the northern bank and a low island, whose forest rises directly from the water. A short hour upon this black stream brought us to Manáos. It was here that we entertained the faint hope of meeting the

Caracas party; but, realizing perfectly the improbability of such a union of the divisions of the expedition, we were prepared for the intelligence that nothing had been heard from them. As we recalled the dangers of our own wanderings, and the one we had left behind, we could not but entertain many apprehensions for the safety of their little party.

CHAPTER XXII.

THE LOWER AMAZONS.

JUST at evening on the 26th of December we stepped aboard the steamer, and started for Pará. We were now upon the last thousand-mile stretch of the Great River. The "Tapajos," our steamer, abounded with monkeys, turtles, anacondas, and other denizens of the forest, presenting the appearance of a floating menagerie. The most observed and observing of all were the monkeys, of which we had a large number aboard; some promenaded the deck with freedom, or climbed the rigging, now and then engaging in sportive play with the passengers, or picking a quarrel with their more unfortunate anthro-.pomorphous companions. One large, serious fellow, allowed the run of the boat, took infinite satisfaction in noting the approach of meal-times; then in stationing himself above in some unobserved position, and, upon the appearance of the steward, bearing upon his head food for the table, in helping himself. Once the dish contained hot soup, which he could not so readily appropriate, and he expressed his chagrin, by maliciously capsizing the vessel, distributing its contents over the steward. Among other species was the little spider-monkey, or *ateles*, the smallest, most beautiful, and interesting of all the monkey-tribes. Its expression bears a startling resemblance to that of a child, and seems almost as indicative of emotion as the human countenance. They are very sensitive to cold, and, upon the lowering of the temperature, if but a few degrees, they may be seen interlocking their long, slender arms and tails, forming a very cozy-looking heap. One of the favorite pastimes of monkeys is to search one another for parasites; the parent, with its offspring between its legs, carefully examines it for any thing of a parasitical nature, and, when successful, gives evidence of apparent gratification.

The day following our departure from Manáos, we passed the mouth of the Madeira, which, after a course of two thousand miles, pours its vast volume of water into the Amazons, yet without causing much appreciable increase either in its width or in the strength of its current. Below the Madeira, the aspect of the Amazons was changed by the great number of floating patches of grass, brought down by that tributary, which was now swollen from the rains of the wet season that was advancing from the south. These tropical rivers are often fringed with wide borders of aquatic vegetation, which, at the time of high water, are torn away, and floated in vast meadow-like islands down the current.

This leads us to speak of the rise and fall of the rivers of the Amazonian Valley. They are not all subject to rises at the same time; for so great is the breadth of the valley, and so widely separated are the head-waters of the northern and southern tributaries, upon opposite sides of the equatorial line, that the periodical rains of the tropics are felt upon the one set of affluents several months before their influence is felt upon the other. Along the line of table-lands and mountains that feed the southern tributaries, the rainy season commences about September, gradually swelling those streams, which slowly roll their floods toward the centre of the valley, reaching the Amazons with their highest waters about the last of February or the first of March. Simultaneous with these contributions from the south, the streams along the slope of the Andes are adding their swollen waters to the great river. At this time the Rio Negro, as we have remarked in speaking of that river, is lowest, and its mouth is dammed up, and its current even turned back by the mass of water from the southern tributaries. By February the rainy season is flooding the highlands of Guiana and the cordilleras of Colombia, when the Rio Negro and the other northern affluents carry down their gathered floods, attaining their greatest rise in June, by which time the southern rivers have fallen. Thus but one set of tributaries is acting at once, to lift the level of the Amazons. Should both simultaneously roll down their accumulated spring floods, the forest in the centre of the valley would be almost submerged. As it is, the Amazons rises between forty and fifty feet above its lowest level, and the valley for several miles either side of the river is laid under water. Some writers, from the manner in which they have spoken of the inundation of the valley, leave the impression that its whole extent is flooded as completely as the Llanos during the spring-tides of the Orinoco. But the portion of the plain overflowed is comparatively small. At the time of the highest rise, the forests are flooded back probably not more than an average of fifteen miles from the banks of the river, while the greatest width of the valley is over seven hundred miles. This is true of the Amazons only between the mouth of the Tapajos and Upper Peru, a distance of seventeen hundred miles. Below the tributary named, the highlands of Guiana on the north, and those of Brazil on the south, crowd closer upon the river, narrowing the valley, so that we no longer find those extensive lowlands so characteristic of the river valley above Santarem. The flooded tract is called *gapo*, and the narrow, overarched channels intersecting the half-submerged forest are termed *igarapés*, which, in the Lingoa Geral of the Indians, means canoe-paths. Some of these run parallel to the Amazons for immense distances. Wallace, in his "Travels on the Amazons," says: "From Santarem to Coari (a distance of eight hundred miles), a person may go by canoe in the wet season without once entering into the main river. He will pass through small streams, lakes, and swamps, and everywhere around him will stretch out an illimitable waste of waters, but all covered with a lofty virgin forest. For days he will travel through this forest, scraping against tree-trunks, and stooping to pass beneath the leaves of prickly palms, now level with the water, though raised on stems forty feet high."

In the lagoons and quiet waters of these flooded regions grows that wonder of the vegetable world, the Victoria Regia, the "Royal Water-Lily of South America." * To Mr. J. F. Allen, a reliable authority in matters relative to its discovery and introduction in the conservatories of Europe and the United States, we are indebted for the following historical material. It was first discovered, in 1801, by the celebrated botanist Hænke, upon the Rio Marmore, a Bolivian tributary of the Madeira, who, as says his fellow-traveller, Father La Cueva, upon first beholding the plant in its native waters, "fell on his knees in a transport of admiration." The plant was next seen,

* This plant is sometimes erroneously termed *Victoria Regina*. Schömberg, believing it to belong to the genus Nymphæa, named it Nymphæa Victoria: it, however, constitutes a distinct genus.

in 1820, by M. Bonpland, near the junction of the Parana and Paraguay Rivers. It was afterward met with by other travellers, but Sir R. H. Schömberg, who found it in Guiana, in 1837, was the first to attempt to introduce it in cultivation in Europe and our own country. The immense leaves are nearly circular, four to six feet in diameter, and float upon the water; the edge being raised so as to form a rim about three inches high. The under-surface presents a remarkably ridged appearance, from the prominence of the ribs which constitute the frame of the gigantic leaf. These veins are nearly an inch in height, and consist of eight main ones radiating from the centre of the peltate leaf, strengthened by cross-ribs, thus forming a strong support. This net-work, with the calyx, is covered with long prickles, as is also the petiole, which is an inch in diameter, and which lengthens rapidly to adapt itself to the deepening waters during the periodical swelling of the rivers. The color above is a vivid green, while below it is a purplish crimson. The beautiful, fragrant flower is twelve to fifteen inches in diameter, with petals six inches in length, and is at first of a pure white color, gradually assuming a rose-tint after its expansion. The leaves will support a great weight. They have been known to uphold one hundred and fifty pounds—a covering being placed upon the leaf to equalize the pressure. The Indians are said, while engaged in gathering the seeds, which they use for food, to cradle their infants upon the leaves, which are first covered with a light skin.*

Two hours after passing the mouth of the Madeira, we reached Serpa, a little Indian village of about seventy houses, located upon a clayey bluff twenty-five feet above the ordinary level of the river. One hundred and thirty miles below Serpa, upon the south bank, stands Villa Bella, where we took on rubber and pirarucu, which, with

* See frontispiece.

cacao and guaraná, are the principal exports of most Amazonian towns. Larger quantities of the last are shipped from Villa Bella than from any other town upon the river. This article, the fifth in importance of the exports of the Amazons, is manufactured from the coffee-like fruit of a spreading shrub (*Paullinia sorbilis*), eight to ten feet in height. These seeds are roasted, ground, then formed into a thickened paste, and pressed into moulds of various and often fantastic shapes. When grated into water and sweetened, it makes an agreeable and refreshing beverage. Its medicinal properties also render it an excellent stimulant, and a good astringent, successfully used in cases of dysenteric diseases.

Before reaching Obidos we were greeted, for the first time since bidding farewell to the Andes, by mountain scenery; for like mountains appeared to us, long accustomed to the dead uniformity of the Amazonian wilderness, what were in fact low hills that occasionally rose above the forest. About three hundred and thirty miles below Manáos are the Straits of Obidos. Here the Amazons, which above this point spreads out three or four miles in width, narrows to less than a mile, with a depth, according to Lieutenant Herndon, of thirty or forty fathoms. The velocity of the current, as it pours through the contracted passage, is about four miles per hour during low water, increasing to upward of five in the rainy season. Although six hundred miles from the sea, the influence of the tides is here perceptibly felt, raising the river several inches. The river never flows backward at this point, but the rise is occasioned by the damming up of the water below, which causes a slackening of the current, and a lifting of the level of the river. At Gurupá, nearly three hundred miles below Obidos, the tide is five feet; at Pará, a distance of seventy miles from the sea, fifteen feet. The higher the tides at any place, the less is the river there affected by the wet season : thus, at three hundred miles from the mouth of the Amazons, there is no perceptible change in the level of the river, except through tidal influence.

At the narrowest part of the strait, upon the north bank, stands posted upon a high bluff the neat little town of Obidos. The village is quite regularly laid out and free from that rank growth of vegetation which defaces the squares and streets of most Amazonian towns. Seventy miles below Obidos we cast anchor off Santarem, located just at the mouth of the Tapajos, one of the great southern tributaries of the Amazons, whose apparently black, yet clear-blue waters, form a strange contrast to the turbid current of the Great River. The town has a mixed Portuguese and Negro population of over two thousand ; being, next to Pará, the largest city upon the Amazons. Grassy plains stretch out from the town, and enable cattle-raising to be carried on extensively. Cacao is largely cultivated ; while recent experiments prove that the sugar-cane can be even more successfully raised here than in our Southern States.

At Santarem we found a large number of rebel emigrants who were there seeking a home. This suggests one word relative to that colonization scheme, which has met with such indifferent success. When recent political movements in our country culminated in emancipation, it was not strange that former slave-holders should look about to see where they might be allowed the privilege of enjoying their favorite institution. Brazil, as an opening field for enterprise, immediately presented itself. The Brazilian Government extended every inducement, defraying expenses of transportation, offering bounties, and giving grants of land. Every thing seemed to favor the plan of colonization ; and large numbers of emigrants from the South, burning with hatred toward the old flag, because it now gave liberty and equal rights to all, established themselves upon the coast of Brazil, and along the banks of the Amazons and its tributaries. But, lacking that energy and persistence indispensable in bringing this new and undeveloped country under cultivation, they soon became dissatisfied, and many abandoned the undertaking and returned home. Besides, there were to them other discouragements. Movements in Brazil point toward a speedy emancipation of her slaves. The probability, and, indeed, certainty, of such an event, deterred these Southern slave-holders from investing largely in a property which might any day be rendered valueless by governmental enactment. They saw that the system was doomed, and that the movement in our country was but a precursor to that which promises speedily to give freedom to the last slave upon both continents. We met some, who, having spent thousands in prospecting the country for selecting a site, were returning home, and who expressed their determination to accept gracefully the situation. Their short tour in the equatorial regions had done them good; it is only to be lamented that more did not make the trip.

Below Santarem the low forest frontage along the northern bank of the river is broken by grassy plains, and upon the south are also spread out quite extensive campos between the rivers Tapajos and Xingu. These savannas are the first break in the great forest which otherwise covers the valley from the slope of the Andes to the Atlantic. Humboldt, relying upon the information of others, speaks of the savannas of the Rio Napo; but we found a dense forest to extend over all that portion of the valley. Messrs. Smith and Lowe were unable to find the Pampas del Sacramento, which we find laid down upon most maps as breaking the forest between the Ucayali and the Huallaga. The eminent explorer Wallace has shown, by his researches upon the Vaupés, that the plains of Caguan, in Colombia, are much less extensive than once supposed. These last hardly interrupt the forest, for we may consider them as lying between the two great valleys of the Amazons and Orinoco. What a grand, unbroken sweep of forest in this vast Amazonian plain!

It requires a little over seven hours to run from Santarem to Monte Alégre, which is situated upon the north bank, a little back from the shore, and partly raised upon a hill, backed by a low, marshy forest, beyond which rises a low range of flat-topped hills. The name of the town means gay mountain, and Mrs. Agassiz's first impression was, that it scarcely deserved its title. Prof. Agassiz's party ascended the river; one must float down the long stretch of the monotonous Amazons, to appreciate the hill-scenery of Monte Alégre. After passing Monte Alégre the Amazons assumes a grand width, its shores separating ten miles, and appearing as indistinctly-traced lines resting upon the water. Nothing impresses one so deeply with the magnitude of this mighty river as to allow the eye to wander over these ocean-like expanses, and watch the white caps as they break along with almost the violence of an open sea. While upon this portion of the river we encountered severe storms travelling up the stream, that often raised so heavy a swell that the movement of our steamer brought on feelings painfully suggestive of ocean experiences. As we neared either shore, occasionally a native's hut or a charming villa would look down from the bluffs, or appear half-buried in the dense vegetation of the river-bank. Along the northern shore extended the table-topped hills of Almeyrim, varying from a few hundred to nearly a thousand feet in height. These were the last hills seen upon the Amazons. Upon the south the grass plains were burning, and by night the reflection of the flames lighted large tracts of the horizon.

The 30th of December we passed the little villages

Prainha, Porto de Moz, and Gurupá, and, three hours below the last, turned into the channel Tajapurú, which leads from the Amazons into Pará River. This channel is, in fact, a maze of deep natural canals joining these two estuaries. We wound about amid innumerable islands, sometimes passing through channels so narrow that the overhanging boughs brushed our steamer as it crowded through. As we crept through these intricate water-paths, we had afforded us a fine opportunity to study the low forests that cover these half-submerged islands. Palms entered more conspicuously into the woods than they had done farther up on the Amazons. Among the many species may be seen the morichi, crowned with its cluster of fan-like leaves; while not less conspicuous are the tall, slender stems of the bacabá and assái. From the berry-like fruit of the latter is made a delicious beverage, the favorite drink of Paráenses. The low islands are inhabited by Portuguese and Indians, whose miserable hovels are posted upon piles, to keep them above high water.

Just before emerging from this labyrinth, we stopped at Breves, a little Portuguese village, located upon the island of Marajó, the last port before reaching Pará. A short run brings us upon the great estuary of Pará, or "Father of Waters," as the word signifies in the Indian language. It is still an open question whether or not this should be considered as one of the mouths of the Amazons. Wallace believes that no water finds its way from the Amazons into the Pará estuary, through the channels that connect the two, and he consequently considers it as forming no part of the Amazons, but as being simply the estuary of the Tocantíns, Capim, Aripana, and other rivers, that empty into it from the south. Agassiz discovers that Marajó, from its geological formation, must not be considered a delta proper, but simply an island, once far up the Amazons, but now brought near its mouth by the encroachment of the ocean, whose currents have worn away the northeastern portion of the continent. Hence he would call the Pará estuary one of the outlets of the Amazons, and would obtain one hundred and eighty miles for the width of the river at its mouth. Rejecting the Pará estuary, we have left a width of one hundred and fifty miles, which is, at least, the smallest estimate that can be given as the breadth of the Great River.

The last day of the year we arrived at Pará, or Belém, as sometimes called.* The city stands upon the right shore of the broad estuary of Pará, seventy miles from the Atlantic, and sixty miles south of the equator. A dense tropical forest crowds upon the city, and half buries the outskirts beneath its encroaching vegetation. Pará was founded in 1615, and now comprises a population of above thirty thousand mixed Negroes and Portuguese. The Indian element, which so largely predominates in most other Amazonian towns, is here sparingly represented. A small number of American and English residents infuse commercial life and enterprise. Pará is destined to become the first city of South America. It is the centre toward which gravitate all those commercial interests springing

---

* The following estimate of distances was obtained from the Amazonian Steamship Companies. The towns left blank we have added, as they are also stopping-places of the steamers:

From Pará	to	Breves	150	miles.
"	"	" Gurupá	252	"
"	"	" Porto de Moz	..	
"	"	" Almeyrim	..	
"	"	" Prainha	375	"
"	"	" Monte Alégre	..	
"	"	" Santarem	466	"
"	"	" Obidos	585	"
"	"	" Villa Bella	626	"
"	"	" Serpa	756	"
"	"	" Manáos	872	"

up on the Amazons and its tributaries; all the immense
resources of that tropic valley will, when developed, form
the material from which will be built up here one of the
largest ports of the New World. Almost all the trade
of the city is carried on with European powers. We
have been strangely indifferent respecting the commerce
of Brazil and the Amazons. Although her next-door
neighbor, we have scarcely any trade with that empire
—Portugal's is larger than our own. According to a
recent estimate, we purchase more than twenty-five million dollars' worth of Brazilian products annually, the
greater part of which come to us by the way of Europe.
This state of non-intercourse between us and Brazil is unnatural; the valleys of the Amazons and Mississippi are
the complements of each other; the products of our
Western States are just such as are demanded by tropical
Brazil, while Brazilian products must find their way,
either by direct or indirect trade, into the Mississippi
Valley. Here, at our very door, lies a country of immense
extent, whose important products are numberless, and such
as we must have; still, we allow the trade of these regions
to be monopolized by countries across the Atlantic. This
anomalous course of trade is the result of a strange indifference and misapprehension, on our part, respecting the
importance to us of Brazilian commerce. Yet even the
trade carried on with Europe is small; and for this fact
we find explanation in the unwise imposition of heavy
tariffs upon exports by the Brazilian Government. Blind
to the immense advantage that would result from unre-
stricted commercial relations with other countries, Brazil
has imposed heavy duties upon the most important exports
of the Amazonian Valley, as coffee, cotton, and wood, preventing free exportation of these great staples, and their
conversion into gold. For illustration, there is a tariff
upon exported wood of fourteen per cent., and, as a result,

the entire duty received at the custom-house of Pará during the year 1868, upon wood exported, including firewood for ships, was only three hundred and fifty dollars! Were duty upon this last article removed, Great Britain alone would ship hundreds of cargoes of the *massaranduba*, or "cow-tree" (*Brosimum galactodendron*), for railway ties and sleepers, in damp situations, where this timber would last for decades. For situations exposed to the weather, the *acapá* is unsurpassed in durability; palisades in Pará, built of this wood, stand at present in as good condition as when constructed forty years ago!

We learn, through James Henderson of Pará, to whom we are indebted for the facts already given, that a Mr. Morrison has recently established a saw-mill and planing-machine on the Amazons. There are two or three other mills of the first character in the valley; so that the valuable woods can be readily put in available form for home use or exportation. There has hitherto been a great scarcity of lumber; boxes in which we transported our collections from Pará to New York were made of boards imported from the States! In order that capital may be led to engage in developing and giving to the world the valuable and inexhaustible natural and cultivated products of the Amazonian Valley, two things are needed: first, that Brazil remove all restrictions to trade, by at once abolishing the absurd tariff upon exports; secondly, that she shall render the waters of the valley virtually, as they are now nominally, open to free competition, by ceasing to subsidize the established lines of steamers, which act, in its practical workings, as effectually discourages competition as though the waters of the river were closed against foreign vessels. With these restrictions removed, the trade of the Amazons would necessarily spring into gigantic proportions. That tropical valley is a vast storehouse, which is destined, when fully opened, to change the commercial relations of the world.

Closely allied to the question of the commerce of the Amazons, is the one of its colonization; for, although the exports of the valley at present are, and for decades must continue to be, in the natural products of its exhaustless forests and great streams, still, the larger part of its trade must ultimately consist in cultivated productions, as cacao, coffee, cotton, tobacco, and sugar, all of which can be successfully raised within the limits of the valley, and with even better returns than in our Southern States. Now, while the native population can be largely depended upon for the collecting of the products of their virgin forests, still, the indolent, unenterprising Indo-Portuguese inhabitants of the valley cannot be hoped to develop the full agricultural capabilities of the country. This, if done at all, must be effected by European or North-American colonists. There are fewer discouragements to a well-conducted scheme of colonization than generally supposed. The climate of the valley is not excessively warm, nor is it insalubrious; the mean annual temperature at Pará is 80°, and Wallace found the greatest variation during four years to be only 25°. One thousand miles inland from Pará it is but one or two degrees warmer than at that point. The open nature of the valley to the east allows the equatorial trade-winds to sweep its entire length, which, while mitigating the heat, render comparatively salubrious the broad river-channels that feel their influence. Our party never enjoyed better health than while upon the Amazons and its tributaries. Intermittent fevers are less frequent on these rivers than on our own Western and Southern waters. The wide tract of forest along the rivers, that is subject to inundation, frequently pushes bluffs above high-water mark, as if purposely to provide sites for villas and towns. The districts periodically flooded receive a rich deposit, and are admirably adapted to the cultivation of the cacao and banana; the finest plantations of these we have observed stood upon ground laid deep under water during the annual overflow of the river. Thus every thing leads us to hope that, as soon as Brazil is sufficiently awakened to her own interests to lift from these regions the incubus of governmental restrictions, a foreign population will spread itself over the shores of the great river, and upon the banks of its tributaries, and secure to the world the immense wealth of this tropical valley.

A pleasant and unexpected event occurred toward the close of our stay at Pará. Upon the 16th of January, the guns of the fort announced the arrival of the steamer from Manáos. Curiosity took us to the wharf, where we watched the little boats, loaded with passengers, as they pushed from the vessel, that had dropped anchor a short distance from the city, and pulled to the shore. All had landed save one, and we had turned away, when a familiar call directed our attention to the boat, that had now neared the wharf. There was the Caracas party! That was a joyous meeting. Paráenses doubtless thought us demonstrative. But that was what Pará had never seen before, and probably never will again—the union of two expeditions across the continent, from the north and west, and their arrival upon the Atlantic within two weeks of the same date. But there were only two of the Caracas division. Where was the third? Attacked by the fever of the lowlands of Venezuela, he had been obliged to return homeward. Then came inquiries for our companions. One had sailed for Rio Janeiro, another for New York. But where the artist? Then we told them of the lonely grave among the Andes. Was it strange that the first night of our meeting we forgot to sleep, and that the morning found us telling of adventures experienced since our parting at New York?

Upon the 18th of January we bade farewell to Pará, and upon the "Tigres" embarked for home. As we passed slowly down the Pará River, the shores became more and more indistinct, and, while we were still upon its turbid waters, land entirely disappeared. From the mouth of the river we sailed directly to Barbadoes, one of the Windward Islands of the West Indies. Here we delayed one day, the Sabbath, and then again weighed anchor. In the gray light of the morning of the 11th of February, we welcomed the snowy hills of Neversink; soon we were pushing through the floes of ice that choked the harbor of New York, and in a few hours the cars were bearing us rapidly along the banks of the ice-locked Hudson, toward our home. Nothing impressed more deeply upon our minds the equatorial scenes we had left, than the strange contrast between the snow-clad banks of our frozen Hudson and the forest-fringed shores of the ever-verdant Amazons. Pleasant were our wanderings, and ever vivid will be our recollections of Nature under the Tropics.

INDEX.

THE END.

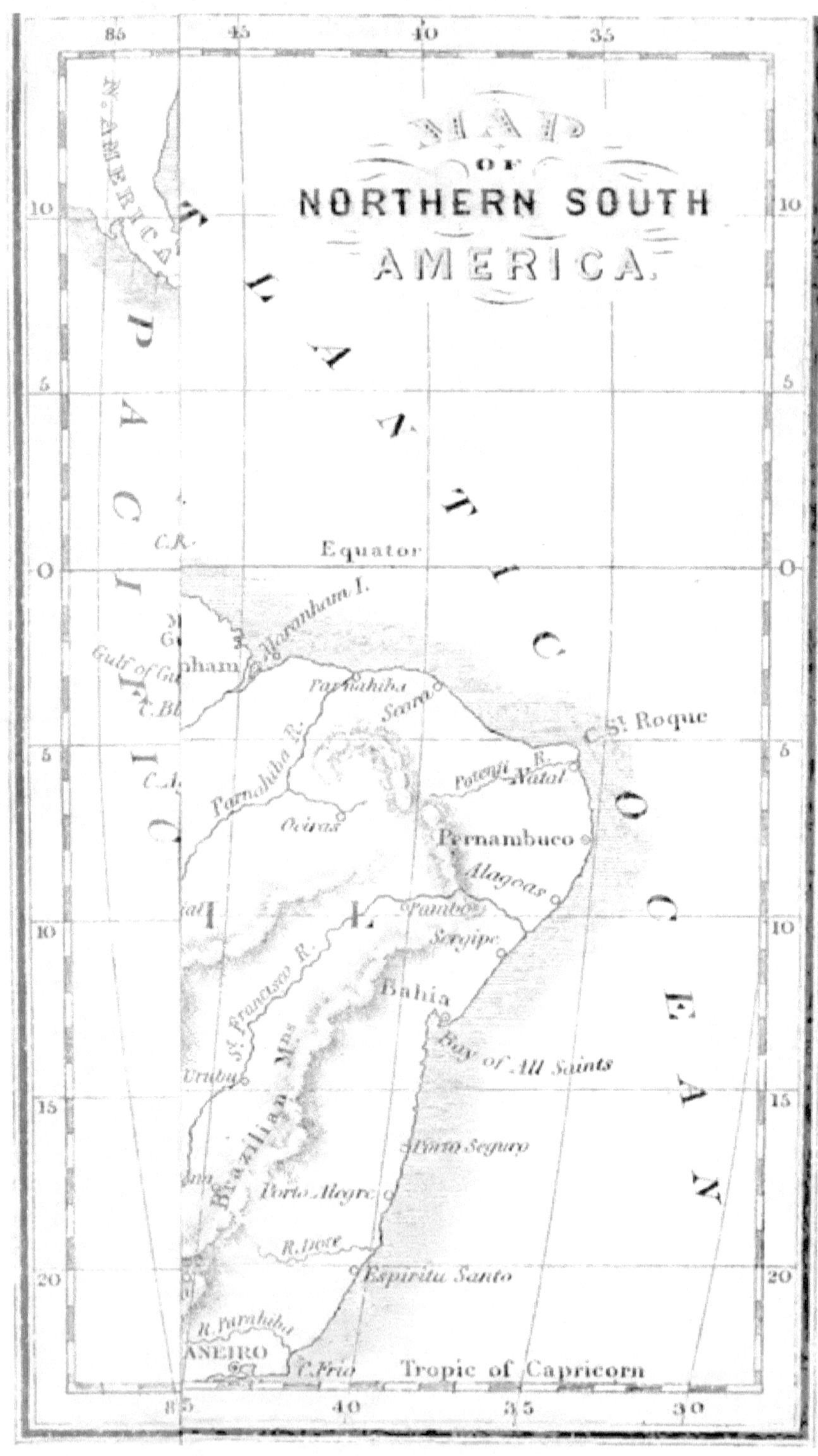
MAP
OF
NORTHERN SOUTH
AMERICA.
N. AMERICA
PACIFIC
ATLANTIC
OCEAN
Equator
Tropic of Capricorn
85
45
40
35
30
10
5
0
5
10
15
20
C.R.
Maranham I.
Gulf of Gu nham
C. Bl
Parnahiba
Searo
C.A.
Parnahiba R.
St. Francisco R.
Oeiras
Potenji R.
Natal
C. St. Roque
Pernambuco
Alagoas
Tamboo
Sergipe
Bahia
Bay of All Saints
Brazilian Mns
Urubu
Porto Seguro
Porto Alegre
R. Doce
Espiritu Santo
R. Parahiba
ANEIRO
C. Frio

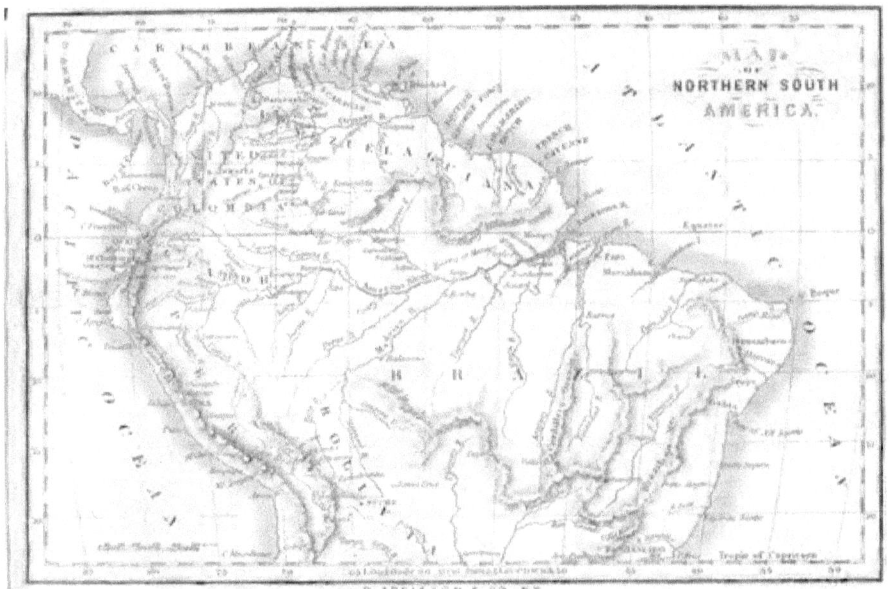

MAP
OF
NORTHERN SOUTH
AMERICA.
CARIBBEAN SEA
UNITED STATES OF COLOMBIA
VENEZUELA
FRENCH GUIANA
B R A Z I L
OCEAN
PACIFIC OCEAN
Equator
Tropic of Capricorn
D. APPLETON & CO. N.Y.